EXAM CRAM™

The Postal Clerk and Carrier Cram Sheet

THE NIGHT BEFORE THE EXAM

1. Relax! You are well prepared and will remain so when you wake up tomorrow morning. This evening, perhaps you can go out to a nice dinner, or take a relaxing walk or bike ride. Or maybe you can catch a movie to help clear your mind of test anxiety. Just be sure you choose a movie that's light-hearted and won't keep you up all night. A four-hour epic can probably wait until tomorrow evening, when you're finished with the exam!

2. Take just a little time to make sure you've accounted for all the non-exam-related (but still very important) details. In other words, make sure you have all your registration information gathered, and thus have all the documentation you will need to get into the test center. A good idea is to gather all this material and put it into a single folder. Then—while you're thinking about it—put that folder in your car or somewhere you know you will not forget it (such as under your car keys).

3. Take a moment to catch the weather forecast for tomorrow. Are you going to need an umbrella? Is it going to be snowing? By all means, do not let something like the weather make you nervous. Of course, if a blizzard is forecast for your area, that is a different story (and if it is, you probably will want to keep an eye on your local TV stations to determine whether the test will be cancelled). Just be prepared for any contingency, so that it doesn't become an issue the morning of the test.

4. At this point in your preparation, it probably won't do you much good to do lots of studying. In fact, trying to cram the night before the exam will probably do more harm than good: It will distract you and raise your anxiety level. If you aren't prepared by now, you aren't going to be, so once again, use this time to relax.

5. After you've covered items 2–4, then return to the first suggestion on this list and...relax!

THE DAY OF THE EXAM

6. Find a good parking spot. At most testing centers, parking will probably not be an issue, but this is not a certainty. Arriving at the testing center early will give you a better chance of finding a good spot. Although distant parking isn't an issue on a nice spring morning, you don't want to be in the position of having to walk a country mile in a torrential downpour or in bone-chilling cold.

7. Hit the restroom! An obvious one, but something to definitely keep in mind. When nature calls, it's amazing how that call can very quickly become the single most important thing on your mind. Don't let this happen to you, especially when you're taking a test as potentially important to your career as this one.

8. Take a few deep breaths...and relax! If you can take care of the previous items in this list and still have several minutes before the exam is scheduled to start, you then will have time for another critical aspect of your test preparation, and that is taking a few relaxing deep breaths. Or you can take a walk around the testing center, or call your spouse or significant other on your cell phone for a last-minute vote of confidence (although use this tip in moderation—sometimes these conversations can end up making you more nervous). The simple point here is that having a few extra minutes to spare will serve you well if—for whatever reason—you need a few extra minutes!

STAY RELAXED DURING THE EXAM

9. The best defense is a good offense. This is especially true when it comes to dealing with text anxiety. Make sure you are well prepared for the test. Study in advance, and don't cram the night before. Bottom line: Walk into the testing center confident that you will perform to the best of

D1566562

10. Take it easy on the caffeine, especially if you are not a morning person to begin with, or if you don't normally drink lots of caffeine. Too much Mt. Dew/coffee/insert-favorite-caffeinated beverage here can make you very jittery. On the other hand, if you always have a cup of java in the morning, don't risk caffeine withdrawal symptoms (translation: very bad headache) by not having it.

11. Don't forget to breathe! Remember that breathing is a necessary component of that thing we call living (!), so if you find yourself panting or hyperventilating, take a few moments to take some deep breaths and relax. Stay focused on the task at hand, and remember how well-prepared you are.

12. Mark some time to get nervous after the test. Yes, you read that right: Give yourself permission to be nervous/freak out/yell/scream/and so on *after* the test. Seriously, if you make part of the test-taking process a "cool down" session, you'll be surprised to find this might take away a great deal of your pre-test (and during the test) anxiety. One idea is to have a favorite CD loaded in your car, so as you drive away from the test center, you can rock out (or mellow out, depending on your preference) and release all that anxiety. Although it's not directly related to the test itself, if you can plan for this type of release, it helps you from becoming overly nervous during the exam.

ADDRESS CHECKING STRATEGIES

- One general strategy worth mentioning is to be sure to not lose your place on your answer sheet. Although that sounds obvious, you could potentially become distracted and start incorrectly marking your answer sheet; that is, you skip over an answer space and thus are "one question behind" in how you've marked your answer sheet. This can lead to a disastrous score, as you will have marked your answers to the wrong questions!

- To counter this possibility, use your finger or pencil to hold your place as you quickly move down the answer sheet, filling in your answers (in this case, either marking them as correct or incorrect). Don't let your eyes wander—you have only six minutes to work through this section of the exam!

- As you're checking addresses, you're loo[king for] differences in street numbers, street nam[e] viations (Dr. versus Rd., for example), c[...] state abbreviations (which can be very si[milar] versus NC, or IN versus IA) and ZIP code[s] as quickly as you can, scanning the addre[ss] from left to right. The absolute smallest de[tail can] make all the difference between whether tw[o] addresses are exactly the same or different. [Pay] attention (!) and work quickly—those are th[e] best strategies you can follow.

MEMORY FOR ADDRESSES STRATEGIES

- Remember that when answering the questions you won't be asked to recall the specific pieces [of] information, but rather the location of where the[y] appear in the grid.

- You should keep in mind that you aren't really expected to answer each one of the 88 questions (five minutes is a very short period of time to give each of these questions a close, focused study). That said, as you work through the questions, answer the ones you know (that is, the ones you can quickly recall from memory) first. Then go back and try to answer the harder or less obvious ones later.

- Another good piece of advice is, as always, to work as fast and efficiently as possible.

- Random guessing, in all probability, will not help your score and might actually hurt it.

- Another strategy you might want to utilize is to eliminate the answers that you know can't be correct. What I mean here is that although you might not be sure of the correct answer, you might still recognize an answer option that is *not* correct. Don't ignore this: It reduces the number of answer choices, which, if anything, can make the question a little less daunting as you try to remember where the address was located in the information grid.

NUMBER SERIES STRATEGIES

- Try to move quickly, but pay attention to detail. Don't skip around; answer the questions in order. You can guess on the ones you didn't get right away at the end. Read the directions very carefully—they will tell you exactly what you need to do.

- Be sure to write some basic information about each question as you study it. That is, take some time to identify patterns and make notes on the page to identify them.

- The great thing is that all the pattern information you need is *right there* in the questions themselves. All you have to do is take the time to write it down. Remember that time is a luxury you don't have with this type of question, and—as mentioned earlier—panic can take over on even the simplest question. So taking the time to write the pattern information will help calm you down, as well as ensure you actually see the pattern that is being used.

Postal Clerk and Carrier Exams

John Gosney

Dawn Rosenberg McKay

Michele Lipson

CERTIFICATION

Postal Clerk and Carrier Exams Exam Cram

International Standard Book Number: 0-7897-3261-0

Library of Congress Catalog Card Number: 2004108920

Printed in the United States of America

First Printing: October 2004

07   06   05   4   3   2

Trademarks

Warning and Disclaimer

Bulk Sales

Que Publishing offers excellent discounts on this book when ordered in quantity for bulk purchases or special sales. For more information, please contact

U.S. Corporate and Government Sales

1-800-382-3419

corpsales@pearsontechgroup.com

For sales outside of the U.S., please contact

International Sales

international@pearsoned.com

Publisher
Paul Boger

Executive Editor
Jeff Riley

Acquisitions Editor
Carol Ackerman

Development Editor
Steve Rowe

Managing Editor
Charlotte Clapp

Project Editor
Jennifer Matlik

Copy Editor
Margo Catts

Indexer
Johnna Dinse

Proofreader
Juli Cook

Technical Editor
Scott Bronnenberg

Publishing Coordinator
Pamalee Nelson

Interior Designer
Gary Adair

Cover Designer
Ann Jones

Dedication

Dedicated to K, R, and M, our inspiration, and A and D, who always support us.

—Dawn and Michele

To DF and WB, who have been trusted companions (in music and spirit) through projects too numerous to mention. Everything must go!

—John Gosney

About the Authors

John Gosney is a consultant, writer, and teacher, working in the fields of information technology and education/test preparation. He has written over a dozen instructional titles, including previous editions on how to pass the USPS and law enforcement exams. John holds a bachelor's degree in professional writing and psychology from Purdue University, and an M.A. in English from Butler University. He is a technology director and instructor at the Indianapolis campus of Indiana University.

Dawn Rosenberg McKay and **Michele Lipson** have masters degrees in Library and Information Science (MLS), and together have a combined total of more than 25 years of professional experience in libaries and research. They are co-owners of Kangaroo Research Mavens, an independant research firm located in New York.

Acknowledgments

. . . .

Thank you to John Gosney, our co-author. It is always a pleasure to work with you. Thanks to everyone at Que for bringing us on board. A tremendous thank you to our families who always stand behind us.

—Dawn and Michele

Thank you to Dawn Rosenberg McKay and Michele Lipson, who make writing more fun (and easy!) than it has any right to be. You both are terrific, and I look forward to more future collaborations. Thanks to everyone at Que, and especially to Carol Ackerman for providing a great writing opportunity. A big thanks (as always) to my family for supporting me in this and all other projects. And a very special thanks to Daisy Jane, who means more to me with each passing day, and is the reason for everything I do.

—John Gosney

About the Technical Editor

Scott Bronnenberg is a letter carrier for the United States Postal Service in Indianapolis, Indiana. After graduating from high school in Anderson, Indiana, Scott joined the Marine Corps and participated in Operation Desert Storm from November 1990 to May 1991. He attended Purdue University and worked several odd jobs before taking the 470 USPS exam in January 1998. Having received a nearly perfect score on the exam, he was one of the first to be hired from his testing group, starting his career at the USPS in March 1998. Not even the long days, the heat and humidity, or the often near-Arctic Indiana weather can daunt Scott's enjoyment of his job. His philosophy is that it beats sitting at a desk, and it keeps him in great physical condition. Scott enjoys sports, his three cats, and visiting his wife's family in Munich, Germany.

Contents at a Glance

Table of Contents

We Want to Hear from You!

As the reader of this book, *you* are our most important critic and commentator. We value your opinion and want to know what we're doing right, what we could do better, what areas you'd like to see us publish in, and any other words of wisdom you're willing to pass our way.

As an executive editor for Que Publishing, I welcome your comments. You can email or write me directly to let me know what you did or didn't like about this book—as well as what we can do to make our books better.

Please note that I cannot help you with technical problems related to the topic of this book. We do have a User Services group, however, where I will forward specific technical questions related to the book.

When you write, please be sure to include this book's title and author as well as your name, email address, and phone number. I will carefully review your comments and share them with the author and editors who worked on the book.

Email: feedback@quepublishing.com

Mail: Jeff Riley
      Executive Editor
      Que Publishing
      800 East 96th Street
      Indianapolis, IN 46240 USA

For more information about this book or another Que Publishing title, visit our web site at www.examcram2.com. Type the ISBN (excluding hyphens) or the title of a book in the Search field to find the page you're looking for.

Introduction

. . . .

Welcome to Postal Clerk and Carrier Exam Cram

Welcome to *Postal Clerk and Carrier Exam Cram (460/470)*, your comprehensive and trusted resource for achieving the highest score!

This guide has been prepared with you—the test-taker—in mind. We have avoided unnecessary jargon and detail to present you with a study guide that is complete yet highly readable. Within its pages you will find insider advice on not only the types of questions you will face, but strategies and tips for answering these questions (as well as general test-taking advice). The guide also contains valuable information about the USPS, including important career and benefit information. So if you are looking for the best resource to score the highest on the 460/470 exams, you have come to the right place.

But more than just wanting to score high on the exam, a great test result furthers your career options with the USPS. That said, this guide also contains helpful information on various career options with the postal service.

Who This Book Is For

This book has been written to guide anyone interested in a career as a postal clerk and carrier, as it not only covers preparing for the 460/470 exams, but also gives practical advice and insight as to the full spectrum of working for the USPS (benefits, advancement opportunities, and so on). Also, this book includes special elements such as a "real world" case study (where you follow along with a fictitious but realistic individual as he works his way through preparing for the exam) and other unique features of the Exam Cram series (for example, the cram sheet), which can truly make it your "one stop" source as you ready yourself for a career with the USPS.

Taking the 460/470 Exams

A terrific general reference for information on the exam is the USPS web site, http://www.usps.com. Although the information about the test is not nearly as inclusive as what you'll find in this book, the site still represents a definitive reference, and you should refer to it often for questions not just about the test, but all facets of your career interest with the USPS.

There is no fee to take the 460/470 exams; however, you must register in advance. To register for the exams online, follow these steps:

1. Within your web browser, navigate to http://uspsapps.hr-services.org/usmapdetail.asp.

2. Select the Examinations option, and from the drop-down list, select the state in which you will take the exam, as shown in Figure Intro.1.

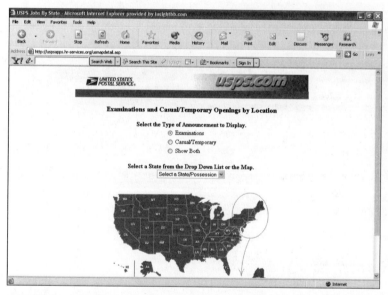

Figure Intro.1   Select the Examinations option, and the state in which you will take the test.

3. After you select your state, you are presented with a list of exam openings for the state you selected. Figure Intro.2 illustrates exam openings for the state of Indiana.

4. Click on the announcement number to be taken to the general information form, which you must complete to finish the registration process. This form is shown in Figure Intro.3.

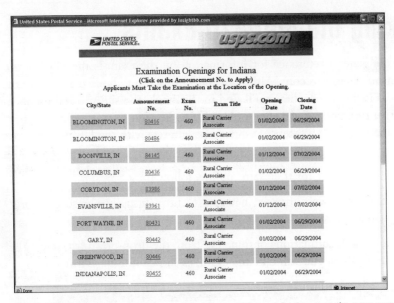

Figure Intro.2   Note that, depending on the state in which you take the exam, the exam may be offered in several cities.

Figure Intro.3   Be sure and complete all the required fields.

5. After you complete this form, you are presented with a confirmation message. Specific information on your test location and date will be mailed to you.

If you have the exam announcement, you can also apply by phone by calling 1-866-999-9777 (or TTY at 1-800-800-8776).

Arriving at the Exam Site

You need to do all types of things to prepare for the exam, up to the night before you take it. All this information is presented to you within the pages of this book.

However, it is important to understand now what specific items you are required to bring to the examination:

➤ *Admission Document*—This is sent to you in your exam scheduling packet.

➤ *Positive Identification*—This can be a driver's license or some other type of picture ID.

➤ *Other Documents*—Depending on specific instructions listed in the scheduling packet you receive in the mail, you may be required to bring other documents. It is very important that you immediately open and review your scheduling packet as soon as you receive it to ensure you understand all the exam requirements, and that you take the proper credentials with you to the exam test center. Do not wait until the night before the exam to review this information!

A driver's license or credit card (with picture) are acceptable forms of identification.

Inside the Exam Room

Again, you will—by reading through this book—learn all kinds of great strategies, tips, and general information on how to score your highest on the exam. From understanding the different question types to learning how to overcome pre-test anxiety, the *Postal Clerk and Carrier Exam Cram (460/470)* has got you covered!

Here's some general information, though, on what to expect inside the exam room/test center:

➤ No unauthorized items are allowed inside the exam room. These items include (but are not limited to) reference books, logarithmic tables, and calculators.

➤ Cheating, obviously, is not permitted; however, you should take special care to not even appear as if you might be cheating. This includes talking to another test taker, passing notes, and so on. If you are caught cheating or just assumed to be cheating, your rating (that is, how your total USPS application is rated) may be cancelled, which will put a serious damper on your future career opportunities with the USPS. The best advice here is to keep your eyes on your own paper, and avoid any conversation after the exam begins.

➤ If you have a need for special accommodations during the exam, these can be considered by the Postal Service. Information addressing this issue will be in your scheduling packet, so again don't wait until the night before the exam to review this information if, in fact, you might have a need for special accommodations during the exam.

Preparing for the Exam

You wouldn't be reading this book if you weren't interested in preparing for the exam. Again, it is worth stating that you've made a wise decision in deciding to utilize a study guide, and especially the one you are now holding in your hands.

As you will see as you work through this book, we will address a wide range of preparatory issues, from the more traditional (such as taking practice exams) to talking about issues you might not generally think of as being "exam preparation" (such as getting a good night's sleep before the exam).

As you work through each chapter of the book, you will also find references to other sources that might prove useful in helping you prepare for the exam. These sources are specific to the topic under discussion in each chapter and have been included in an effort to make this book as comprehensive as possible in helping you score your highest.

About this Book

Postal Clerk and Carrier Exam Cram (460/470) utilizes a variety of special elements to help you best understand the material being tested, as well as ensure you are comfortable with the format of the test and other issues or concerns you might face during the testing process (for example, how to overcome test anxiety).

The special elements you will find within the book are described as follows:

 Notes will give you supplementary information on a topic at hand, and in some cases point you to other information resources.

 Tips are useful tidbits of advice, and—like notes—are used to supplement the current topic of discussion. Look to the Tip elements to give general pointers or hints about the information being discussed.

Sidebars

Sidebars are designed to give you more extensive supplementary information.

 Exam alerts are to help you score better on the exam, which they do by providing you with "insider information" for the particular question type/section that is being discussed where the exam alert appears.

Each chapter also contains additional special elements that are designed to help you succeed. These elements include

➤ *"Terms you need to understand"* and *"Concepts/Techniques you'll need to master"*—These two lists appear at the beginnings of several chapters and can be seen as "must know" listings of key terms/concepts you should be very familiar with if you intend to get the best score possible on the exam.

➤ *Exam Prep Questions*—You are going to get a lot of practice questions in this book, both in the form of sample quizzes and full-length practice exams. Practice questions are not only listed, but detailed answer explanations are also provided.

Self-Assessment

No matter how confident you may feel about any given situation (regardless of whether or not a test is involved), you might feel a sense of uncertainty, and maybe even start asking yourself questions such as, "Am I up to this?" or "Am I qualified to do this?"

This type of second-guessing is natural, and should not discourage you from pursuing your intended goal. In fact, you can turn what appears to be negative self-reflection into a positive by using this uncertainty as an impetus to keep studying and thus avoid getting over-confident.

Although describing your psychological profile is not a goal of this book, it is important—with regard to these types of questions you might be asking yourself—to perform a realistic self-assessment. You should not just examine how you feel about your abilities, but you should also reflect on such issues as the current job market for the career you are interested in, the qualifications of the "ideal candidate," and the experience (either educational or work) you should have (or plan on getting soon) to make yourself an attractive candidate.

The purpose of this short self-assessment is to get you thinking—now!—about these questions as they relate to your own personal situation. In turn, you can use your answers to target areas in which you might be deficient, and/or to further explore various areas of (in this case) the USPS in which you might have additional questions or concerns.

Although the following list of questions is not meant to be exhaustive (that is, other questions may be applicable to your own specific situation), you should nevertheless take some time to answer/think about them as you read through the information presented in this self-assessment. Keep in mind that for many of these questions, there is no right or wrong answer, but you should honestly answer each one to best gauge how you will address the issues and requirements of working with the USPS that are presented here:

➤ Are you prepared to put a great deal of time and effort into passing the exam, with the understanding it could be months (or longer) before you have the chance to apply for an opening with the USPS?

➤ Depending on how you answered the first question, does your personal, family, and/or financial situation allow you the flexibility to deal with this situation?

➤ How will you address the challenging schedule and mental/physical demands that are unique to a position with the USPS?

➤ *Postal Clerk and Carrier in the Real World*—Becoming a postal clerk and carrier is not usually something you do overnight. Although you may have a strong interest and desire to work for the USPS in this capacity, there is strong competition to becoming a postal clerk and carrier; moreover, there can be (on average) a waiting period of 1–2 years (or more) after you successfully pass the 460/470 exams before you are presented with a work opportunity. That said, most people who become postal clerks and carriers come from a different occupation. (In other words, they continue to work in that other profession until an opportunity to work for the USPS presents itself.)

Overall employment of postal clerks and carriers remains somewhat flat, with just a modest increase in the number of available jobs expected through the next few years. Various factors are expected to contribute to this. Clearly, the increased use of technology in the USPS (featuring a variety of automated mail sorting/handling technologies) will decrease the amount of time carriers spend sorting mail for their routes. Also, continued use of the "ZIP + 4" system and the larger initiative of the Postal Service to move toward centralized delivery are expected to increase carrier productivity and thus reduce the need for the number of actual carriers.

Another interesting factor contributing to the job outlook for postal clerks and carriers is that because it is such an attractive job, those individuals who are able to obtain a position often work until retirement. That said, retirement of existing workers should not be viewed as a significant (in terms of the number of open positions available) opportunity for vacant positions.

Although you can read the above information as discouraging in terms of your own job prospects, it would probably be a mistake to do so. Again, a position with the USPS carries very attractive benefits, so you can (fairly) say it is worth the wait, especially if you are truly interested in a career with the USPS. More good news is that full-time postal clerks and carriers have never been laid off. When there is a high volume of mail, additional workers are brought in to help; in turn, when mail volume drops, overtime is cut back, part-time employees work fewer hours, and casual workers are released.

You will find more general information about working for the USPS in Chapter 1.

➤ *The Ideal Postal Clerk and Carrier Candidate*—What makes the perfect candidate? That is a difficult question. As you will see as you work through this book, an attention to detail and good memorization skills are very important; however, in addition to these skills, a friendly demeanor and the ability to keep a strong "customer-focused" attitude are just as important. That said, nearly any previous occupation might help to prepare you for a career as a postal clerk or carrier because—all things considered—nearly any occupation is going to ask you to listen closely, follow directions, pay attention to detail, have a good memory and (usually) project a good customer-focused attitude. As you will see in Chapter 1, "Career Options As a Postal Clerk or Carrier," different positions within the USPS require varying physical skills (the ability to stand for long periods of time, the ability to lift heavy packages) as well as other abilities. Although previous work experience that would speak directly to these skills would obviously be a benefit, these physical skills are required in many occupations.

It's worth noting here, however, that because of the proud history (and obvious importance) of the USPS, candidates of exemplary personal character, and who demonstrate a high level of responsibility and dedication, are also going to stand above the crowd. And of course, achieving a high score on your exam is a critical factor in making you a very attractive candidate, if not a perfect one!

➤ *Put Yourself to the Test*—So you've read a bit about the job outlook for postal clerks and carriers, and you have a general idea of what makes a strong candidate. But, what if you are still asking yourself those same questions that were mentioned at the beginning of this assessment? ("Am I up to this" or "Am I qualified to do this?") As you prepare to work through this book, take a moment to compare your own situation/ experiences/educational and work experiences with both the actual requirements and the "best candidate" attributes in the following list. If you are honest with yourself, you will be able to more effectively address any deficiencies and, as a result, do a better job of preparing for the exam itself.

>   ➤ *Educational background requirements*—There are no specific educational requirements to become a postal clerk and carrier. However, as already indicated, an aptitude for memorization, the ability to listen to and follow direction, and attention to detail are required of any position with the USPS.

➤ *Hands-on experience*—Although you will review these and other qualification requirements in Chapter 1, documenting employment history for the past 10 years, or from 16 years of age is a requirement. As already mentioned, many (if not most) people come into the clerk and carrier positions via another occupation, so providing a history of work experience is not only a requirement (as listed here), but that experience should be useful in building the customer-centric traits that are so important to all positions with the USPS.

The ability to successfully pass a pre-employment drug screen is also a requirement for working at the USPS.

➤ *Testing your exam readiness*—Clearly, you know the importance of preparing for an exam; otherwise you would not be reading this book. However, the importance of studying and preparing for the 460/470 exams cannot be understated, as a high score can often (and will often) set you apart from other applicants, or—in the event you score very poorly—disqualify you from the outset. Careful study of the material presented in this book is a requirement, and you should take time to familiarize yourself with the question types and to take the practice exams. Just as important, though, is understanding the intangible (but important) elements of test taking, which include such things as how to avoid text anxiety. (This and related issues are discussed in Chapter 3.) Bottom line: There is no substitute for good preparation, so use this book and be prepared!

➤ *Assessing Your Readiness for Exams 460/470*—After reading through this self-assessment, you should have some idea of your level of readiness for the exam. You also might now be aware of some areas (either in your mental abilities or work experience) that you need to improve upon to both score high on the exam and be viewed as an ideal candidate. The important thing to remember is to not let any discrepancy or "weak area" discourage you. The whole point of purchasing a book like this one is to identify the areas in which you need to improve, and to give you plenty of opportunity to practice what is required. So again, use these "weak areas" as encouragement and motivation to better prepare and to in turn achieve your highest score.

You might use the following additional questions to help you better assess your exam readiness. As with the questions presented to you earlier in this self-assessment, the important thing is that you honestly answer each question as it relates to your specific situation/skill set, so that you can more effectively use the information presented in this book to target and improve the areas in which you might need some extra work:

➤ Do you have trouble focusing on a specific task, especially if you are given a short period of time to complete the task? In other words, how well do you deal with stressful situations?

➤ What is your level of attention to detail? Can you spot subtle differences when comparing, for example, two different numbers and quickly note those differences?

➤ Do you have a good memory? Can you quickly memorize a set of information and then answer questions based on your ability to recall that information?

➤ When presented with a mathematical problem, do you tense up? Although these exams don't ask you to know algebra, they do test your ability to detect mathematical patterns when comparing sets of numbers.

➤ Can you listen to and follow spoken directions?

Career Options with the United States Postal Service

Terms You'll Need to Understand

✓ Salary
✓ Health insurance
✓ Leave time
✓ Step program

Concepts/Techniques You'll Need to Master

✓ Structure of federal civilian employment
✓ USPS positions requiring Exam 470
✓ Requirements of the postal clerk and carrier position

A career in the United States Postal Service (USPS) is an exciting one. Various career opportunities are available, from postal clerk and carrier (the focus of this book, of course) to machine operator. This chapter gives you a brief introduction to these opportunities, and the benefits of working for the USPS. You'll also take a look at the larger federal civilian employment sector, and how postal workers fit into this framework.

This chapter

➤ Examines the benefits the USPS has to offer, including salary, health insurance, leave time (including holidays) and discusses the "step" program used to determine these benefits

➤ Discusses the structure of federal civilian employment, including how to find information on federal job vacancies and the job salary classification

➤ Provides an overview of USPS positions that require Exam 470 (the focus of this book), as well as a general description of these positions and their qualification requirements

➤ Discusses the accepted requirements of the postal clerk and carrier positions, with a focus on specific things to know regarding the job

Working for the USPS: Advantages and Benefits

There are several good reasons to be envious of those who work for the USPS (and in turn, these same reasons can motivate you to do well on your qualifying exam). From excellent pay to perks that come with seniority, the USPS offers an attractive compensation and benefit package, wrapped in a exciting career-growth opportunity.

Having a career with the USPS usually means starting as a part-time flexible worker. Part-time flexible (PTF) workers are paid an hourly rate and work only as many hours as the workflow requires. Eventually, part-time flexible workers can move into a full-time position. At that time, the employee will be paid an annual salary.

NOTE City carriers always start as PTF. Craft employees may be technically paid a salary, but all pay is calculated by hours worked. Moving from PTF status to "regular" status does not mean moving from hourly to salary work.

A typical workweek includes 40 hours of work in intervals of eight hours per day. Those who work more than eight hours a day are paid overtime at the rate of one and one-half times the hourly rate. Workers who work between the hours of 6 p.m. and 6 a.m. are paid a night differential, which varies by grade and step.

Compensation for Postal Workers

Compensation of postal workers varies by job title as well as by number of years in service. Employees move between steps after completing a specified amount of time (measured in weeks) in a position. For example, an employee can move from Step A to B after 96 weeks, from Step B to C after another 96 weeks, and then from Step C to D after an additional 44 weeks.

USPS employees are represented by labor unions that include the National Association of Letter Carriers (NALC), the National Postal Mail Handlers Union (NPMHU), the National Rural Letter Carriers Association (NRLCA), and the American Postal Workers Union (APWU). These unions negotiate contracts with the USPS on behalf of their members. These negotiations include, but aren't limited to, establishing pay schedules.

The salary examples in the list here are based on the most recent contracts negotiated by the respective labor unions.

Employees are not required to join the union.

The following represent some sample earnings for full-time and part-time flexible employees working in different USPS jobs:

➤ Joe was just hired to be a mail handler on a part-time flexible schedule. He will earn $14.02 per hour. Currently on Step A, if he stays in this position for 96 weeks, he will move to Step B, where he can earn $16.54 per hour.

➤ Amy is a city carrier. She has just moved into a full-time schedule where her annual salary is $28,047 ($13.48/hour). If she works more than eight hours a day or more than 40 hours a week, she will be paid $20.22 per hour in overtime pay.

➤ Paul is a rural carrier who works part-time flexible hours. He has worked in this position for about four years. He is on Step C. Paul earns $18.44 per hour.

➤ Joanne has been a full-time clerk for a few years. She is a Grade 2 employee at Step D. Her regular annual salary is $30,728. Joanne is considering changing her schedule from a day schedule to a night schedule. If she does this, her hourly rate will increase by $1.07 because of the night differential given to employees who work between the hours of 6 p.m. and 6 a.m.

➤ Gertie has worked as a mail handler for 15 years. Her annual salary is $42,993. When she works more than eight hours a day or more than 40 hours a week, she earns $31.01 per hour, which is one and one-half times her regular hourly rate of $20.67.

In addition to monetary compensation, USPS employees also receive excellent benefits, including

➤ Health insurance (but not dental)

➤ Retirement benefits

➤ Life insurance

➤ Flexible spending accounts

➤ Annual and sick leave

➤ Ten annual paid holidays

The following sections describe these benefits in more detail. Note that these benefits are inclusive to the entire USPS and not just the clerk and carrier position.

Health Insurance: Federal Employee Health Benefits Program (FEHB)

USPS employees and their families are eligible for the FEHB. Available options include

➤ Fee-for-service plans, with or without a PPO (Preferred Provider Organization) option

➤ Plans offering a POS (Point-of-Service) product

➤ Participation in an HMO (Health Maintenance Organization)

In regard to eligibility for the FEHB, "families" are defined as spouses and/or unmarried dependent children under 22 years of age, and unmarried dependent children over 22 years of age if they are incapable of supporting themselves because of physical or mental incapacities that existed before their 22nd birthdays.

Retirement: Federal Employees Retirement System (FERS)

Employees first hired after December 31, 1983 are eligible for participation in the FERS.

Components of the FERS include

➤ Social Security benefits (employee pays Social Security taxes)

➤ Basic Benefit Plan (based on contributions from the employee)

➤ Thrift Savings Plan (a tax-deferred savings plan, similar to a 401[k])

Life Insurance: Federal Employees' Group Life Insurance Program (FEGLI)

Through this program, the USPS pays for basic coverage; however, the employee can purchase additional coverage through payroll deduction. Coverage is available for both the employee and his or her family.

Eligibility definitions and requirements for family are identical to participation in the health benefits program (FEHB). That is, families are defined once again as spouses and/or unmarried dependent children under 22 years of age, and unmarried dependent children over 22 years of age if they are incapable of supporting themselves because of physical or mental incapacities that existed before their 22nd birthdays.

Flexible Spending Accounts

Career employees, after one year of service, may make tax-free contributions that can be used to cover most out-of-pocket health care and dependent day care expenses.

Leave Benefits

USPS employees have available to them several leave benefit options. These options include

➤ *Annual Leave*—Full-time employees earn annual leave. During the first three years of service, 13 days of annual leave are granted. After three years of service, the number of annual leave days increases to 20 days. Finally, after fifteen years of service, this number increases to 26 days of annual leave.

➤ *Sick Leave*—Full-time employees earn 13 days of sick leave per year, as insurance against loss of income due to illness or accident.

➤ *Family and Medical Leave*—The United States Family and Medical Leave Act (FMLA) allows employees to take up to 12 weeks of unpaid leave because of a serious illness to care for a spouse or child with a serious illness, or because of the birth or adoption of a child.

➤ *Court Leave*—Full-time and part-time regular employees may be absent from work without losing pay or accrued leave time, or credit for time or service, to serve on jury duty or to be a witness in a nonofficial capacity on behalf of a state or local government.

➤ *Military Leave*—Authorized absences are granted to full-time, part-time regular, and part-time flexible employees who are members of the National Guard or reservists of the armed forces. These employees are not subject to loss or reduction in pay or credit for time or service.

➤ *Leave Sharing*—Employees may donate earned, unused annual leave to another employee when that employee has exhausted his or her own leave.

➤ *Holiday Leave*—As of this writing, the USPS observes 10 holidays per year. These holidays include

  ➤ Martin Luther King Jr. Day

  ➤ President's Day

  ➤ Memorial Day

  ➤ Independence Day

  ➤ Labor Day

  ➤ Columbus Day

  ➤ Veteran's Day

  ➤ Thanksgiving Day

  ➤ Christmas Day

  ➤ New Year's Day

Working for the Federal Government

Total civilian employment for the U.S. government includes over 2.7 million people, including both U.S. and non-U.S. citizens, as well as those civilians working within the United States and overseas. Specifically, the total civilian employment breaks down as follows:

➤ U.S. citizens: 2,694,520

➤ Non U.S. citizens: 31,428

➤ Total civilian employment: 2,725,948

 An interesting fact: Over 92,000 overseas civilian employees work for the federal government.

Generally speaking, the civilian occupations available within the federal government are divided into two groups: *white-collar occupations* and *blue-collar occupations*. White-collar occupations include such positions as accountants, engineers, lawyers, and clerical workers. Blue-collar occupations include such positions as electricians, carpenters, and machinists.

All occupations—both blue- and white-collar—that exist in private industry also exist in the federal government.

Learning About Federal Job Vacancies

Job vacancies in federal agencies are listed on the USAJOBS Web site: http://usajobs.opm.gov. This database is also available by phone at (703) 724-1850 or TDD (978) 461-8404. Figure 1.1 shows the USAJOBS Web site.

Entrance Requirements

Entrance requirements vary from job to job just as they do in the private sector. A college degree is required for some occupations, whereas technical training is required for others.

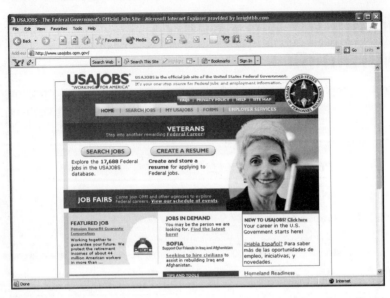

Figure 1.1 The USAJobs Web site allows you to search for current job openings with various federal agencies, as well as post an online resume.

Some jobs require you have only experience or a particular skill. Some—but very few—agencies administer exams. Often, prospective employees must complete an extensive application called the OF-612. They are then rated based on the knowledge, skills, and abilities (KSAs) shown on that application.

More information and direct links for downloading the OF-612 and other forms can be found at http://www.opm.gov/forms/html/of.asp.

Earnings

Federal jobs are classified by *grade*: GS-1 through GS-15. There are also in-grade salary increases called *steps*. Table 1.1 breaks down the different grades and salary ranges associated with the different grades.

Table 1.1 General Pay Schedule for Federal Employment, Effective January 2004	
Grade	**Range**
GS-1	$15,625–19,543
GS-2	$17,568–22,109
GS-3	$19,168–24,919
GS-4	$21,518–27,971

(continued)

Table 1.1 General Pay Schedule for Federal Employment, Effective January 2004 (continued)	
Grade	Range
GS-5	$24,075–31,302
GS-6	$26,836–34,891
GS-7	$29,821–38,767
GS-8	$33,026–42,935
GS-9	$36,478–47,422
GS-10	$40,171–52,222
GS-11	$44,136–57,375
GS-12	$52,899–68,766
GS-13	$62,905–81,778
GS-14	$74,335–96,637
GS-15	$87,439–113,674

Where Do Postal Employees Fit Within the Federal Employment Scheme?

The U.S. Office of Personnel Management website states that, "Postal Service employees serve under excepted appointments. They do not acquire competitive status or reinstatement eligibility for competitive service jobs."

NOTE
In addition to the federal government, many people also work, of course, for state or local governments in various capacities. Pay scales vary from municipality to municipality and employees may or may not be members of unions.

In a nutshell, the USPS has specific requirements (including, of course, Exam 470, in which you are undoubtedly most interested) as well as specific benefits/compensation packages as described in the opening pages of this chapter. Still, you should be familiar with how the USPS fits into the larger federal government employment sector, and understand the differences between working for the USPS and another federal agency. Figure 1.2 highlights the employment section of the USPS website. As you move through your study of this book—and ideally, your career with the USPS—you should visit this site frequently for the latest updates, information, and job/career opportunities available to you.

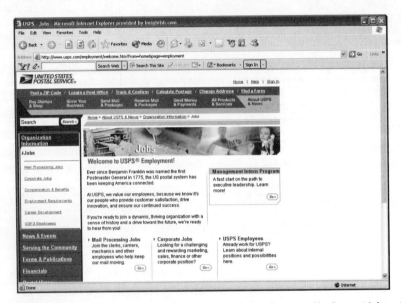

Figure 1.2   The employment section of the USPS Web site offers a wealth of current information, including career opportunities for existing USPS employees.

USPS Positions Requiring Exam 470: Descriptions and Qualifications

All the positions described in the following sections require Exam 470. Additionally, all applicants for the positions described must

➤ Be prepared to take and successfully pass a pre-employment drug screening and physical exam.

➤ Undergo a criminal conviction history check.

➤ Be prepared to document employment history for 10 years, or from 16 years of age.

➤ Be a U.S. citizen or have permanent resident alien status.

➤ Be competent in the English language.

Job training is, in most cases, specific to each position; however, the following apply to all job descriptions covered here:

➤ Most new postal workers receive on-the-job training by experienced workers.

➤ In many situations, classroom instruction is offered on defensive driving and safety.

➤ Workers always receive updated training when new equipment or procedures are introduced.

➤ Workers are expected to maintain the trust of the public by adhering to safety and privacy rules. Additionally, they are expected to maintain the security and reliability of the mail, as demonstrated by their actions, work performance, demeanor, and commitment to a level of excellence required for all USPS positions.

NOTE | Other positions aside from clerk and carrier are described in the following sections, including flat sorting machine operator, mail handler, and mark-up clerk. These positions are described because Exam 470 is a requirement for all of them.

City Carrier: Position Description and Qualifications

Carriers travel predetermined routes to deliver and collect mail, and may cover these routes either by vehicle or on foot. Deliveries can be made to houses, roadside mailboxes, businesses, or apartment buildings.

The carrier position is probably the most recognizable of the USPS positions, both in regard to the visibility of the position (that is, everyone has an image of his mail carrier), as well as the obvious importance of the position. Think about the last time—probably recently—that you were waiting anxiously for some important letter or package to arrive in the mail and you can quickly judge why the position carries with it (sorry, no pun intended) such importance. It's worth noting, too, that carriers must often work in adverse weather conditions. Depending on what part of the country you live in, this can range from sub-zero temperatures to extreme heat (or both)!

General requirements for the city carrier position include the following:

➤ Carriers are responsible for collecting money for COD (cash-on-delivery) fees and obtaining signatures for registered, certified, and insured mail.

➤ At the end of the day, a carrier is required to return to the post office to turn in any cash collected, receipts, and mail gathered during the day.

➤ Carriers must be prepared to answer questions regarding postal regulations or services and provide change-of-address cards or other postal forms.

➤ This job often requires the employee to report to work early in the morning, but the workday often ends early in the afternoon.

Specific job qualifications/application requirements for the city carrier are as follows. Note that, as with all USPS positions, the list includes a minimum age requirement, which ensures that carriers can understand (and protect) the essential security and reliability of mail service:

➤ Postal Service workers must be at least 18 years old.

➤ All applicants must be prepared to take and pass a pre-employment drug screening.

➤ Carriers must be U.S. citizens or have permanent resident alien status.

➤ Males must have registered with the Selective Service by the age of 18.

➤ Applicants must have a basic competency of English.

➤ Carriers must have a valid state driver's license.

➤ Carriers must have a clean driving record and a minimum of two years driving experience.

➤ Qualification is based on successfully passing Exam 470.

➤ Applicants can expect to take a physical exam and might be asked to demonstrate that they can lift sacks of mail that weigh up to 70 pounds.

Postal Clerk: Position Description and Qualifications

Postal clerks are responsible for using automated mail processing equipment to process incoming and outgoing mail in both plant and post office facilities. While perhaps not as potentially physically demanding as the carrier position, the position can be mentally taxing and—depending on the work environment—involve continuous standing, stretching, and reaching.

Fox River Valley Public Libraries
Dundee Library - Check 1
Check your account 847-428-3661
  or online at www.frvpld.info

Items that you checked out

Title: Postal clerk and carrier exams.
ID: 31192012897565
Due: 4/18/2019
Messages:
Item checkout ok.

Total items: 1
Account balance: $0.00
3/28/2019 9:09 AM
Checked out: 3
Ready for pickup: 0
Messages:
Patron status is ok.

A clerk should also expect to sort mail that is not handled by automatic equipment. In addition, clerks sell services at the window of the Post Office and distribute mail to carriers.

 Although automation has replaced many clerk duties, clerks are expected to sort mail according to a scheme. Ability to learn the scheme is essential for any clerk. Operating a machine is of secondary importance (which is why the USPS has Flat Sorting Machine Operators, who are generally paid less than clerks).

Clerks are responsible for selling stamps, money orders, and, of course, mailing envelopes and packages. In the process of this work, they are required to weigh packages and determine that such packages are in satisfactory condition (that is, properly packaged) to be sent through the mail. As a result of this process, clerks also are required to register, certify, and insure mail and answer questions about postage rates, Post Office boxes, and any number of assorted questions that may arise when dealing with the public.

Given such a direct involvement with the public, strong customer service skills are an absolute requirement for this position.

Flat Sorting Machine Operator: Position Description and Qualifications

Flat sorting machine operators are responsible for keying data into a machine, either from memory or by ZIP code, to distribute large, flat pieces of mail. The job requires the ability to maintain close visual attention for extended periods of time. Additionally, because of the nature of the job, the flat sorting machine operator must load and remove mail from machines.

 A flat sorting machine operator may have to work at night or on the weekends.

Given the need for accuracy in sorting mail, close attention to detail and consistent accuracy—especially over long work shifts—is an absolute requirement. Also, in dealing with the time of year (such as during the holidays), tight deadlines, and established quotas, the flat sorting machine operator must be able to effectively deal with stress.

Mail Handler: Position Description and Qualifications

A mail handler, on any given day (or night!), must be prepared to load and unload containers and sacks of mail, often from postal trucks. As part of the general handling process, the employee may sometimes be required to use small forklifts, electric tractors, and/or hand-pushed carts.

Given the strenuous nature of this position, the mail handler must be in good physical condition and be able to lift mail packages/bundles/containers weighing up to 70 pounds. Additionally, mail handlers often work outside on loading docks in all types of weather.

Mark-up Clerk: Position Description and Qualifications

A mark-up clerk's responsibilities include typing change-of-address information into a computer, which in turn is used to generate labels and forward a customer's mail to a new address. Assorted other clerical responsibilities may also be required.

Because the job involves such a high degree of data entry, the mark-up clerk must be very detail oriented, and have the ability to focus on repetitive tasks for long shifts. As condition for employment, the mark-up clerk is required to pass a typing test.

Exam 460: Rural Carrier Associate

The rural carrier associate position is similar in many ways to that of the city carrier, however Exam 460—not 470—is required of all applicants. In addition to achieving a satisfactory score on Exam 460, all applicants must be prepared to take and successfully pass a pre-employment drug screening. Also, all applicants must be U.S. citizens or have permanent resident alien status.

What does a rural carrier associate do? The following lists many of the daily requirements of the job:

➤ Sorts mail into sequence for an assigned route.

➤ Responsible for delivering and collecting all classes of mail (to a maximum of 70 pounds).

➤ Must have a valid driver's license, and a safe driving record (with at least two years of driving experience).

➤ Deliveries are made to a house or roadside mailbox.

➤ Carriers are responsible for collecting money for COD (cash on delivery) fees and obtaining signatures for registered, certified, and insured mail.

➤ At the end of each day, the carrier is expected to return to the Post Office to turn in any cash collected, receipts, and mail gathered during the day.

➤ The job often requires the employee to report to work early in the morning, but the workday often ends early in the afternoon.

Unlike the city carrier position, the rural carrier must often be able to provide other postal services to their customers. For example, a rural carrier is often asked to sell stamps and money orders, or to register, certify, and insure mail (responsibilities that are more inline with those of a postal clerk). Generally speaking, rural carriers might be asked to provide more information/forms (for example, change of address cards) to their customers than their city carrier counterparts, although both types of carrier may certainly be required to address these and other customer service requests. Finally, rural carriers should expect to use their own automobiles for their work.

Postal Workers: General Things to Know

There are several general issues you should be aware of in regard to many of the positions described in this chapter. Although the following list is not meant to be exhaustive, it does highlight several important elements of working for the USPS, the availability of jobs, specific and recommended skill sets, and so on:

➤ Part of the job of both clerks and carriers is to answer questions and field complaints—employees are expected to be courteous and pleasant at all times.

➤ There is a lot of competition for positions as clerks and carriers, so expect to work your way up to these jobs. The typical waiting period is 1–2 years or more after passing the exam.

People who take the exam are put on a list in the order of their exam scores. The higher the score, the sooner one will be interviewed for a job. Because most Post Offices give the exam only every 2–4 years, it is possible to wait on the list for years before being called. The Postal Service does have a program where they encourage clerks and other craft employees to "change crafts"; that is, become carriers. They do so because automated processes require fewer human employees. However, clerk, mail handler, and flat sorting machine operator positions are not just "waiting rooms" for people to become carriers and therefore should not be thought of as such.

➤ A good memory and ability to read and retain information quickly is essential.

➤ Good interpersonal skills are very important because postal workers tend to work closely with one another.

➤ Postal workers usually begin their careers as part-time or flexible employees and attain full-time employment in order of seniority, as vacancies occur.

➤ Carriers can anticipate getting preferred routes as seniority increases. This applies to craft employees who "bid" on jobs (and are awarded according to seniority) as well.

➤ Postal workers fall into one of four categories: casual, part-time flexible, part-time regular, or full-time. Casual employees are hired for 90 days, during the busiest times, to help with processing and delivering mail. Part-time flexible employees are called upon as the need arises; they don't have permanent hours. Part-time regular workers have regularly scheduled hours that equal less than 40 hours per week. Full-time employees work 40 hours per week.

Casual positions are not career positions and do not lead to career positions. Anyone can become a casual employee for 90 days; however, permanent employment always depends on your test score, which is yet another (big!) reason to study the material presented in this book!

460/470 Postal Carrier and Clerk Pre-Test

If you read through the self-assessment at the beginning of this book, you might have already formed some ideas about what you think your strengths and weaknesses are at this point—in regard to both your test-taking ability and specifically the 460/470 exam. Although the self-assessment presented you with some general questions, it also asked you to consider various aptitudes and skill sets that are being tested with this exam. This chapter—and the mock exam it contains—will help you continue that self-assessment, so you can better target areas for improvement.

Why Take the Mock Exam?

Many professional training programs begin with a more detailed self-assessment. This is sometimes called a "pre-test." Given this is only the second chapter in the book, why are we hitting you already with a test and why should you take time to complete it now before reading further? By taking the pre-test now, you will

➤ *Get an early snapshot of your strengths and weaknesses*—As we'll reiterate in this book, the 460/470 exam is not going to ask you to write an essay on the history of western civilization or to solve a complex mathematical problem. Rather, this exam is designed to test your aptitude in a variety of areas (memory, following oral instructions, logic) as well as your ability to perform under pressure and to work quickly and efficiently (something all exams test, in one fashion or another). You might find you have a strong aptitude for all the question types on the exam; on the other hand, you may really struggle with each one. More than likely, you'll fall somewhere in the middle: That is, you'll do very well on one section, but have some difficulty with another. Regardless of how well you do, remember that this is only a pre-test, and that its sole purpose is to introduce you to the exam question format and, ideally, put you at ease with the concept of taking an exam. This is especially true if it's been a while since you've been asked to take a test.

➤ *Develop a sense of the test format*—The 460/470 exam is not anything terribly unique in regard to the format of its questions. You are asked to answer different sets of question types, and are asked to do so in a limited amount of time. What is unique about this exam, however, is that, again, it is primarily an aptitude test concerning your ability to memorize, follow instructions, and think logically. The questions, in and of themselves, are not difficult. Indeed, in many cases, the difficulty is simply staying focused on the task at hand: You have lots of easy questions to answer in a very short period of time. (This pressure can lend those questions a certain degree of difficulty, but that's a subject left for discussion in Chapter 3, "General Test-Taking Strategies.") At any rate, the more you practice and become familiar with how this exam is put together, the higher the score you can expect to achieve.

What Is being Tested on the Pre-Test?

The 460/470 exam consists of four major question types, described in the following list. You are going to have plenty of opportunity to learn about and practice these different question types as you focus on them individually (Chapters 4–11), as well as in four full-length practice exams (Chapters 13–20).

The four question types are as follows:

➤ *Address Checking*—This question type tests your ability to compare two different addresses and determine whether they are exactly alike, or are different in *any* way. Often, the differences between the two addresses will be very minor, so you need to pay very close attention. The challenging part about this question type is that you have to compare nearly a hundred pairs of addresses in a very short period of time, so you need to work quickly.

➤ *Memory for Addresses*—For this question type, you need to memorize a block of address information, then—drawing on your memory—determine where in that block a specific address would be placed. The key focus of this question type is to test your memory by seeing how quickly you can memorize information and then apply it.

➤ *Number Series*—This is probably the question type that gives the largest number of test takers the most concern. In reality, however, this just might be the easiest if you take the time to sort through what the question is asking you and apply some fairly straightforward critical thinking and logic. I'm not going to say much more about this question type because, as I wrote earlier, I don't want you to be overly nervous or concerned about your abilities (or your perceived lack thereof) to answer this question type.

➤ *Following Oral Instructions*—Perhaps the most unique question type on the exam is the Following Oral Instructions question. For this section of the exam, instructions will be read to you, and in turn you will need to closely follow these instructions to answer the questions correctly. Testing your ability to listen and pay attention is a key aspect of this question type.

Again, the point of this mock exam is not to trick you with question formats you're not comfortable with. Rather, the idea with presenting you with an exam right off the bat is to see how well you do with these question formats before you've had a chance to develop any preconceived ideas about how well you think you'll do on them.

What do I mean by that? Not to give away too much information here, but many people will get nervous when they really start to dig in to the number series questions because they hear the word "number" and they think "mathematics." No offense intended to all you math wizards out there, but for many people math is not their strongest subject. So, if you take the mock exam now—before you've had a chance to discover how "awful" the number series questions really are—you might find you achieve a decent score on this section of the exam. And what does that mean? This is a general aptitude test and you might just have more "general aptitude" than you think, so don't let your nerves (or preconceived notions of what you think you can't do) get in the way of your natural abilities.

Preparing for the Mock Exam

Although we've tried to prepare this mock exam so it resembles an actual real-world test, you should be aware of a few critical differences:

➤ First, the "flow" of this mock exam will be interrupted by explanatory/other text that you won't see on the real exam. We've done this to provide some additional introduction and guidance, as well as provide a more detailed explanation of each answer key.

➤ Second, you will see fewer questions here than you will on an actual exam. Although we could have hit you with a full-length exam, the primary goal of the mock exam is not so much to mimic an actual test question for question, but rather give you a "cold start" introduction to the type and format of the questions. For those of you who are worried that you aren't being presented with enough questions (and thus, practice), you can put those fears to rest: This book is chock full of practice questions, quizzes, and full-length exams!

➤ Finally, you will be able to work through this mock exam at a more leisurely pace than an actual test. Although we'll give you some general time parameters in which to work, you will have considerably more time to complete each section than you will on the real exam.

Before you begin the mock exam, you'll need to gather a few things. Specifically, you will need

➤ The answer sheet for this pre-test, which is included at the back of the book.

➤ A few pencils.

➤ A quiet room to work.

➤ For the "Following Oral Instructions" section, you'll need a partner to read you the instructions. Although it's possible to read them yourself, you won't get the same necessary introductory experience to this specific question format.

Finding a quiet place to study and work through this book is a critical component to your success, not just for this mock exam but for all the preparation that you do. If you lead a hectic life finding a quiet place to study—even for a short period of time—can prove to be one of the more challenging aspects of self-study. But, it is essential. Although there are people who claim they can study with the television or radio blaring, those who really can are few and far between. Turn off the tube, and turn down the tunes to help you concentrate and focus on what you are studying.

A quick note regarding how to work through this mock exam: You can either work through the entire set of questions in one sitting, or you can visit each section individually over the course of multiple sessions. If you are looking to get an early (and more complete) introduction to the actual testing environment, working through the entire mock exam in one session might be a good idea. However, the point is to introduce you to the question types and help you better assess your abilities. As you move into the chapters dealing with each specific question type, you can then know where to focus.

We've probably said too much already in regard to the mock exam, so the only thing left to do is get started!

Section One: Address Checking

This section of the exam tests your ability to compare two sets of addresses, to determine whether they are exactly alike or different.

Instructions:

For each pair of addresses, compare to determine whether they are exactly alike or different (in even the slightest way). If they are exactly alike, write "A" in the space on your answer sheet for that question. If they are different in any way, mark a "D" for that answer.

An answer key follows the questions.

For this and all other sections of the mock exam, the amount of time you have to complete each section is considerably more than on an actual exam. However, that being said, you should still try to move through these questions as quickly as possible because this will be a major requirement on the actual exam.

Ready? Allow yourself two minutes to read the following addresses and determine whether they are alike or different.

1.	Birmingham, AL 42251	Birmingham, AL 42251
2.	5726 Lowell Ave	5276 Lowell Ave
3.	286 E 26th Street	286 E 86th Street
4.	9656 Forest Pkwy	9656 Forest Pkwy
5.	37 Deering Rd	37 Deering St
6.	Denver, CO 30335	Denver, CO 30035
7.	635 Poplar Ln	635 Poplar Ln
8.	9787 Lawrence Ct	9787 Lawrence Ct
9.	2002 Senate	202 W Senate
10.	547 Oak St	547 Oak St
11.	36 Fullerton Dr	36 Farmington Dr
12.	54557 Apple Ave	54557 Apple Ave
13.	Torrence, CA 22424	Torrence, CA 24224
14.	6555 Pine St	6655 Pine St
15.	968 Cinnamon Ln	968 Cinnamon Ln
16.	4581 S Broadway	4581 E Broadway
17.	6458 Third St	6458 Third St
18.	8558 Temple Ave	8585 Temple Ave
19.	2584 State Street	2584 State Street
20.	Indianapolis, IN 46865	Indianapolis, IN 46865

Answer Key for Address Checking

Use the following answer key to determine how well you did. See Chapters 4 and 8 for more specific information on this question type.

Your score on this section is determined by the number of questions you answer correctly minus the number of questions you answer incorrectly.

1.	A	11.	D
2.	D	12.	A
3.	D	13.	D
4.	A	14.	D
5.	D	15.	A
6.	D	16.	D
7.	A	17.	A
8.	A	18.	D
9.	D	19.	A
10.	A	20.	A

Section Two: Memory for Addresses

The Memory for Addresses question type asks you to first memorize a set of information, and then answer a set of questions based on what you've been able to memorize.

Instructions:

There are two specific aspects to working with this section of the exam:

➤ First, you will have time to memorize the information grid you'll need to use before you have to answer the questions.

➤ After you've memorized the grid, you will be presented with the actual questions you'll need to answer.

 On an actual exam, you'll be given some additional practice exercises (not counted toward your score) to help you memorize the information grid. Be sure to see Chapter 5 for specific, detailed information about this question type, as well as strategies/tips/techniques for better approaching this section.

For this mock exam, you should do the following:

1. Give yourself three minutes to memorize the information grid.

2. After that time has expired, give yourself another three minutes to answer the questions. Each question presents you with a segment of an address that fits into one of the columns (lettered A–E) in the information grid. The challenge with this question type is that you can't refer back to the information grid when answering the questions! In other words, the question type lives up to its name in that you literally have to memorize the information and then answer the questions.

 To best assess your abilities with this type of question, it is imperative that you do *not* refer back to the information grid when answering the questions. On the actual exam you won't be allowed to refer back to the grid, so you shouldn't do it with this mock exam, either.

An answer key follows the questions.

Ready? Allow yourself three minutes to memorize—to the best of your ability—the following information grid. When you are finished, flip to the next page and give yourself an additional three minutes to answer the questions presented by noting on your answer sheet the column in which the address fragment would be placed. Again, do *not* refer back to the information grid as you answer the questions.

A	B	C	D	E
1000-1499 Oak	1500-2099 Oak	2100-2299 Oak	8300-8499 Oak	4500-4699 Oak
Jennings	Farnsworth	Deering	Fountain	Sirus
2300-2599 Elm	2600-2899 Elm	2900-3099 Elm	6500-6799 Elm	4400-4599 Elm
Flint	Maple	Long	Dalbert	Woodlawn
3600-3799 Bethel	3800-4099 Bethel	1200-1499 Bethel	9300-9499 Bethel	5200-5299 Bethel

STOP! As you now give yourself three minutes to answer the following questions, do NOT refer back to the information grid.

1. Flint
2. 4400-4699 Elm
3. 3800-4099 Bethel
4. Sirus
5. 6500-6799 Elm
6. 1200-1499 Bethel
7. 1000-1499 Oak
8. 2300-2599 Elm
9. Woodlawn
10. 2900-3099 Elm
11. 9300-9499 Bethel
12. Jennings
13. 2600-2899 Elm
14. Dalbert
15. 2100-2299 Oak
16. 3800-4099 Bethel
17. 2300-2599 Elm
18. Sirus
19. 2600-2899 Elm
20. 5200-5299 Bethel

Answer Key for Memory for Addresses

Use the following answer key to determine how well you did. See Chapters 5 and 9 for more specific information on this question type.

 Scoring for this section is a little different compared to the others: For every question you answer incorrectly, 1/4 point is deducted from your total score.

1. A	
2. E	
3. B	
4. E	
5. D	
6. C	
7. A	
8. A	
9. E	
10. C	
11. D	
12. A	
13. B	
14. D	
15. C	
16. B	
17. A	
18. E	
19. B	
20. E	

Section Three: Number Series

Ah, the dreaded number series—your time has come, as they say.

Enough of the joking. In reality, there is absolutely nothing to be afraid of or nervous about when working with these questions, if you can look past the somewhat intimidating title of this question type.

Instructions:

You should give yourself 10 minutes to work through the questions. Your task is simple: For each question, you are given four answer choices. The correct answer represents the pair of numbers that would follow next in the number series. The challenge with this question type is determining the pattern that is being utilized to generate the number series. If you can identify that pattern, you can answer the question correctly.

 There are specific strategies you can use in working through this type of question. These strategies are discussed in later chapters.

Ready? Allow yourself 10 minutes to answer the following 12 questions.

1. 3 8 13 18 23 28 33 __ __
   - ❏ A. 38 43
   - ❏ B. 37 45
   - ❏ C. 39 42
   - ❏ D. 36 42

2. 63 56 49 42 35 28 21 __ __
   - ❏ A. 15 7
   - ❏ B. 11 1
   - ❏ C. 29 32
   - ❏ D. 14 7

3. 1 2 4 2 16 2 64 __ __
   - ❏ A. 128 256
   - ❏ B. 2 128
   - ❏ C. 2 256
   - ❏ D. 128 256

4. 4 5 45 6 7 67 8 __ __
 - ❑ A. 9 10
 - ❑ B. 9 89
 - ❑ C. 68 89
 - ❑ D. 68 9

5. 89 88 87 86 85 84 83 __ __
 - ❑ A. 81 82
 - ❑ B. 82 81
 - ❑ C. 84 85
 - ❑ D. 80 79

6. 11056 11059 11062 11065 11068 11071 11074 _____ _____
 - ❑ A. 11077 11080
 - ❑ B. 11075 11076
 - ❑ C. 11077 11078
 - ❑ D. 11078 11079

7. 12 24 36 48 60 72 84 __ __
 - ❑ A. 90 92
 - ❑ B. 100 109
 - ❑ C. 96 108
 - ❑ D. 94 104

8. 1 2 4 8 10 20 22 __ __
 - ❑ A. 44 46
 - ❑ B. 24 48
 - ❑ C. 23 23
 - ❑ D. 45 46

9. 256 128 64 32 16 8 4 __ __
 - ❑ A. 3 2
 - ❑ B. 2 1
 - ❑ C. 8 3
 - ❑ D. 4 2

10. 11 8 22 9 33 10 44 __ __
 - ❑ A. 22 33
 - ❑ B. 46 48
 - ❑ C. 54 22
 - ❑ D. 11 55

11. 3 2 7 12 13 4 103 22
   - ❏ A. 55 40
   - ❏ B. 33 55
   - ❏ C. 66 24
   - ❏ D. 30 43

12. 92 88 86 81 79 73 71 __ __
   - ❏ A. 72 74
   - ❏ B. 69 60
   - ❏ C. 64 62
   - ❏ D. 70 69

Answer Key for Number Series

Use the following answer key to determine how well you did. See Chapters 6 and 10 for more specific information on this question type.

 NOTE

Scoring for the Number Series question type is very simple: You get points only for the questions you answer correctly. This is a question type where guessing is a good idea if you either don't have a clue as to what the answer might be or you are running out of time and want to mark at least something down for each question.

1. **A**—The numbers in this series increase by 5, for example, 3+5=8, 8+5=13.

2. **D**—The numbers in this series decrease by 7, for example, 63–7=56, 56–7=49.

3. **C**—There are two alternating patterns at play here: Every other number, beginning with the first one, is multiplied by 4, for example, 1×4=4, 4×4=16; the number in between those numbers is always a 2.

4. **B**—There are two alternating patterns: The first counts up by one beginning with 4, for example, 4 5 6 7; every third number puts together the two numbers that precede it to make a new number, for example, 4 5 45.

5. **B**—This is a simple pattern that counts down by 1.

6. **A**—The numbers in this pattern increase by 3, for example, 11056+3=11059, 11059+3=11062.

7. **C**—The numbers in this series increase by 12, for example, 12+12=24, 24+12+36.

8. **A**—The pattern here is ×2 +2, for example, 1×2=2, 2+2=4, 4×2=8, 8+2=10.

9. **B**—Divide each number by 2 to get the next number in the series, for example, 256÷2=128, 128÷2=64.

10. **D**—There are two alternating patterns: The first one keeps increasing by 11, for example, 11+11=22, 22+11=33; the alternating pattern increases by 1, for example, 8+1=9, 9+1=10.

11. **A**—In this pattern even numbers alternate with odd numbers, beginning with an odd number, for example, 3 2 7 12.

12. **C**—There are two alternating patterns in this series: In the first pattern the differences between the numbers increase by 1; in the second pattern the difference is always –2, for example, 92–4=88, 88–2=86, 86–5=81, 81–2=79, 79–6=73.

Section Four: Following Oral Instructions

The Following Oral Instructions section is a unique section of the exam, in that it will require you to listen to an examiner who reads you instructions for answering the questions.

As was noted at the beginning of this chapter, you'll need someone to help you with this portion of the mock exam. This person needs to "role play" the test examiner and read you the necessary information for answering the questions.

1. Refer to the following information to work through this section of the exam. The questions will refer to this information as your "worksheet":

    1. 20 4 15 2 8

    2. 9:30 1:20 4:50 12:00 6:30

    3. RED BLUE ORANGE GREEN YELLOW

    4. 1 2 3 5 7

    5. A B E F G H

    6. 1:00 2:00 7:00 11:00 4:00

    7. EAST WEST NORTH SOUTH

    8. 98 99 55 22 44

    9. LEFT RIGHT MIDDLE UP DOWN

    10. A B A B A B A C A C A C

2. Hand the book to your partner who will be reading the instructions to you.

3. Remind your partner to read each question only one time.

TO THE PERSON READING THE INSTRUCTIONS: You should read quickly and clearly. You do not have to read the words in parenthesis; these have been provided for your guidance in allowing the test taker time to think about/answer each question.

READ THE FOLLOWING TO THE TEST TAKER: You need to mark your answer sheet according to the specific instructions I read to you. I'll pause for a few seconds after each instruction, so you have time to mark your answer sheet.

The test begins now.

➤ **Look at line 1 of the worksheet (pause slightly).** Draw a line under the fourth number in the list. Now, on your answer sheet, darken the oval for the letter of the alphabet for which this number corresponds (pause five seconds).

➤ **Look at line 2 of the worksheet (pause slightly).** Draw a line under the first time and last time. Subtract the last time from the first time to get a whole number. For question #3 on your answer sheet, darken the oval for the letter of the alphabet for which this number corresponds (pause five seconds).

➤ **Look at line 2 of your answer sheet (pause slightly).** Darken the oval for this same letter in the space for question #2 on your answer sheet (pause five seconds).

➤ **Look at line 3 of the worksheet (pause slightly).** If the word "orange" is the second color listed, darken the "A" oval for question #4 of your answer sheet. If the word "orange" is not the second color, darken the "B" oval for question #4 on your answer sheet (pause five seconds).

➤ **Look at line 4 of the worksheet (pause slightly).** Find the even number listed and, for question #5 on your answer sheet, darken the oval for the letter of the alphabet to which this number corresponds (pause five seconds).

➤ **Look at line 5 of the worksheet (pause slightly).** Find the letter of the alphabet you answered for answer #5, and darken this same oval in the space for question #6 on your answer sheet (pause five seconds).

➤ **Look at line 6 of the worksheet (pause slightly).** Darken the "c" oval in the space for question #7 on your answer sheet (pause five seconds).

➤ **Look at line 7 of the worksheet (pause slightly).** Draw a line under the word "North" and write the number 3 next to it. Now, look at line 8 of your answer sheet. Subtract the first number listed from the second, then add the number you come up with to the number you wrote down next to the word "North" on line 7 of your answer sheet. Finally, darken the oval for the letter of the alphabet to which the position of this number corresponds in the space for question #8 (pause 10 seconds).

➤ **Look at line 9 of the worksheet (pause slightly).** Draw a line under the word "up," and then draw another line under the word "down." Subtract the number position of the word "up" from that of "down," and subtract that number from 5. Finally, darken the oval for the letter of the alphabet to which the position of this number corresponds in the space for question #9 on your answer sheet (pause 10 seconds).

➤ **Look at line 10 of the worksheet (pause slightly).** Draw a line under each letter "C," and then count the number of lines you draw. Add this number to 6, and then subtract 8. Finally, darken the oval for the letter of the alphabet to which this number's position corresponds in the space for question #10 on your answer sheet (pause 10 seconds).

Answer Key for Following Oral Instructions

Use the following answer key to grade and evaluate how well you did on the practice test:

1. B	2. C	3. C	4. B	5. B
6. B	7. C	8. D	9. A	10. A

NOTE

Scoring for the Following Oral Instructions question type is based on the number of questions you answer correctly.

Mock Exam Wrap-Up: Assessing Your Score

Congratulations (yes, congratulations are definitely in order)! You've taken a brave and bold step in working through a mock exam this early in your test preparation process.

How did you do? If you scored very high in one or more of the question areas, then you should most definitely be encouraged. In fact, you might have a "natural ability" with the skills tested in one or more sections of the exam. That confidence should enable you to relax a bit and focus on the other areas where you didn't do as well.

But even if you scored low (or didn't score as high as you thought you would) on one or all of the sections, that is no reason to be disheartened. Again, the whole point of the mock exam is to give you a flavor for what the actual exam will be like in terms of the format of the questions. Although the number of questions in this mock exam are not indicative of a full-length exam, you should have still received an idea of what it will be like to "work under pressure" (that is, only having a limited amount of time to answer each section).

You should refer back to your score on this mock exam as you work through each of the chapters that deals specifically with each of the question types. In Chapters 4–11, each question type is given two chapters: First, a chapter generally describes the question type and offers strategies/tips/techniques for how best to address it, and then another chapter offers a practice exam for just that question type. Specifically:

➤ Chapters 4 and 8 cover Address Checking

➤ Chapters 5 and 9 cover Memory for Addresses

➤ Chapters 6 and 10 cover Number Series

➤ Chapters 7 and 11 cover Following Oral Instructions

Additionally, Chapter 3 provides general test-taking strategies and Chapter 12 offers you a "real world" case study in preparing for the actual day of the test.

General Test-Taking Strategies

Terms You'll Need to Understand

✓ Planning
✓ Preparation
✓ Focus
✓ Test Anxiety

Concepts/Techniques You'll Need to Master

✓ Parts to the test-taking strategy
✓ Getting a good night's sleep
✓ Knowing your route to the test center
✓ Arriving early to the test center
✓ Listening to and reading instructions carefully
✓ Marking your answers correctly
✓ Avoiding cheating (or the appearance of cheating)
✓ Paying attention and staying focused
✓ Working as quickly and accurately as possible
✓ Checking your answers
✓ Avoiding test anxiety

No matter how seasoned of a test taker you happen to be, there is no getting around the fact that even the best "cool and collected" test takers can get nervous. Actually, this can be to your advantage because (sometimes) a little case of the nerves can keep you alert and at the top of your test-taking game. On the other hand, if you get too inside your own head (so to speak), it can distract from your ability to do your best, and all of the preparation and studying you have done can go out the window.

The good news is that you can keep your anxiety in check. The fact that you are reading this book, and taking the time to prepare is going to really help you, perhaps more than you are aware: The bottom line is that if you take the time to prepare, you'll be…well…prepared and far less likely to let your nerves get the better of you.

This chapter gives you not only some practical tips on how to beat test anxiety, but also good advice on general test-taking strategies. It's our bet that as you read this chapter, you'll find yourself saying, "Gee, I never considered that as a test-taking tip!" (for example, knowing the route you are going to take to the testing center). It's also our bet you'll say to yourself, "Well, yeah, now that they mention it, that is a really good point!" So we'll give you some good test-taking pointers, and you can in turn use this chapter as you read further into the book to calm any nagging fears or concerns that you aren't a good test-taker. Indeed, within every person lies a great test-taker just waiting to come out. This chapter can put you in touch with that person!

A General Test-Taking Strategy

Some people think that the actual test day is the only real part of the test-taking process. In reality, of course (as you probably already know because you are reading this book) it is a two-step process, with preparation being just as important as actually taking the test.

But what does "test preparation" really entail? The obvious is understanding the exam questions and taking practice exams. But there are also some other very important elements to test preparation that go far beyond the work you'll do with the practice exercises that compose most of this book.

What are these elements? They vary from person to person, but generally speaking, we can call them the "night before the test" preparations, and they consist of such things as getting a good night's sleep and being sure you have your route mapped out to the testing center (nothing like getting lost the morning of the exam to really get those nerves hopping)! We're going to talk quite a bit about these special preparations in this chapter, through the introduction of your fictitious (but realistic) "test-taking partner," Bill Roberts.

The second component of the test-taking process is, of course, taking the test. You'll have done lots of great preparation heading into the test, but you aren't going to be able to refer to your notes (or this book, for that matter). That said, there are several tips and tricks you can use to keep your mind focused, and to help you achieve the highest score. Some of these are obvious (for example, don't cheat), whereas some might seem obvious on the surface (for example, listen to and read directions carefully), but they are in fact more complicated than they might otherwise seem. We take a look at all of these elements in this chapter as well.

Test-Taking Process, Part I: The Night Before the Exam

Although we're referring to this step of the process as "the night before the exam," it actually involves more preparation than waiting until the night before. You should be thinking of these things the night before the exam, but if you really want to be prepared, you need to consider them well in advance of that night, as well. After all, you'll want to try and relax as much as you can the night before the exam, and not wait until the last minute to gather your registration materials, find a babysitter for the kids, and so on.

Okay, what are these "night before the exam" tips? We want to focus on a few in the following sections.

Take some time to think about the following tips in regard to your specific situation. Everyone is different, and, that being the case, not everyone needs eight hours of sleep a night. Still, generally speaking, the following tips apply to most people in the position of taking of a major test.

Night Before the Exam: Get a Good Night's Sleep

You may recall (I know I do) the "all-nighters" you pulled in high school or college, waiting until the last minute to study for a big exam and then literally staying up all night. And you might fondly recall these all-night cram sessions, as they were (at least as I remember them) sometimes a lot of fun: You could study with friends, and laugh about your situation as much as you did any actual studying.

But at the risk of sounding melodramatic, those are probably bygone days of youth. The exam you are studying for is not for a grade, but rather will have a serious impact on your career. In other words, it is not something to be taken lightly, and not something to wait until the last minute to study for.

So although not everyone needs eight hours of sleep a night, the vast majority of people need at least six hours of sleep to really feel alert. Moreover, studies have shown that your ability to retain what you study is not going to be significantly aided by staying up all night and trying to cram everything in at the last minute. In fact, new research suggests that sleep helps you "sort out" what you have learned so that if you get your studying done early and get a good night's sleep you will do much better on the exam than you will if you pull the infamous "all nighter." In fact, this type of studying, in addition to making you tired, might actually be detrimental to your success on the test. Taking the time to prepare in advance of the night before the exam, then using the night to relax (a bit of advice we're going to repeat many times in this chapter) is your best bet for doing well. Final words on the subject: Don't feel compelled to go to bed at sundown, but at the same time don't stay up for the late-late movie.

Night Before the Exam: Know Your Route to the Test Center

As we mentioned at the beginning of the chapter, this might be one of those pieces of advice where you say to yourself, "Wow, that is a really good point." And if you are saying that as you read this, then our purpose for including this information has been served: that is, you are thinking about it now, rather than waiting until the last minute!

I remember when I took the graduate record exam (GRE), which is the standard test everyone takes as part of the application process for graduate school. I was set to take the exam in my hometown of Indianapolis, and I was sure (or so I thought) of the exact route I was going to take to get to the testing center. Well, if you aren't familiar with the Midwest, Indianapolis is a reasonably large city, and even if you grew up there, many places—although you *think* you know where they are—prove to be just a little more elusive when you get in the car and try and drive to them. As it turned out, I fell victim to not thinking about how I would get to the test center, and while I wasn't late, I got there with only 10 minutes to spare instead of my planned 30. I also managed to dump a large McDonald's coffee in my lap that morning, as well as slipping and sliding in some unexpected (and not fore-casted) bad weather.

There wasn't much I could do about the coffee , but the two other things—knowing where I was going and planning for the unexpected—were defi-nitely issues I should have considered. Although you probably don't need to have maps and charts for the route you are going to take to the testing cen-ter, it might be a good idea to do a pre-test "drive-by" to ensure you not only know how to get to the test center, but have considered other issues as well: Is there free parking? Are there convenience stores nearby where you can grab some coffee? These are just a few things to keep in mind as you plan your route.

 Don't forget about the weather, especially if you live in an area of the country that is prone to unpredictable weather (like the Midwest)! Know the forecast for the morn-ing of the exam so that if bad weather is expected you can build this into your planned travel time to the test center.

The Night Before the Exam: Plan to Arrive Early

Unlike the days you might have spent camping out in front of the box office window for front-row seats to your favorite concert, chances are quite good you won't need to pitch a tent in front of the testing center the night before the exam.

All kidding aside, though, getting to the test center early can go a long way toward helping calm your nerves and generally putting you more at ease with the actual test-taking process. Consider the following issues that, although perhaps not parts of the actual test-taking process, can nevertheless go a long way in helping you to relax prior to the test:

➤ *Find a good parking spot*—Parking will probably not be an issue at the testing center, but this is not a certainty. Arriving at the test center early gives you a better chance of finding a good spot. Distant parking isn't an issue on a nice spring morning, but you don't want to be in the position of having to walk a country mile in a torrential downpour or in bone-chilling cold.

➤ *Hit the restroom*—An obvious one, but something to definitely keep in mind. When nature calls, it's amazing how that call can very quickly become the single most important thing on your mind. Don't let this

happen to you, especially when you're taking a test as potentially important to your career as this one.

➤ *Take a few deep breaths…and relax*—If you can take care of the previous
items in this list and still have several minutes before the exam is scheduled to start, you then will have time for another critical aspect of your
test preparation, and that is taking a few relaxing deep breaths. Or, you
can take a walk around the testing center, or call your spouse/significant
other on your cell phone for a last-minute vote of confidence. (Use this
tip in moderation, though—sometimes these conversations can end up
making you *more* nervous.) The simple point here is that having a few
extra minutes to spare will serve you well if, for whatever reason, you
need a few extra minutes!

Test-Taking Process, Part II: Taking the Test

Imagine yourself on the morning of the test. You've followed all the tips in
the previous section, and you are rested, have made it to the testing center
with no problem, have found a good parking space, and had a few minutes to
spare to relax. And, because you've read this book, you are well prepared for
the types of questions you are going to see.

You are, in a nutshell, very well prepared.

So how do you make sure all this preparation doesn't go out the window
when the actual test begins? Again, every test-taker is going to react differently, based on previous experiences with tests of this nature, as well as general personality. Still, there are—just as with the night before the exam—
some good "taking the test" tips you can follow. The following sections talk
about those very tips.

Taking the Test: Listening and Reading Carefully

After working through this book, you will be very familiar with the types of
questions asked of you on the exam. That being the case, you still need to
take time to carefully read the instructions for each section, and for the "listening to directions" component of the exam, to be sure to listen carefully to
the instructions being read to you. Although you might be tempted to skip

over the instructions out of familiarity, don't! Take your time for this all-important component of the exam.

Taking the Test: Marking Your Answers Correctly

Knowing the right answer is one thing; making sure you mark it correctly on your answer sheet can be just as important. This is one of those little tips that can save you a lot of time, frustration, and potentially panic: Be sure you are marking the answer sheet for the question you are being asked (that is, don't mark an answer for question #5, when in reality you are answering question #4). Also, be sure you fill in your answer completely to avoid any confusion or scoring errors.

Taking the Test: Don't Cheat

An obvious tip, right? You obviously are not going to cheat outright on your exam, but don't put yourself in the position where it appears you are cheating when in reality you are not. Put simply, don't let your eyes wander or do anything that would make it appear in any way that you are trying to look at another test taker's answer sheet. You don't want to be placed in a situation where you have to defend yourself against a charge of cheating. Best case, this takes away previous test-taking time. Worse case, your score is cancelled (and your career options potentially seriously jeopardized).

Taking the Test: Pay Attention

Similar to being sure you listen to and read instructions carefully, avoid letting your mind wander to anything other than the task at hand, which is taking the test and scoring as high as possible. Although some general "outside thoughts" are normal (thinking about how great it will be when the test is complete), don't dwell on these things; they will again waste your time and otherwise distract you from the test itself.

By following the advice in the "Night Before the Exam" sections, you will fare much better in many of these "Taking the Test" areas, especially when it comes to paying attention and staying focused on the task at hand.

Taking the Test: Focus on One Question at a Time

You may be tempted to read ahead and try to answer more than question at a time. Or you may fall victim to becoming overwhelmed by the number of questions and start to read ahead (and thus start to panic) as you think to yourself, "There is no way I can answer all these questions." Again, take a few deep breaths and keep your mind focused on the question at hand. The test is designed so that you have time to answer all the questions, so don't feel you have to read ahead to finish on time.

Taking the Test: Work As Quickly and Accurately As You Can

Although you shouldn't rush your answers, you shouldn't—on the other hand—take an inordinate amount of time on each question. You do need to work quickly, but there is a difference between this approach and rushing. If you follow the tips in this section, including listening carefully and following directions, you should be able to work quickly but at the same time feel confident you are giving each question a thorough read.

Taking the Test: Check Your Answers

This final tip is one that should be used with extreme caution. It is good (indeed, great!) to finish each section of the test with time to spare, but don't put yourself in the position where you begin to second-guess yourself and, as a result, start changing all your answers. If you relax, listen/read carefully, and work quickly (but accurately), there is no reason why you should make so many mistakes the first time through the questions that you would need (or want to) go back and make significant changes to several questions. Again, it's a great idea to do some "spot checking" of your answers, but don't go overboard with this, and don't feel overly concerned if you have time to check only a few of your answers, and not all of them.

Overcoming Test Anxiety

We've talked a lot in this chapter about not falling victim to a case of the nerves, or becoming so anxious/nervous that you can't utilize—to your maximum potential—all the great preparation and work you've put into studying for the test.

Although there is no guarantee you won't be nervous, remember again that a little nervousness can be a good thing: It can keep you focused on the task at hand. Still, consider the following suggestions for overcoming test anxiety:

➤ *The best defense is a good offense*—This is especially true when it comes to dealing with text anxiety. Make sure you are well prepared for the test. Study in advance, and don't cram the night before. Bottom line: Walk into the testing center confident that you will perform to the best of your ability.

➤ *Avoid caffeine overdose*—Take it easy on the caffeine, especially if you are not a morning person to begin with, or if you don't normally drink lots of caffeine. Too much Mountain Dew/coffee/insert-favorite-caffeinated-beverage-here can make you very jittery. On the other hand, if you always have a cup of java in the morning, don't risk caffeine withdrawal symptoms (translation: very bad headache) by not having it.

➤ *Don't forget to breathe*—Remember that breathing is a necessary component of that thing we call living, so if you find yourself panting or hyperventilating, take some deep breaths and relax. Stay focused on the task at hand, and remember how well prepared you are.

➤ *Make some time to get nervous after the test*—Yes, you read that right: Give yourself permission to be nervous/freak out/yell/scream/and so on *after* the test. Seriously, if you make part of the test-taking process a "cool down" session, you'll be surprised to find this might take away a great deal of your pre-test (and during the test) anxiety. One idea is to have a favorite CD loaded in your car, so as you drive away from the test center, you can rock out (or mellow out, depending on your preference) and release all that anxiety. Although not directly related to the test itself, if you can plan for this type of release—and in turn it keeps you from becoming overly nervous during the exam—then it will be well worth it.

Introducing Bill Roberts, Your Test Partner

As you read through the book, you will see in many chapters a special element on your "test partner," who we've named Bill Roberts. The purpose of this element is to present you with a realistic (albeit fictitious) test-taker, who more than likely shares many of your concerns about taking the test. You can reflect on Bill's experiences as potential examples of what you might be feeling/experiencing as you prepare for the test, and—ideally—draw positive reinforcement from how Bill deals with these concerns. The point of this special element is not to say you have to feel/react the exact same way as Bill does, but rather to give you a real world example of how someone might actually address typical concerns in both preparing for and taking the test. So, moving forward, look to this special element as a great way to review the specific information presented, and as an illustration of how you can practically synthesize the specific chapter's information to best prepare for the test.

Exam Prep Questions

This chapter doesn't really lend itself to practice questions. Nevertheless, the tips and suggestions presented here can significantly enhance your exam score; that said, you should practice (or think through, as they relate to your own specific situation) these tips and suggestions so as to achieve the highest score possible.

Consider the following short (fictitious) vignettes that highlight test-takers who did not follow the strategies presented in this chapter, and fell victim to the consequences.

➤ Kathy Smith has always been a good test-taker, having scored well on her college entrance exams with very little preparation (not to mention very little sleep). Although she gets to the test center in plenty of time, she stayed up late into the night before the exam, watching movies with a friend. Given that this exam requires attention to detail, her lack of sleep causes her mind to wander, and as a result she misses several questions she otherwise would have easily answered correctly.

➤ Kirk Jeffries lives in the northeastern United States and is well accustomed to unpredictable weather, especially in the winter months. Moreover, he's taking the exam in the city where he works, so he's not worried about getting lost on the way to the test center. But the morning of the test, an unexpected winter storm blows into town, turning the streets into sheets of ice. Kirk, not "planning for the unexpected," must rush through bad weather to make it to the test on time. After he arrives, he is so anxious from barely avoiding sliding into another vehicle (and, in general, worrying about being late), that he has trouble concentrating on the questions at hand.

➤ Jennifer Kirkpatrick has done everything right in preparing for the exam. From studying for several weeks in advance to learning (and practicing) relaxation techniques, she is confident of her abilities to do well on the exam. The morning of the exam, she gets up very early and heads out to the testing center, arriving nearly an hour and a half in advance. She thinks this extra time will allow her a chance to do some last-minute cramming, but this strategy actually backfires: She becomes overly nervous about the impending exam and begins to second-guess her thorough preparation. Rather than feeling confident (and enjoying the benefits of a good night's sleep), she begins the test with feelings of anxiety and insecurity as to her abilities to perform well.

Address Checking

Terms You'll Need to Understand:
✓ Address Lists
✓ Sorting Mail
✓ Verifying Correct Addresses

Concepts/Techniques You'll Need to Master:
✓ Address checking with long address lists
✓ Attention to detail
✓ Working quickly

When you think of the necessary skill set for a postal worker, the ability to accurately check an address must be on the top of your list. Think about it: You are a postal carrier and prior to heading out on your route, you sort the day's mail. Inevitably, many of the addresses are going to be similar, especially those that are on the same street (for example, 4151 Rockville Road compared to 4115 Rockville Road). Keen attention to detail is critical because your customers aren't going to be pleased if they receive someone else's mail (or worse still, if someone else receives their mail)!

Not surprisingly then, address checking is a central component of the exam, and careful address checking is a skill you need to master if you want to not only score high on the exam, but perform well in your postal duties.

What Is Being Tested with Address Checking Questions?

Simply put, the address checking portion of the exam is used to determine the applicant's attention to detail. As we noted at the beginning of the chapter, this is a very important skill for a postal clerk/carrier because of the possible similarity between addresses and the danger of sending mail to the wrong location if addresses are confused.

Of course, another important component being tested in this section is the applicant's ability to work quickly. There are very few jobs that allow you to work at a leisurely pace (or even your own pace), and the postal clerk/carrier position is most definitely no exception. Speed is a critical skill that is being tested on the exam: You will be asked to compare 95 addresses in just 6 minutes, so obviously you'll need to work quickly. The good news is that, by working through this book, you'll get plenty of opportunity to practice, not just with this question type but all the others as well.

Address Checking Strategies

The most important strategy for these types of questions is to work as quickly as you can and to be sure you pay very close attention.

Be sure to review Chapter 3, "General Test-Taking Strategies," for ideas on how to clear your mind and stay relaxed and focused. You can then apply these general skills when trying to work as quickly and as accurately as you can through the address checking questions.

One general strategy worth mentioning is to be sure you don't lose your place on your answer sheet. Although that sounds obvious, you could potentially become distracted and start incorrectly marking your answer sheet; that is, you skip over an answer space and thus are "one question behind" in how you've marked your answer sheet. This can lead to a disastrous score, as you will have marked answers to the wrong questions!

To counter this possibility, use your finger or pencil to hold your place as you quickly move down the answer sheet, filling in your answers (in this case, either marking them as correct or incorrect). Don't let your eyes wander you have only six minutes to work through this section of the exam!

As you're checking addresses, you're looking for differences in street numbers, street names, abbreviations (Dr. versus Rd., for example), city names, state abbreviations (which can be very similar: NY versus NC, or IN versus IA), and ZIP codes. Work as quickly as you can, scanning the addresses from left to right. The absolute smallest detail can make all the difference in whether two addresses are exactly the same or different. Pay attention and work quickly—those are the two best strategies you can follow.

 Be aware that "exactly the same" even applies to whether the thoroughfare is abbreviated or written out.

 Another strategy might be to compare the addresses by reading right to left. This can be time-consuming because you are not accustomed to reading right to left. However, when you read more slowly, you might spot differences you would otherwise miss in reading from left to right.

Address Checking Scoring

Scoring for the address checking section is very simple: Your score is calculated by the number of questions you answer correctly minus the number of questions you answer incorrectly. Random guessing is not going to help your score, so it will be to your benefit to get through as many questions as possible, and giving each question your full attention (that is, no random guessing).

 It is not expected that you will answer all questions in the time allowed. That said, random guessing remains a bad idea, as questions you leave blank are not counted as wrong answers. So if you find yourself running out of time, don't just start wildly filling in answers (that is, random guessing): Unless you are a very lucky—in other words, randomly guessing correctly!—this random guessing will hurt your score.

Exam Prep Questions

The following list of 50 questions represents a sample of the address checking question format.

To get the most out of this practice quiz, follow this procedure:

1. Locate a pencil to darken the correct oval on the answer sheet. You can find an answer sheet for this practice quiz in the back of the book. It is labeled "Chapter 4 Answer Sheet."

2. For this practice quiz, you should give yourself four minutes to answer the 50 questions provided. Ask a friend or family member to time you, or if you have a timer (a stopwatch with an alarm, for example) that will suffice as well.

3. As you mark your answers, mark "A" if the two addresses are exactly the same, and mark "D" if you notice any difference.

4. When the four minutes are up, stop work immediately even if you are not finished. In a real exam situation, you will also be asked to stop work when time expires.

When you are ready, work through the following questions. Remember to give yourself only four minutes to answer all the questions to make this practice quiz as realistic as possible.

1. 108 Maple St.	180 Maple St.
2. 130 S Middle Neck Rd.	130 N Middle Neck Rd.
3. 1981 Marcus Ave.	1981 Marcus St.
4. 45 North Station Plaza	45 South Station Plaza
5. 1 Bellingham Lane	1 Bellingham Lane
6. 14 Steven Lane	14 Steven Lane
7. Brooklyn NY	Brooklyn NY
8. 48035 Clinton Township	48036 Clinton Township
9. 48080 Saint Clair Shores	48008 Saint Clair Shores
10. 8 Sycamore Drive	8 Sycamore Drive
11. 41 Farm Lane	41 Farm Lane
12. 182 Grace Ct. N	182 Grace Rd. N
13. 60 Knightsbridge Rd.	60 Knightsbridge Dr.
14. 1979 Tuddington Rd.	1979 Tuddington Rd.
15. 233 East Shore Rd.	233 East Shore Rd.

16. 15 Sutton Place   15 Sutton Place

17. 250 Schenck Ave. SW   250 Schenck Ave. SW

18. 1010 Northern Blvd.   1010 Northern Blvd.

19. Bloomfield Hills, MI 48304   Bloomfield Hills, MI 48304

20. Evergreen, CO 80437   Evergreen, CO 80439

21. 39 School House Lane   39 Schoolhouse Lane

22. 15 Hill Park Street   15 Hillpark Drive

23. 125 Knightsbridge Rd.   125 Knightsbridge Rd.

24. 35 Somer Blvd.   35 Somer Blvd.

25. 1872 Terrace Circle   1872 Terrace Circle

26. 95 Beech Court   95 Beech Court

27. Point Washington, FL   Point Washington, FL

28. Gainesville, FL 32611   Gainesville, FL 32601

29. Steamboat Springs, CO 80487   Steamboat Springs, CO 80477

30. Bethania, NC 27010   Bethania, NC 27010

31. 1983–56 Cambridge Rd.   1933–56 Cambridge Rd.

32. 6 Ascot Rdg.   6 Ascot Rdg.

33. 87 Poplar Court   87 Poplar Court

34. 108 Forest Row   108 Forest Row

35. 534 Lakeville Rd. W   534 Lakeville Rd. E

36. 73 Cumberland Lane   73 Cumberland Lane

37. White Plains, NC   White Plains, NY

38. Winston Salem, NC 27117   Winston Salem, NC 27199

39. Lexington, KY   Lexington, NC

40. Limerick, ME   Limington, ME

41. Auburn, ME 04212   Auburn, ME 04212

42. 254-08 West End Dr.   254-08 West End Dr.

43. 61 Jayson Ave.   61 Jayson Ave.

44. 5003 Madelyn Place   5003 Madeline Place

45. 2862 Rebecca Road   2862 Rebecca Road

46. 7341 Katie Court   7431 Katie Court

47. Boothbay, ME   East Boothbay, ME

48. Glen Cove, ME   Glen Cove, NY

49. Phoenix, AZ 85034   Phoenix, AZ 85014

50. Superior, AZ 85273   Superior, AZ 85273

Exam Prep Answers

Use the following answer key to grade and evaluate how well you did on the practice test:

1. **D**—The first address is 108, whereas the second is 180.

2. **D**—The first address is south (S) Middle Neck Rd., whereas the second address is north (N) Middle Neck Rd.

3. **D**—The first address is Ave., whereas the second lists the address as St.

4. **D**—The first station is North, whereas the second address is South.

5. **A**

6. **A**

7. **A**

8. **D**—The first address is 48035, whereas the second address is 48036.

9. **D**—The first address is 48080, whereas the second is 48008.

10. **A**

11. **A**

12. **D**—The first address is Ct., whereas the second lists the address as Rd.

13. **D**—The first address is Rd., whereas the second is Dr.

14. **A**

15. **A**

16. **A**

17. **A**

18. **A**

19. **A**

20. **D**—The ZIP codes are different.

21. **D**—The first address is spelled School House, whereas the second is Schoolhouse.

22. **D**—The first address is spelled Hill Park, whereas the second is Hillpark.

23. **A**

24. **A**

25. A

26. A

27. A

28. D—The ZIP codes are different.

29. D—The ZIP codes are different.

30. A

31. D—The street addresses are different.

32. A

33. A

34. A

35. D—The first address is west (W), whereas the second is east (E).

36. A

37. D—The states are different.

38. D—The ZIP codes are different.

39. D—The states are different.

40. D—The names of the towns are different.

41. A

42. A

43. A

44. D—The street name is spelled differently.

45. A

46. A

47. D—The city names are different.

48. D—The states are different.

49. D—The ZIP codes are different.

50. A

Bill Roberts Case Study: Address Checking Questions

In my current job at a bank, I have to scan through long lists of numbers every day, comparing one list to another to make sure there are no discrepancies. Given that I have this experience, I felt pretty good about my chances with the address checking questions: After all, if I make a mistake in comparing numbers in my current job, it can mean missing not just a difference in two numbers, but a difference in thousands of dollars. I definitely know the need for attention to detail.

One thing that did make me nervous, though, was being timed on these questions. I know it's an exam, and I know I can't take my sweet time working through the questions, but at least at the bank, I can work slowly and methodically, to be sure that I am not making inaccurate comparisons. I know I can't do this with address checking (or any aspect of the exam) and that I'm going to have to step up the pace if I want to get all the questions answered in six minutes, and if I want to get them answered correctly!

So how did I do on the practice test? Well, honestly, I didn't do that great, only getting 35 of the questions correct. I think I maybe went a little too fast (I finished in three minutes, instead of taking all four that were available for the practice quiz), and I also didn't consider that—unlike my job at the bank in comparing numbers only—the address checking questions ask you to compare all types of different abbreviations (especially city and state) and to be aware of—and be able to spot the difference between—the different types of thoroughfare abbreviations.

I've already decided I'm going to frequently review Appendix B included in this book, so I can become more familiar with all the different thoroughfare abbreviations. I was talking to a friend of mine who has worked for the USPS for several years, and he told me that recognizing those thoroughfare abbreviations is, in a way, like learning how to read in that you can quickly learn to recognize the correct abbreviation (and quickly spot when it is wrong).

So, address checking might turn out to be a little more difficult than I had originally thought. But ultimately, I know that it's a question of just buckling down and paying attention to what I'm doing. I admit that, during the practice quiz, I found myself thinking more about how much time I had left when I should have been paying closer attention to the questions, especially considering I finished the quiz with a minute to spare!

Memory for Addresses

Terms You'll Need to Understand

✓ Memory
✓ Short-term versus long-term memory
✓ Remote Memory

Concepts/Techniques You'll Need to Master

✓ Memorization strategies
✓ Memory-enhancement techniques

You now understand from working through Chapter 4 that attention to detail is a primary attribute for any successful postal clerk and carrier. The accurate and efficient delivery of mail is obviously important. Carelessness with noting what letters/packages go to a specific address results (obviously!) in some very angry customers, with the possibility of disciplinary action being taken against the carrier who repeatedly makes delivery errors.

But aside from attention to detail, a keen memory is also an absolute must for this position. Imagine the postal clerk who can't remember where Main Street is, and spends an hour (or more!) wandering or traveling in the wrong direction. It is critical, then, that you develop and maintain a strong memory. Coupled with your attention to detail (and other skill sets you will be asked to develop, as evidenced by the other exam question types still to be discussed), your sharp memory will prove an invaluable on-the-job tool.

What Is Being Tested with Memory for Addresses Questions

There's no getting around it: This section of the exam is testing your memory!

If you read that sentence and get a sense of foreboding, it is only partially intended; however, many people struggle with memorization, and especially when they know they are going to be tested specifically on it. The memory for addresses questions are obviously testing your ability to remember but— as you'll see in a moment—they are also testing your ability to focus on a specific task at hand (once again, attention to detail comes into play) and to apply that focus to memorizing (in a short time) what is arguably a complex set of information.

Now, if after reading the above paragraph, you are really getting nervous about this section of the exam, try to relax! Memory is something we all have, obviously, and that we use on a daily basis. You "remember" things all the time, and do so subconsciously. Certainly there are times when you make a more pointed effort to remember important items (for example, your anniversary, an important meeting with your boss, and so on), but for any given situation, your brain runs on autopilot, memorizing essential pieces of information you will need later.

The key, then, to doing well on the memory for addresses question type is to tune in to your brain's natural ability to memorize, and to focus that ability on quickly memorizing a set of information so that you can just as quickly (and accurately) retrieve that information as you answer the questions presented to you.

Specifically, the memory for addresses section of the exam consists of 88 questions that you need to complete in five minutes. You will be asked to memorize the locations of addresses from a 5×5 grid (that is, five rows and five columns). Each cell in the grid contains five specific pieces of information, for a total of 25 pieces of information (or entries) per question.

Fortunately, you don't have to jump into this section of the exam cold. You are given three exercises to help you with your memorization tasks. Specifically, these three exercises focus on the actual grid that you will be asked to draw from when you answer the 88 questions, so you have a good opportunity to focus in on the information before you are asked to recall it from memory. Another bit of good news is that you aren't asked (for each of the 88 questions) to actually recall what the information is. Rather, you are only asked to recall in which section of the grid the specific piece of information (such as an address) was placed.

Don't let this confuse you. The actual test procedure isn't as difficult as it sounds. You will have the chance to practice this type of question in a mini-quiz at the end of this chapter; then you will get a full-length quiz in Chapter 9, too (not to mention the four full-length exams that are also included in this book).

Memory for Addresses Strategies

Improving one's memory is probably one of the most fundamental challenges facing any professional (or anyone, for that matter). A good memory can be a very powerful tool regardless of the task you are facing. If nothing else, it allows you to quickly address a question/problem/situation with your existing knowledge/skill set. Put simply, a good memory often greatly reduces the amount of time you have to "think about" a situation because it (quickly!) provides you with the information you need!

> In reality, the ability to quickly recall facts is different from memory. But it probably goes without saying that you can't recall facts if you don't have them memorized in the first place, so the two abilities go hand-in-hand.

From (proclaimed, but usually not validated) memory-enhancing drugs to the simple advice of getting enough sleep, the methods and strategies for improving your memory vary wildly.

Be wary of any drug's claim that it can improve your memory. Many of these drugs you see advertised on television are nothing more than natural herbal extracts combined in some random fashion. Worse still, very few (if any) of these drugs have been tested or approved by the Food and Drug Administration as to their effectiveness or safety. Bottom line: Avoid them!

Where to begin with memorization strategies? The discussion is divided into two parts. First we discuss strategies for approaching the actual process of how these questions are presented on the exam. Then we look at a few memory-enhancement strategies and techniques.

Approaching the Memory for Addresses Question Type

As you read above, you have three opportunities to practice memorizing the information you'll need to draw from as you answer the questions asked of you. The best piece of advice regarding these practice opportunities is to take full advantage of them! Don't get nervous worrying about the "real questions," how much you have to memorize, how much time is left, and so on. Stay focused on the task at hand. Remember that, when answering the questions, you won't be asked to recall the specific pieces of information but rather the location of where they appear in the grid.

Aside from taking advantage of the practice time, there are other things you can do to help with this question type. You should keep in mind that you aren't really expected to answer each one of the 88 questions (five minutes is a very short period of time to give each of these questions a close, focused study). That said, as you work through the questions, answer the ones you know (that is, the ones you can quickly recall from memory) first; then go back and try to answer the harder, less obvious ones. Another good piece of advice is, as always, work as fast and efficiently as possible.

 Random guessing, in all probability, will not help your score and might actually hurt it (answers left blank are not considered wrong answers). You'll read more about how this question type is scored later in this chapter, at which time you'll see why random guessing is not a good idea.

 Another strategy you might want to utilize is to eliminate the answers that you know can't be correct. What I mean here is that although you might not know which is the correct answer, you might still recognize an answer option that is not correct. Don't ignore this: It reduces the number of answer choices, which can make the question a little less daunting as you try and remember where the address was located in the information grid.

Strategies for Enhancing Your Memory

What is memory? In simple terms, memory is the ability to retain and recall specific events and information. Three basic types of memory classification are often used:

➤ *Short-term memory*: This is "temporary" memory, or information that you need for only a short period of time. For example, when you are on vacation you might put your hotel room number in your short-term memory. This is valuable information to retain while you are staying at the hotel, but after you return from vacation, remembering your hotel room number will probably do you little good. Your brain instinctively recognizes this, and places the room number in your short-term memory.

➤ *Long-term memory*: Information that you need for the "long haul" is placed in long-term memory. The names of your family members or even your telephone number are things you want to retain for a long period of time, so long-term memory proves useful for retaining this type of information.

➤ *Remote memory*: This type of memory is usually referenced in regard to your ability to speak, read, and so on. In a way, this is long-term memory (that is, you "remember" how to speak for your entire life) but because it is so deeply embedded in our everyday experiences and needs, it has its own classification.

Memory for Addresses Scoring

Guessing on the memory for addresses questions is not a good idea. Why? Because for every question you answer incorrectly, 1/4 point is deducted from your total score. Again, you aren't expected to answer all of the 88 questions in the allotted five minutes, so work as quickly and efficiently as you can, answer the easier questions first (that is, the ones you immediately can recall from memory), and work through the harder ones as time allows.

Take the Memory for Addresses Practice Test

For this practice test, you have three minutes to answer as many of the following questions as possible. Your score is determined in the following manner:

Total number of correct answers minus 1/4 point for each wrong answer.

There are some additional rules you will need to follow for this test (note these are the same rules by which you will need to abide on the actual exam, too):

➤ During the exam, you cannot refer back to the address grid.

➤ During the memorization period, you cannot write down the addresses/any other information (that is, you truly have to memorize the information, and answer the questions based solely on your memory).

 The "memorization period" is a short period (a few minutes) of time, which will be administered by the individual proctoring the exam.

Finally, remember that your goal is to determine from which column (A, B, C, D, or E) the address came. You don't need to memorize where the addresses are placed within the grid, but just in what column they are.

1. Locate a pencil to darken the correct oval on the answer sheet. You can find an answer sheet for this practice quiz in the back of the book. It is labeled "Chapter 5 Answer Sheet."

2. For this practice quiz, you should give yourself 1 1/2 minutes for the "memorization period." Ask a friend or family member to time you, or if you have a timer (a stopwatch with an alarm, for example) that will suffice as well.

 You are given 1 1/2 minutes for this practice test. On the actual exam, you will be given more time (three minutes) for the "memorization period."

3. For each question, mark you answer sheet with either A, B, C, D, or E to correspond to the column in which the address would be placed.

4. After your memorization period, you will have three minutes to answer as many of the 25 questions as possible. When your time is up, stop work immediately even if you are not finished. In a real exam situation, you will also be asked to stop work when time expires.

Remember that on the actual exam, you will have three practice exercises to help you memorize the location of each address shown in the five columns.

For the next 1 1/2 minutes, study the following table, noticing how the addresses are organized in each of the columns.

A	B	C	D	E
1300–1359 Ash	7450–7460 Ash	1200–1399 Ash	5644–5744 Ash	6000–7399 Ash
Inglewood	Whittier	Cypress	Norwalk	Stanton
5000–6050 Fir	1250–1359 Fir	5000–5800 Fir	2050–3500 Fir	4200–4399 Fir
Glendale	Claremont	Upland	Oceanside	Barstow
6500–7399 Cedar	8050–9000 Cedar	7300–7499 Cedar	9000–9200 Cedar	1500–2500 Cedar

STOP! DO NOT TURN THE PAGE TO VIEW THE TEST QUESTIONS UNTIL YOU HAVE COMPLETED THE MEMORIZATION PERIOD AND ARE READY TO BEGIN THE THREE-MINUTE TIMED TEST.

1. Oceanside

2. 4200–4399 Fir

3. 1300–1359 Ash

4. Claremont

5. 9000–9200 Cedar

6. Barstow

7. 1250–1359 Fir

8. Whittier

9. 5000–5800 Fir

10. 6000–7399 Ash

11. 8050–9000 Cedar

12. Glendale

13. Upland

14. 5644–5744 Ash

15. Cypress

16. 7300–7499 Cedar

17. Norwalk

18. 6500–7399 Cedar

19. 7450–7460 Ash

20. Stanton

21. 1200–1399 Ash

22. Inglewood

23. 1250–1359 Fir

24. 2050–3500 Fir

25. 7300–7499 Cedar

Exam Prep Answers

Use the following answer key to grade and evaluate how well you did on the practice test:

1. D	2. E	3. A	4. B	5. D
6. E	7. B	8. B	9. C	10. E
11. B	12. A	13. C	14. D	15. C
16. C	17. D	18. A	19. B	20. E
21. C	22. A	23. B	24. D	25. C

Bill Roberts Case Study: Memory for Addresses Questions

I don't have a good memory. I know it, my co-workers know it, and my family knows it (yes, I've been guilty of unintentionally forgetting a birthday/anniversary now and again). On the other hand, though, I've always been pretty good with numbers (I do work at a bank, after all), and if I can clear my head before sitting down to do serious work, I usually don't have a problem concentrating and getting the job done.

Still, these memory for addresses questions really threw me for a loop. I think it was more the style/process of how the questions are presented, though, than the actual questions themselves: When I first worked through this chapter and the practice test, I got so hung up on trying to mimic the test process (that is, first review the question grid, then try to remember everything for the questions themselves), I found I really couldn't remember much at all. Not surprisingly, my score on the practice exam was nothing to write home about.

But, I'm committed to a career with the USPS, and I know that being able to rely on a sharp memory is going to be an essential part of that career. The web sites that were listed in this chapter are good. If nothing else, they help you to realize that memorization is something we all do every day, and something we all do without realizing it. And, as with all things related to this test, knowing how to relax and concentrate seems to go a really long way. After all, the memory for addresses and address checking questions aren't really anything you can study for in terms of content. However—and I think this is really an important point—if you can become familiar with the format in which the questions are presented and the testing procedure for each exam (that is, how much time you have to complete each section), then you can "study." Practice is essential, and especially with the memory for addresses, I think practice is even more critical to success.

So, I'm definitely going to keep working to improve my memory, both by reviewing the web sites presented in this chapter and by just practicing, practicing, practicing. I'm hopeful that as I continue to work through the full-length practice tests (and the full-length, question-specific Chapter 9), I'll start to feel more confident and relaxed. As soon as that happens, my scores on these practice exams are sure to improve.

Number Series

Terms You'll Need to Understand

✓ Addition
✓ Subtraction
✓ Multiplication
✓ Division

Concepts/Techniques You'll Need to Master

✓ Work with a Number Series
✓ Comprehend Number Patterns

Many people panic when they hear there is a math component to Exams 460 and 470. Not to worry—it isn't a math test per se, but rather is intended to test your skill at figuring out number patterns.

Some postal workers are responsible for keying in numbers quickly and need to be able to type accurately and with speed. As with backgammon or chess, when you're familiar with common moves, it improves your chances of winning. Well, so it goes with number series and patterns: If you can quickly recognize and adapt to these patterns (especially recurring patterns), you'll be able to perform your job tasks more efficiently.

Number series questions may involve determining patterns involving addition, subtraction, multiplication, or division. You should also be aware that some of them involve alternating patterns.

Scared and confused yet? Don't be. Of all the question types you are going to encounter on the exam, this is—at first glance—the most intimidating. But like all the question types, after you are familiar with the format and what is being asked, you can learn (with some practice!) how to master it.

What Is Being Tested with Number Series Questions

Number series questions are designed to test your ability at discerning number patterns. You will be presented with four types of number series questions:

➤ *Addition*—These questions ask that you determine how addition is being used to generate the pattern. For example, 1, 3, 5, 7, 9 might be a pattern, and you are asked to determine the next number in the sequence. In this case it would be 11, as the pattern shown increases by 2 for each number presented.

➤ *Subtraction*—The subtraction questions ask you to determine the pattern when subtraction is involved. For example, 40, 35, 30, 25, 20 might be a pattern, where the next number in the series would be 15, as each number in the pattern decreases by 5.

➤ *Multiplication and Division*—These questions ask you to utilize multiplication in determining the correct answer. For example, in the pattern 4, 8, 16, 32, each subsequent number in the pattern is the product of the previous number multiplied by 2. So the next number in this series would be 64.

➤ *Alternating number series*—Perhaps the most difficult (at least at first glance) are the alternating number series questions. These questions use (in an alternating fashion) different types of mathematical operations and ask you to determine the pattern that is evolving. For example, the series 1, 8, 4, 8, 16, 8, 64 utilizes two patterns: Every other number is multiplied by 4, whereas the number between the two numbers is always an 8. So, the next numbers in this series would be 8, 256.

The good news about this question type is that you are asked to answer only 24 questions. The bad news is that, in turn, you are given only 20 minutes to answer them. Of course, the term "bad news" is relative only if you let your nerves get the better of you or you are unprepared. Fortunately, you can address both of these test-taking problems by carefully studying this book. So, as you read further into this chapter, don't let all the numbers concern you, or the idea of having to "do math" on the exam. You are asked to perform only simple addition, subtraction, and multiplication—no algebra or calculus necessary!

Number Series Strategies

There has been much written about how to successfully pass this section of the exam. So much, in fact, that the explanations are more complicated than the actual questions!

Try to move quickly, but pay attention to detail. Don't skip around—answer the questions in order. You can guess on the ones you're stuck on at the end. Read the directions very carefully—they will tell you exactly what you need to do.

For the Number Series questions, there is no penalty for guessing, so be sure to provide at least some answer for each question on your answer sheet.

Although this is good basic advice, the best strategy you can use in answering these questions is to be sure you write some basic information about each question as you study it. Consider the following series:

5, 7, 4, 6, 3, 5, 2

Admittedly, this is not that difficult of a question from which to determine the pattern. But then again, imagine yourself in a real exam situation: Rather than being able to review each question at a leisurely pace, you have to move quickly (remember, you only have 20 minutes). As we said earlier, there is no need to let panic set in. But all those numbers can start melting into one if the nerves take over. There is a very simple way to avoid this confusion, and that is to make the questions work for you and answer themselves.

What do we mean? Take another look at the series in the preceding paragraph, but notice the additional information that is now included:

$$5,_{(+2)}7,_{(-3)}4,_{(+2)}6,_{(-3)}3,_{(+2)}5,_{(-3)}2$$

As you can see, the additional information that is provided in this example (that is, the subscript numbers placed below and between each of the numbers in the series) tell you the pattern that is being used to develop this series. Although this is once again a simple pattern, having this additional information is quite valuable.

Taking the time to write out this pattern information becomes very useful when you are asked to identify alternating patterns. Consider the following example:

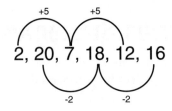

Again, this is not a difficult pattern, but in a high-pressure exam situation, even easy patterns can be difficult to spot. So take the time to mark this extra information (that is, the extra marks you place on the question, as illustrated here) on the question, and in turn let the question work for you by answering itself.

If you think we keep using the phrase, "This is not a difficult pattern" in this chapter, then kudos to you for having a sharp eye for detail. We are using that phrase quite a bit, and for good reason: If you remain calm and follow the strategies presented here, you will have no problem identifying the patterns in the number series questions because they really aren't that difficult to figure out. Or, in other words, they are not difficult patterns!

The great thing is that this additional information is *right there* in the questions. All you have to do is take the time to write this additional information within the question. Remember that time is a luxury you don't have with this type of question, and panic can take over on even the simplest question. So, taking the time to write this pattern information on the question will help calm you down, as well as ensure you actually see the pattern that is being used.

 Don't spend too much time on any one question because you don't have much time for this question type. Work as quickly as you can, and if you simply cannot determine the pattern for a specific question, move on to the next question in the exam.

Number Series Scoring

Unlike other sections of the exam, only the right answers count in the Number Series portion of the exam. That said, it is worth answering every question, even if you have to guess.

Given the fear that many people have of anything math-related, one other thing is also worth repeating: Remember, you are not taking a math test. In fact, you are using no more complicated math (indeed, probably less) than you do in your everyday life. So remain focused, and do not get frustrated if you can't figure out the pattern. Move on to the next question, and if you have extra time, go back and take a look at the questions you skipped.

Take the Number Series Practice Test

For this practice test, you have 20 minutes to answer as many of the following questions as possible. Your score will be determined in the following manner:

Total number of correct.

1. Locate a pencil to darken the correct oval on the answer sheet. You can find an answer sheet for this practice quiz in the back of the book. It is labeled "Chapter 6 Answer Sheet."

2. For each question, mark your answer sheet with A, B, C, or D to correspond to the set of numbers that would follow next in the pattern.

3. When your time is up, stop work immediately even if you are not finished. In a real exam situation, you will also be asked to stop work when time expires.

Addition and Subtraction

1. 11 13 15 17 19 21 23 ___ ___
    A. 9 14
    B. 27 29
    C. 25 27
    D. 31 33

2. 101 96 91 86 81 76 71 ___ ___
    A. 65 59
    B. 66 61
    C. 65 60
    D. 66 60

3. 29 30 32 35 39 44 50 ___ ___
    A. 53 56
    B. 57 65
    C. 52 55
    D. 65 57

4. 14 12 11 9 8 6 5 ___ ___
    A. 3 2
    B. 4 5
    C. 4 4
    D. 6 5

5. 2 4 1 6 8 1 10 ___ ___
    A. 1 12
    B. 12 14
    C. 12 1
    D. 11 13

6. 7 10 13 11 14 17 15 ___ ___
    A. 18 21
    B. 16 17
    C. 18 17
    D. 14 13

7. 160 134 110 88 68 50 34 ___ ___
    A. 8 20
    B. 24 4
    C. 27 16
    D. 20 8

Multiplication and Division

8. 7 21 28 35 42 49 56 ___ ___

   A. 63 70
   B. 62 68
   C. 63 71
   D. 65 74

9. 1 1 2 2 4 4 8 ___ ___

   A. 8 16
   B. 16 8
   C. 8 8
   D. 16 16

10. 6561 2187 729 243 81 27 9 ___ ___

    A. 5 3
    B. 3 1
    C. 1 3
    D. 6 1

11. 1 1 2 6 24 120 720 ___ ___

    A. 820 920
    B. 1440 2880
    C. 5040 40,320
    D. 5040 35,280

12. 9 18 9 27 9 36 9 ___ ___

    A. 45 9
    B. 9 45
    C. 45 54
    D. 54 9

13. 1 8 4 8 16 8 64 ___ ___

    A. 8 256
    B. 72 80
    C. 8 256
    D. 72 8

14. 15 10 20 15 30 25 50 ___ ___

    A. 45 90
    B. 90 45
    C. 40 100
    D. 15 75

15. 1 6 2 12 4 24 8 ___ ___

    A. 20 6

    B. 36 4

    C. 32 8

    D. 48 16

Miscellaneous

16. 101 11 102 12 103 13 104 14 105 ___ ___

    A. 16 106

    B. 15 106

    C. 106 107

    D. 15 16

17. 2 3 4 4 5 6 6 ___ ___

    A. 6 8

    B. 7 8

    C. 8 8

    D. 9 10

18. 2 22 122 2 22 122 2 ___ ___

    A. 22 122

    B. 122 22

    C. 2 122

    D. 22 2

19. 10 1 11 2 12 3 13 4 ___ ___

    A. 14 15

    B. 4 5

    C. 5 6

    D. 14 5

20. 1 2 3 2 1 2 3 ___ ___

    A. 2 1

    B. 4 5

    C. 2 1

    D. 1 2

21. 1 4 9 16 25 36 49 ___ ___

    A. 54 63

    B. 64 81

    C. 100 121

    D. 66 74

22. 39 38 8 11 39 38 8 ___ ___
- A. 11 39
- B. 39 11
- C. 29 7
- D. 37 8

23. +1 -2 -3 +4 -5 -6 +7 ___ ___
- A. -8 -9
- B. +8 -9
- C. +8 +9
- D. -9 +8

24. 1 4 10 19 31 46 64 ___ ___
- A. 72 95
- B. 80 92
- C. 85 109
- D. 81 110

Exam Prep Answers

1. C. The numbers in the series increase by 2, for example, 11+2=13, 13+2+15.

2. B. The difference between each number in the series is 5, for example, 101–5=96, 96–5=91.

3. B. The series follows the rule +1 +2 +3..., for example, 29+1=30, 30+2=32, 32+3=35.

4. A. The differences between numbers alternate between 2 and 1, for example, 14–2=12, 12–1=11, 11–2=9.

5. C. Two patterns are at work here: The number 1 is inserted every third number in the series; the rest of the series follows a +2 pattern, for example 2+2=4, 1, 4+2=6, 6+2=8, 1.

6. A. The numbers in the series follow the pattern +3 +3 –2 +3 +3 –2, for example, 7+3=10, 10+3=13, 13–2=11.

7. D. The differences between the numbers keep decreasing by 2, for example, 160–26=134, 134–24=110.

8. A. The multiplier throughout the series is 7, for example, 7×1=7, 7×2=14, 7×3=21.

9. A. The multiplier alternates between 1 and 2, for example, 1×1=1, 1×2=2, 2×1=2, 2×2=4

10. B. The divisor throughout the series is 3, for example, 6561÷3=2187, 2187÷3=729, 729÷3=243.

11. C. The multiplier keeps increasing by 1, for example, 1×1=1, 1×2=2, 2×3=6, 6×4=24.

12. A. This series uses a pattern of alternating the number 9 with a number multiplied by 9, and that multiplier keeps increasing by 1, for example, 9×2=18, 9×3=27.

13. C. This number has two alternating patterns: Every other number is multiplied by 4, and the number in between those two numbers is always an 8, for example, 1×4=4, 4×4=16.

14. A. This series uses a pattern that alternates subtraction (–5) with multiplication (×2), for example, 15–5=10, 10×2=20, 20–5=15, 15×2=30.

15. D. This series alternates multiplying by 6 with dividing by 3, for example, 1×6=6, 6÷3=2, 2×6=12.

16. **B.** This series simply uses a pattern that alternates the number that has a zero in the middle with a number that lacks a zero in the middle; arithmetic isn't used.

17. **B.** This series counts up by one, repeating the third number along the way.

18. **A.** This pattern just repeats a series of three numbers.

19. **D.** In this series, every other number is the sum of the digits in the number before it.

20. **C.** The numbers ascend from 1 to 3 and then descend; the pattern then repeats itself.

21. **B.** Each number in this series is a number squared. That number keeps increasing by 1, for example, 1×1=1, 2×2=4, 3×3=9.

22. **A.** This series of four numbers repeats itself.

23. **A.** The numbers ascend by 1 throughout the series; the signs form a pattern: + – –, + – –.

24. **C.** The numbers in this series increase when multiples of 3 are added, for example, 1+3=4, 4+6=10, 10+9=19.

Bill Roberts Case Study: Number Series Questions

I've always been comfortable with numbers (I work at a bank, after all). I was having dinner with a friend who is a postal clerk, and he said that of all the questions on the exam, the number series was the most difficult. I asked him why this was the case, and he said very simply, "Because of the math." Although numbers have never really bothered me (in fact, I sort of enjoy them), it wasn't surprising to hear that. I guess there is a reason math is a four-letter word—it can really strike fear into the hearts of the test-taker.

So, keeping in mind that I like numbers, I was still somewhat surprised at how easy the number series questions seem to be. I mean, compare them to the memory for addresses questions (which I happen to think are the most difficult). In those questions, you are really pressured to do something very difficult, and that is memorize a good deal of information in a very short time. Then, to make matters worse you have to quickly and accurately recall that information to answer specific questions on the exam. At least with the number series questions you have everything you need right in front of you, so you don't have the added pressure of having to memorize.

Admittedly, some people might find memorization easy. But to me, having the information right in front of me is a huge advantage to answering questions quickly and—how should I put this—calmly. Yes, it's true: I'm still battling with some nerves (even on these practice tests). Don't know if it's just the idea of having to take a test (you know, the idea of being evaluated) or that I'm thinking how important this exam is to my future career opportunities. At any rate, I'm going to keep on working through all the practice exams in this book (working through them a few times, as a matter of fact) and just getting as comfortable as I can with the format of the questions and the time I have for each section.

Following Oral Instructions

Terms You'll Need to Understand

✓ Verbal instructions
✓ Attention focus
✓ Active listening

Concepts/Techniques You'll Need to Master

✓ Following instructions
✓ Listening for specific detail
✓ Understanding spoken content

This section of the exam is designed to test your ability to follow oral directions. After the directions are given, they will not be repeated, so you have to listen carefully to each question.

The only way to prepare for this type of exam is to practice (with a partner) so that you are familiar with the types of questions asked. This presents a somewhat unique study challenge as compared to the other sections of the exam (and thus this book), which allow you to study on your own. However, to most accurately prepare for the real testing situation, you should definitely have a partner read you the instructions. Technically it is possible to study this on your own (that is, read the directions out loud to yourself, and read them only once) but again this won't present you with nearly as accurate of an actual testing environment.

What Is Being Tested with Following Oral Instructions Questions?

This section of the 460 and 470 seeks to determine how well you can listen to and follow directions. The examiner reads instructions to you, and in turn you must follow said instructions to correctly mark your answer key. Don't worry: The examiner isn't going to ask you history questions or how to conjugate verbs. Indeed, the questions themselves will refer to what is presented on a worksheet (more on this in the practice quiz of this chapter), and you will in turn have to listen to the instructions the examiner gives for how to mark your answer sheet.

Some procedural notes about this section of the exam

➤ You will have time after each question to mark your answer sheet. Don't be concerned that you'll have to answer a question while trying to listen to the next one being asked.

➤ You will need to listen closely to the examiner; your success on this section of the test is absolutely dependent on how well you can focus your attention on the spoken instructions of another person.

➤ After the examiner reads the question, it cannot be repeated.

➤ You are not allowed to ask questions at any time during this section of the exam.

Following Oral Instructions Strategies

I remember a trick one of my elementary teachers played on the class to test how well we were able to follow instructions (both written and verbal) and pay attention. One day, the teacher distributed a test that consisted of several pages. As she was passing out the test, she emphatically told the class not to begin working on the test until she said it was okay to do so. Well, naturally, some of the kids immediately jumped in to taking the test and were asked to turn in their tests with a grade of 0 (not really—this was just an exercise, but it scared them nonetheless).

But the real trick (and the one that got me, I admit!) was saved for those of us who listened to the directive not to begin work until we were told to do so. When we could finally look at the exam, what we saw, in big bold letters, was the instruction to read the last question of the exam before beginning work. Remember, I said this was several pages of questions, so even taking the time to flip to the back of the test would have been an effort (at least for an impatient fourth-grader). Well, I didn't bother flipping to the last question and started work on the difficult exam. To my amazement, other students started walking up to the front of the class to turn in their exam after just a minute. How could they be finished so quickly? Were they throwing in the towel on this difficult test before they even gave it a chance? After several minutes, those of us who were still working were told by the teacher to stop work and flip to the last question of the test. This is what we found waiting for us:

"This test is designed to evaluate your ability to read closely and follow directions. Please write your name on the test, and turn it in at the front of the room. Congratulations—you are done!"

I don't know if they still do this kind of thing in elementary schools (my daughter hasn't mentioned it, but she's a lot smarter than I ever was), but, in retrospect, it was a good exercise. The ability to follow written and spoken directives is a key attribute for any job, and postal clerks and carriers are no exception. Although you (unfortunately) won't find this kind of quick and easy question on the 460/470 exam, the point remains the same: To do well on this section of the test, you have to bring your "A" game for listening to directions, and you must be able to pay close attention and focus on what is being said.

The following tips can prove useful strategies for doing well in regard to following oral instructions:

➤ You need someone to practice with you. This person must read slowly and carefully, pausing where the directions indicate a pause.

➤ These questions aren't difficult; you just need to listen very carefully. Unlike the rest of the exam, you won't be answering the questions in order—in fact, your answers will be all over the answer sheet, and some of the spaces may even be left blank!

➤ Always work from left to right, unless you're told to do otherwise.

➤ Pay attention—you'll need to listen closely and do exactly as you're told.

➤ Because you're not working sequentially, it is easy to get confused. Don't try to go back to correct an answer; you are likely to fall behind. Just skip it and listen for the next instruction.

Note the warnings here about not answering questions in sequential order. If you don't pay very close attention, you can very easily get confused, and after that happens—especially on this section—you could be in very deep trouble. Although the strategies presented in this chapter are general, you might want to refer to the general test-taking strategies presented in Chapter 3, especially those concerning how to remain calm and not let those "day of the exam jitters" get the best of you.

Following Oral Instructions Scoring

Your score on this section of the exam is based on the total number of questions you answer correctly. There is not a time limit in the traditional sense because you are listening to questions read to you by an examiner; however, the questions will be read to you only once.

Be sure that, when you finish this section of the exam, you have only one space marked for each question. If more than one space is marked for a specific question, it will be counted as wrong. If you can't answer a question, you should definitely guess because there is no point deduction for wrong answers.

Remember, paying close attention is the name of the game here. Although incorrect answers do not subtract from your score, if you get really lost in the process of answering this section of the exam, you'd have to be a very lucky guesser to answer the questions correctly (if you can answer them at all). As you will soon see in the practice test, these are not multiple choice questions; indeed the "answers" are often specific instructions told to you by the instructor, so the only way to get them correct is to correctly hear what the examiner instructs you to do. (In other words, you probably couldn't guess—even if you wanted to—at a question for which you didn't hear the instructions.)

Finally, don't forget that the instructions can be read only one time, so there won't be a second chance. How many more times can we say this? Okay, we'll say it one more time: You simply must pay close attention. The questions asked of you are not hard (in fact, they are very simple), but you must pay close attention so you can hear them correctly. Otherwise, this section of the exam will be a very difficult one—if not impossible—on which to score high.

Exam Prep Questions

To best utilize this practice test (and all Following Oral Instructions practice tests in this book) you should enlist the help of a friend to read the instructions to you, as this will more accurately mimic the actual testing environment.

There are some additional rules you need to follow for this test (note these are the same rules you will need to abide by on the actual exam, too):

➤ Questions are read only once.

➤ You are not allowed to ask any questions during this portion of the exam.

➤ When you finish the test, have no more than one space marked for each number. If more than one space is marked for a number, the item is counted as wrong.

1. Locate a pencil to darken the correct oval on the answer sheet. You can find an answer sheet for this practice quiz in the back of the book. It is labeled "Chapter 7 Answer Sheet."

2. Find a blank piece of paper and copy each of the following 10 questions exactly as you see them presented here:

   1. 20 4 15 2 8

   2. 9:30 1:20 4:50 12:00 6:30

   3. RED BLUE ORANGE GREEN YELLOW

   4. 1 3 5 7 4

   5. A B D F G H

   6. 1:00 2:00 7:00 11:00 4:00

   7. EAST WEST NORTH SOUTH

   8. 98 99 55 22 44

   9. LEFT RIGHT MIDDLE UP DOWN

   10. A B A B A B A C A C A C

3. Hand the book to your partner, who will be reading the instructions to you.

4. Remember to have your partner read each question only one time.

TO THE PERSON READING THE INSTRUCTIONS: *You should read slowly and clearly. You do not have to read the words in parentheses; these have been provided for your guidance in allowing the test taker time to think about/answer each question.*

READ THE FOLLOWING TO THE TEST TAKER: *You need to mark your answer sheet according to the specific instructions I read to you. I'll pause for a few seconds after each instruction, so you have time to mark your answer sheet.*

The test begins now.

1. Look at line 1 of the worksheet (pause 2–3 seconds). Draw a line under the fourth number in the list. Now, on your answer sheet, darken the oval for which this number corresponds (pause five seconds).

2. Look at line 2 of the worksheet (pause 2–3 seconds). Draw a line under the first time and last time. Subtract the last time from the first time to get a whole number. For question #3 on your answer sheet, darken the oval for which this number corresponds (pause five seconds).

3. Look at line 2 of your answer sheet (pause 2–3 seconds). Darken the same oval on your answer sheet for question #2 (pause five seconds).

4. Look at line 3 of the worksheet (pause 2–3 seconds). If the word "orange" is the second color listed, darken the "A" oval of your answer sheet. If the word "orange" is not the second color, darken the "B" oval next to question #4 on your answer sheet (pause five seconds).

5. Look at line 4 of the worksheet (pause 2–3 seconds). Find the even number listed and, for question #5 on your answer sheet, darken the oval for which the position of the number corresponds (pause five seconds).

6. Look at line 5 of the worksheet (pause 2–3 seconds). Find the letter of the alphabet you wrote for answer #5, and darken the oval that corresponds to the same letter you answered for question #6 (pause five seconds).

7. Look at line 6 of the worksheet (pause 2–3 seconds). Simply darken the oval that corresponds to choice "C" for question #7 on your answer sheet (pause five seconds).

8. Look at line 7 of the worksheet (pause 2–3 seconds). Draw a line under the word "North" and write the number 3 next to it. Now, look at line 8 of your work sheet. Subtract the first number listed from the second, then add the number you come up with to the number you wrote down next to the word "North" on line 7 of your answer sheet. Finally, darken the oval of the letter of the alphabet for which the position of this number corresponds in the space for question #8 (pause 10 seconds).

9. Look at line 9 of the worksheet (pause 2–3 seconds). Draw a line under the word "up," then draw another line under the word "down." Subtract the number position of the word "up" from that of "down," and subtract that number from 5. Finally, darken the oval of the letter of the alphabet for which the position of this number corresponds in the space for question #9 on your answer sheet (pause 10 seconds).

10. Look at line 10 of the worksheet (pause 2–3 seconds). Draw a line under each letter "C," then count the number of lines you draw. Add this number to 6, then subtract 8. Finally, darken the oval of the letter of the alphabet for which this position of this number corresponds in the space for question #10 on your answer sheet (pause 10 seconds).

You have completed the practice quiz for Following Oral Instructions. Please check your answers against the answer key provided in the next section of this chapter.

Evaluating Your Score

Use the following answer key to grade and evaluate how well you did on the practice test:

1. B	2. C	3. C	4. B	5. D
6. D	7. C	8. D	9. D	10. A

Bill Roberts Case Study: Following Oral Instructions

My wife tells me (from time to time) that I don't listen to her. I don't understand it—I hear everything she says, and amazingly, it is only the things I want to hear. How could I be so lucky to have such a perfect wife? Probably because I am such a perfect husband, and obviously have a real knack for paying close attention.

Seriously, I know I don't always listen closely enough, and it's not just when my wife lists the chores she wants me to perform on Saturday morning. I've found my attention can wander at work, too. I guess I have become so used to working alone and "following my own mental voice" (so to speak) that when I really need to actively listen to other people, it can be, well, difficult.

Not surprisingly, I've asked my wife to help me prepare for this section of the exam. The first time through the practice quiz, I was really distracted by just the format of the section: that is, having someone read to you while you follow instructions. I have to admit it was a little unsettling because it took on a real "exam atmosphere." It didn't help that I knew—per the exam rules—that she could read each instruction only one time. I'd have to say that my first warning about these questions is to assume that the format of the questions will be a little unusual.

Even though you might follow oral directions all the time (driving instructions, the advice of your doctor...the list goes on), knowing that you are being tested on those instructions can be a bit unnerving. Although the questions aren't difficult at all, don't let that fool you into thinking this section of the exam is really easy. It is not as challenging (on one level) as, for example, the Number Series questions, but it is very challenging (on a whole other level) in the mental demands it places on you to really "focus in" on what is being said to you.

At any rate, I am getting better at paying attention (both inside and outside a testing environment, thank you very much). But I know I have to practice with this question format several more times. I'm going to review the general test-taking strategies that were presented in Chapter 3, "General Test-Taking Strategies," especially in regard to staying focused and not losing track of my primary goal, which is, of course, achieving the highest score possible.

Address Checking Practice Test

You should be familiar with address checking questions from Chapter 4, where you were presented with strategies for tackling this type of question, as well as taking a short practice test. This chapter gives you the opportunity to take a more extensive and complete practice test that focuses solely on address checking, prior to moving into the full-length exams in Chapters 13–16.

You should approach this chapter in the same way you do the following three chapters (that is, each of the question-specific practice test chapters), which is by using the time to focus on each of these individual question types. As you know from Chapter 4, there is not a tremendous amount of "strategizing" you can do in regard to the address checking questions; that said, the more familiar you are with this type of question and the format in which it is asked (that is, comparing two addresses) the more comfortable you will be when you take the real exam.

Be sure to note the "Bill Roberts Case Study" element at the end of this chapter, as well as the other question-specific chapters, to get a "real world" perspective on how a typical exam taker both approaches these questions/exams, and in turn deals with the resulting score in an effort to do better on the real exam.

Take the Address Checking Practice Test

For this practice test, you have six minutes to answer as many of the following questions as possible. Your score will be tabulated by the number of correct answers minus the number of wrong answers or unanswered questions.

Don't worry about completing every question in this section of the exam. The exam is not necessarily designed so that it's impossible to finish all the questions in the allotted time, but it certainly isn't designed so that you *can* finish, either (at least not in the Memory for Addresses and Address Checking sections).

How's that for advice?!? Seriously, the tip here is to work as quickly and efficiently as you can, keeping in mind that you will be penalized for questions you answer incorrectly, so wild guessing (if you are running out of time) is not a good strategy in this section. Note that answers left blank are not considered wrong answers. You don't get any points for blank answers, but you don't get any points deducted either, so, once again, it is better to leave them blank than guess randomly. Remember, though, that scoring differs from section to section: Some sections of the exam don't subtract points for incorrect answers, so guessing is something to consider in those sections.

Detailed information on scoring for each section of the exam will be given in the chapters specific to each question.

Work as quickly and efficiently as possible. As you learned in Chapter 4, avoid letting your eyes (and attention!) wander: Differences in the two addresses you are asked to compare can be very minor, and thus easily missed if you are not paying close attention.

1. Locate a pencil to darken the correct oval on the answer sheet. You can find an answer sheet for this practice test in the back of the book. It is labeled "Chapter 8 Exam Answer Sheet."

2. For this practice quiz, you should give yourself six minutes to answer the 50 questions provided. Ask a friend or family member to time you, or if you have a timer (a stopwatch with an alarm, for example) that will suffice as well.

3. As you mark your answers, mark "A" if the two addresses are exactly the same, and mark "D" if you notice any difference.

4. When the six minutes are up, stop work immediately even if you are not finished. In a real exam situation, you will also be asked to stop work when time expires.

1.	1226 Harbor Ave	1262 Harbor Ave
2.	Fort Jefferson NY	Port Jefferson NY
3.	672 Michigan Ave	672 Michigan Ave
4.	12432 14th St	12432 14th St
5.	Albany GA	Albany NY
6.	Cleveland OH 44101	Cleveland OH 44107
7.	6564 Pinelawn Ave	6564 Pinecone Ave
8.	1443 Dial Rd	1443 Dial Rd
9.	Miami Beach FL	Miami FL
10.	85 Manchester Dr	85 Manchester Dr
11.	25 East Marion Blvd	25 West Marion Blvd
12.	7274 Farley Ave NW	7274 Farley Ave NW
13.	44a Washington Ter	44a Washington Ter
14.	34 Pontiac Plz	34 Pontiac Pl
15.	21326 Devon Ct	21325 Devon Ct
16.	1256 Dorchester Rd	1256 E. Dorchester Rd
17.	Decatur IL	Decatur AL
18.	17 Candlestick Ln	17 Candlestick Ln
19.	New London CT	New Britain CT
20.	8182 N. Chester St	8118 N. Chester St
21.	Pembroke Pines FL	Pembroke Pines FL
22.	5342 Hemlock Ln	5342 Hemlock Ln
23.	704 Crane Ave SW	704 Crane Ave SW
24.	20 Petunia Ct.	20 Petunia Dr
25.	Union Valley Rd.	Union Valley St.
26.	56 Paris Ln	58 Paris Ln
27.	32 Capri Ct	32 Capri Ct
28.	88824 Rhodes Hwy	88824 Rhodes Hwy
29.	2221 Fanshaw St	2221 Fanview St
30.	Warwick RI	Warwick RI
31.	Portland ME	Portland OR
32.	Montgomery AL 36102	Montgomery AL 36120
33.	254 Central Dr NW	254 Central Dr SW
34.	Billings MT 59106	Billings MT 59106
35.	847 Oak Tree Rdg	847 Oak Tree Rdg

(continued)

36.	93292 SW 45 Ave	93292 SW 45 Ave
37.	69 Peppertree Lane	69 Pepperday Lane
38.	35 Belle Ct	35 Bella Ct
39.	2232 Mondale Rd	2232 Mondale Rd
40.	94 Crenshaw Ave	94 Cranberry Ave
41.	566 Swallow Ln	566 Swallon Ln
42.	901 Berto Pl	901 Berto Pl
43.	58 Jennifer Hts Rd	58 Jennifer Rd
44.	8989 Pane St	8989 Pane St
45.	42003 Argyle Ct	42030 Argyle Ct
46.	77 Cameron Plz	77 Cameroon Plz
47.	Brooklyn NY 11236	Brooklyn NY 11236
48.	Tewksbury MA	Tewksbury MA
49.	50 Otis St	50 Otis Rd
50.	North Chicago IL 60064	North Chicago IL 60063
51.	Groton CT 06340	Groton CT 06340
52.	4125 Premier Dr	4225 Premier Dr
53.	Wilmington DE 19898	Wilmington DE 19897
54.	1313 Levin Path	1313 Levine Path
55.	543 Browning Ln	543 Browning Ln
56.	Frederick MD	Frederick MD
57.	6041 Variel Ave	6141 Variel Ave
58.	111 Bauer Dr	111 Bauer Dr
59.	Providence RI 02906-3323	Providence RI 02907-3333
60.	830 S Greenville Ave	830 N Greenville Ave
61.	Janesville WI 53546	Janesville WI 53546
62.	9822 Fallard Ct	9822 Fallan Ct
63.	8550 Balboa Blvd	9550 Balboa Blvd
64.	Langhorne PA 19053	Langhorne PA 19053
65.	Saint Paul, MN 55114	Saint Paul, MN 55115
66.	400 Winans Ave	400 Winars Ave
67.	Santa Fe Springs CA	Santa Fe Springs CA
68.	954 Crayfish Dr	954 Crawfish Dr
69.	Upper Marlboro MD	Upper Marlboro MD
70.	698543 Penny Ln	695843 Penny Ln

(continued)

71.	24534 Barking Rd	24534 Barking Rd
72.	875 Dogwood Cir	875 Dogwood Cir
73.	Marietta GA 30067	Marietta GA 30067
74.	2920 Red Hill Ave	2920 Reid Hill Ave
75.	100 S Milwaukee Ave	100 SE Milwaukee Ave
76.	Simpsonville KY 40067	Simpsonville KY 40067
77.	327 Daniel Webster Hwy	327 Daniel Webster Hwy
78.	403 N Levee Rd	413 N Levee Rd
79.	Greenville SC	Greenville NC
80.	6610 Cabot Dr	6610 Carbon Dr
81.	Milford IN	Milford CT
82.	New Rochelle NY 10801	New Rochelle NY 10801
83.	857 N Central St	857 N Central St
84.	Denver CO 80202	Denver CO 80102
85.	120 W 45th St	120 W 45th St
86.	5330 Dijon Dr	5330 Dilon Dr
87.	633 N Barranca Ave	633 N Barranca Ave
88.	267 A Ory St	257 A Ory St
89.	26 N Middletown Rd	26 W Middletown Rd
90.	Peoria IL 61616	Peoria IL 61616
91.	101 Highway 11 N	101 Highway 11
92.	Philadelphia MS	Philadelphia PA
93.	1925 Enterprise Pkwy	1925 Enterprise Pkwy
94.	308 Canal St	308 Canal St
95.	887 Pearlman Rd	887 Pearlment Rd
96.	26433 Southwest Fwy	26433 Southwest Hwy

Exam Prep Answers

Use the following answer key to grade and evaluate how well you did on the practice test. Remember your total score should be the number of correct answers minus the number you answered incorrectly or did not answer.

1. D	2. D	3. A	4. A
5. D	6. D	7. D	8. A
9. D	10. A	11. D	12. A
13. A	14. D	15. D	16. D
17. D	18. A	19. D	20. D
21. A	22. A	23. A	24. D
25. D	26. D	27. A	28. A
29. D	30. A	31. D	32. D
33. D	34. A	35. D	36. A
37. D	38. D	39. A	40. D
41. D	42. A	43. D	44. A
45. D	46. D	47. A	48. A
49. D	50. D	51. A	52. D
53. D	54. D	55. A	56. A
57. D	58. A	59. D	60. D
61. A	62. D	63. D	64. A
65. D	66. D	67. A	68. D
69. A	70. D	71. A	72. A
73. A	74. D	75. D	76. A
77. A	78. D	79. D	80. D
81. D	82. A	83. A	84. D
85. A	86. D	87. A	88. D
89. D	90. A	91. D	92. D
93. A	94. A	95. D	96. D

Bill Roberts Case Study: Address Checking Questions Practice Test

When I first worked through the address checking intro chapter, I was a little surprised to find these types of questions are harder than I thought. At the bank where I work, I have time to review stuff: I mean, I can't dawdle, but at the same time my customers expect me (demand of me!) to be accurate and careful when reviewing their financial documents, so if I have to compare figures, I can take time to make sure my work is accurate. So again, with these questions, I know I don't have that luxury of time, and that I have to rely on my abilities to concentrate and not let my attention drift away.

Like I said earlier, I didn't do that great on the initial sample test covering this type of question. But this time around on the practice test, I really "cleared my mind" before sitting down to take the test. Like with the short test in Chapter 4, I finished these questions in less than six minutes (although just by about twenty seconds!) but I really focused in and didn't let other thoughts creep into my head. I've actually been practicing "concentrating" in what I think is an interesting way. I give myself a category of something to think about—for example, rock music and more specifically my favorite band, the Beatles—and then I give myself six minutes (just like the amount of time I have to take this section of the exam) to think of nothing but Beatle song titles. At the first thought of a song (or anything) that is not Beatle related, I stop as I have "failed" the test. Admittedly, this is really hard when you are just thinking and you have to be honest with yourself to "stop the test" when you think of something off subject, but it is a great little mental exercise.

So, before I sat down to take this practice test, I got myself in the same frame of mind: Before I took the test, I tested my concentration level, this time thinking of nothing but Elvis song titles for six minutes. You should try this, as it's harder than you think! At first, the song titles flood your brain, but then you have to really think about them, and (this is where things get difficult) not think of anything else!

At any rate, I did very well on this practice test, getting 88 of the 96 questions correct. I am becoming more confident in my ability to do well on this section of the exam, if I can just keep my attention focused.

9

Memory for Addresses Practice Test

This chapter makes its focus the memory for addresses question type. You will recall from Chapter 5 several web sites giving practicing tips on how to improve your memory. As you work through this sample test, you should keep in mind the same "strategies" from the address checking test, which are—quite simply—clear your mind as much as you can, and relax and focus on the task at hand. However, unlike the address checking questions, there are proven ways to enhance your memory. Again, refer to the strategies/tips listed in Chapter 5 for more information.

Note the "Bill Roberts Case Study" element at the end of this chapter and the other question-specific chapters to get a real-world perspective on how a typical exam taker both approaches these questions/exams, and in turn deals with the resulting score in an effort to do better on the real exam.

Take the Memory for Addresses Practice Test

For this practice test, you have five minutes to answer as many of the following questions as possible. Your score will be determined in the following manner:

Total number of correct answers minus 1/4 point for each wrong answer.

As with the Address Checking section, random guessing is not a good strategy with these questions. Note that you will be penalized 1/4 point for each wrong answer. Better to leave an answer blank (and not have it counted as incorrect) than to wildly guess.

There are some additional rules you will need to follow for this test (note these are the same rules you need to abide by on the actual exam, too):

➤ During the exam, you cannot refer back to the address grid.

➤ During the memorization period, you cannot write down the addresses or any other information (that is, you truly have to memorize the information, and then answer the questions based solely on your memory).

 The "memorization period" is a short period (a few minutes), which will be administered by the individual proctoring the exam.

Finally, remember that your goal is to determine which box (A, B, C, D, or E) the address came from. You don't need to memorize where the addresses are placed within the address box, but just from what box they are in.

1. Locate a pencil to darken the correct oval on the answer sheet. You can find an answer sheet for this practice test in the back of the book. It is labeled "Chapter 9 Answer Sheet."

2. For this practice quiz, you should give yourself five minutes for the "memorization period." Ask a friend or family member to time you, or use a timer (a stopwatch with an alarm, for example).

3. For each question, mark your answer sheet with either A, B, C, D, or E to correspond to the column in which the address would be placed.

4. After your memorization period, you will have five minutes to answer as many of the 88 questions as possible. When your time is up, stop work immediately even if you are not finished. In a real exam situation, you will also be asked to stop work when time expires.

For the next five minutes, study the following table, noticing how the addresses are organized in each of the boxes.

A	B	C	D	E
6500-7400 Talbot	3300-3900 Talbot	5400-6100 Talbot	2100-2999 Talbot	7200-8000 Talbot
Marlin	Magnolia	Hillside	Jeanette	Davis
8300-8999 Yale	6100-6999 Yale	1200-1999 Yale	4200-5000 Yale	3500-4000 Yale
Liberty	Roger	Lawrence	Roselle	Charles
9300-9999 Northern	6399-6999 Northern	3300-4000 Northern	1200-2000 Northern	5500-6200 Northern

STOP! DO NOT TURN THE PAGE TO VIEW THE TEST QUESTIONS UNTIL YOU HAVE COMPLETED THE MEMORIZATION PERIOD AND ARE READY TO BEING THE FIVE-MINUTE TIMED TEST.

1. Magnolia	45. Lawrence
2. 6399-6999 Northern	46. 3300-4000 Northern
3. 1200-2000 Northern	47. 7200-8000 Talbot
4. Jeanette	48. Charles
5. 4200-5000 Yale	49. Roger
6. Charles	50. 1200-1999 Yale
7. 7200-8000 Talbot	51. 6500-7400 Talbot
8. 3500-4000 Yale	52. Liberty
9. Davis	53. Roselle
10. 8300-8999 Yale	54. 5400-6100 Talbot
11. Marlin	55. Jeanette
12. 5400-6100 Talbot	56. 2100-2999 Talbot
13. Hillside	57. 8300-8999 Yale
14. 9300-9999 Northern	58. Hillside
15. Liberty	59. Davis
16. 2100-2999 Talbot	60. 6399-6999 Northern
17. Roger	61. 3500-4000 Yale
18. 3300-4000 Northern	62. Magnolia
19. 1200-2000 Northern	63. Marlin
20. Lawrence	64. 5500-6200 Northern
21. 4200-5000 Yale	65. 6100-6999 Yale
22. Roselle	66. Roger
23. Magnolia	67. Lawrence
24. 7200-8000 Talbot	68. 9300-9999 Northern
25. 6399-6999 Northern	69. Roselle
26. Charles	70. Liberty
27. 1200-2000 Northern	71. 3300-4000 Northern
28. 8300-8999 Yale	72. Hillside
29. Jeanette	73. Roger
30. Hillside	74. 7200-8000 Talbot
31. 4200-5000 Yale	75. 1200-1999 Yale
32. 3300-4000 Northern	76. 2100-2999 Talbot
33. 5500-6200 Northern	77. Charles
34. 8300-8999 Yale	78. Jeanette
35. Liberty	79. 6399-6999 Northern

(continued)

36. Marlin	80. Marlin
37. 4200-5000 Yale	81. Davis
38. Davis	82. 8300-8999 Yale
39. Lawrence	83. 3500-4000 Yale
40. 9300-9999 Northern	84. Magnolia
41. 1200-2000 Northern	85. Hillside
42. 4200-5000 Yale	86. 6100-6999 Yale
43. Rogor	87. 6300-6999 Northern
44. Marlin	88. 7200-8000 Talbot

Evaluating Your Score

Use the following answer key to grade and evaluate how well you did on the practice test. Remember your total score should be the number of correct answers minus 1/4 point for each wrong answer.

1. B	23. B	45. C	67. C
2. B	24. E	46. C	68. A
3. D	25. B	47. E	69. D
4. D	26. E	48. E	70. A
5. D	27. D	49. B	71. C
6. E	28. A	50. C	72. C
7. E	29. D	51. A	73. B
8. E	30. C	52. A	74. E
9. E	31. D	53. D	75. C
10. A	32. C	54. C	76. D
11. A	33. E	55. D	77. E
12. C	34. A	56. D	78. D
13. C	35. A	57. A	79. B
14. A	36. A	58. C	80. A
15. A	37. D	59. E	81. E
16. D	38. E	60. B	82. A
17. B	39. C	61. E	83. E
18. C	40. A	62. B	84. B

(continued)

19. D	41. D	63. A	85. C
20. C	42. D	64. E	86. B
21. D	43. B	65. B	87. B
22. D	44. A	66. B	88. E

Bill Roberts Case Study: Memory for Addresses Questions Practice Test

Well, memory has never been one of my greatest assets. If you asked my wife, she would tell you (on a bad day) my memory is terrible, and that I can't remember anything. Or, she would tell you (on a good day!) that I have "selective memory," where I can't for the life of me remember to take the trash out, but I have no problem remembering the score of every football game for the entire season. I suppose she has a point, although I certainly don't intentionally try to forget things. It's just that some things seem to "stick in my head" better than others.

This is all fine and good when it comes to good-natured arguments with my wife, but for the exam—and as a result, my career—improving my memory is a crucial issue. When I first worked through the introductory chapter (Chapter 5) that covered memory for addresses, I was very concerned at my ability to perform even moderately well on this portion of the exam. When I first glanced at that address box, I tensed up and just could not imagine having to memorize all that information and then answer so many questions revolving around it.

However, as with all things related to this exam (or so it seems, the more I study and prepare for it), just taking a deep breath, clearing my head, and taking a few minutes to calm down really made (and continues to make) a huge difference. First of all, if I had to give advice on this section of the exam, I would say—other than what I just said above about relaxing—that the information isn't as difficult to memorize as it first appears. After all, there is quite a bit of similarity to each column in the address box (for example, the same street name but just a different range of house numbers for each address in the box). So, you can put the street name out of your mind as it will always be the same. When you do, this leaves just the range of house numbers you have to memorize.

But hey, I'm not going to kid you: this is not the easiest part of the exam for me, and even after reading/working through some of the techniques for memory enhancement presented in Chapter 5, I did pretty poorly on this practice test, only answering 50 of the 88 questions correctly (I didn't finish in time, either, so I had many blank answers). Still, Chapter 5 presented some good strategies for memory enhancement, so I'm going to be spending quite a bit of time reviewing those, as well as (of course!) working through this sample test again, and working through the full-length sample exams in this book.

Number Series Practice Test

You've already been exposed to the number series question type in previous chapters, with a chance to preview your aptitude for this question type in Chapters 2 (the mock exam) and 6.

With this chapter, however, you'll be presented with a full-length practice test of 24 questions and asked to answer them as if you were actually taking this portion of the exam. You'll have 20 minutes to complete as many questions as possible.

As you work through the sample test, be sure—as with all other sections of the exam—to keep a clear and focused mind on the task at hand. And remember what we've said from the very beginning about this question type: Don't let the inclusion of the word "numbers" throw you or otherwise make you apprehensive. The questions are tolerable (indeed, can be quite easy) if you can stay focused and apply a little logic to each question. This is not calculus, but rather the questions will ask you to use addition, subtraction, multiplication, and division to "solve" the pattern being presented. Be sure to refer specifically to Chapter 6, which provides some strategies and techniques for approaching these types of questions.

Also, be sure to note the "Bill Roberts Case Study" element at the end of this chapter (as well as the other question-specific chapters) to get a real-world perspective on how a typical exam taker approaches these exams and then deals with the resulting score.

Take the Number Series Practice Test

For this practice test, you have 20 minutes to answer as many of the following questions as possible. Your score will be determined in the following manner:

Total number of correct answers.

 Remember, there is no penalty for guessing in this section, so be sure to provide an answer for each question presented.

Although strategies for this question type are again discussed in Chapter 6, you should keep the following in mind as you work through this practice test:

➤ Stay as relaxed as possible, concentrating on the questions themselves (in other words, don't let your mind wander)!

➤ If you are working on a question and you can't immediately recognize the pattern, utilize the tips you were presented with in Chapter 6, most notably drawing in your test booklet to help you visualize the pattern.

➤ More than likely, there will be some easy questions ("easy" in the sense that you immediately can identify the pattern). Answer these questions first, then go back and tackle the harder ones. Don't forget there is no penalty for guessing, so be sure to provide an answer for every question, even if you are guessing.

1. Locate a pencil to darken the correct oval on the answer sheet. You can find an answer sheet for this practice test in the back of the book. It is labeled "Chapter 10 Answer Sheet."

2. For each question, mark your answer sheet with A, B, C, D, or E to correspond to the correct answer.

3. You will have 20 minutes to answer as many of the 24 questions as possible. When your time is up, stop work immediately even if you are not finished. In a real exam situation, you will also be asked to stop work when time expires.

Ready to begin? Use a stopwatch and set it for 20 minutes, or ask a friend to time you. When you are ready, start the clock and begin work on the following 24 questions.

1. 3 2 7 12 13 4 103 22__ __
    A. 55 40
    B. 33 55
    C. 66 24
    D. 30 43

2. 92 88 86 82 80 76 74 __ __
    A. 70 68
    B. 69 60
    C. 64 62
    D. 70 69

3. 20 26 34 44 56 70 86 ___ ___
    A. 90 94
    B. 96 106
    C. 107 110
    D. 104 124

4. 21 29 37 45 53 61 __ __
    A. 65 70
    B. 69 77
    C. 64 70
    D. 62 63

5. 12 21 13 31 14 41 15 __ __
    A. 16 17
    B. 16 55
    C. 51 16
    D. 42 15

6. 76 69 62 55 48 41 34 __ __
    A. 26 19
    B. 27 20
    C. 30 28
    D. 32 29

7. 11 17 23 29 35 41 47 __ __
    A. 53 59
    B. 51 67
    C. 48 49
    D. 55 56

8. 25 31 39 49 61 75 91 __ __

    A. 99 100

    B. 109 129

    C. 92 119

    D. 110 121

9. 18 25 32 39 46 53 60 __ __

    A. 61 66

    B. 72 77

    C. 65 66

    D. 67 74

10. 22 30 38 46 54 62 70 __ __

    A. 77 78

    B. 76 81

    C. 78 86

    D. 72 74

11. 75 66 57 48 39 30 21 __ __

    A. 20 4

    B. 19 1

    C. 17 3

    D. 12 3

12. 26 30 34 38 42 46 50 __ __

    A. 54 58

    B. 52 57

    C. 55 59

    D. 58 62

13. 2 0 4 2 6 4 8 __ __

    A. 5 12

    B. 6 10

    C. 10 8

    D. 10 12

14. 21 3 31 4 41 5 51 __ __

    A. 52 53

    B. 54 57

    C. 5 61

    D. 6 61

15. 96 94 90 84 76 66 54 __ __
   A. 40 32
   B. 50 45
   C. 55 62
   D. 42 54

16. 7 7 3 8 8 2 9 __ __
   A. 8 3
   B. 9 1
   C. 7 2
   D. 6 5
   E. 9 2

17. 25 28 31 34 37 40 43 __ __
   A. 47 51
   B. 46 48
   C. 44 47
   D. 46 49
   E. 50 53

18. 6 13 13 6 14 14 6 __ __
   A. 15 15
   B. 6 15
   C. 15 6
   D. 7 7
   E. 16 16

19. 5 7 10 14 19 25 32 __ __
   A. 39 46
   B. 41 50
   C. 38 45
   D. 40 49

20. 18 20 22 18 20 22 18 __ __
   A. 18 20
   B. 20 20
   C. 20 22
   D. 22 22
   E. 18 22

21. 94 92 94 90 94 88 94__ __
    A. 86 94
    B. 90 94
    C. 86 92
    D. 94 94
    E. 84 94

22. 32 9 33 10 34 11 35__ __
    A. 36 11
    B. 38 10
    C. 12 26
    D. 11 36
    E. 12 35

23. 88 85 82 88 84 80 88__ __
    A. 85 50
    B. 88 88
    C. 83 77
    D. 83 78

24. 67 59 52 44 37 29 22__ __
    A. 18 11
    B. 14 7
    C. 14 8
    D. 16 11
    E. 15 8

Evaluating Your Score

Use the following answer key to grade and evaluate how well you did on the practice test. Remember, your total score should be the number of correct answers (no penalty or point deduction for incorrect answers).

1. **A.** In this pattern even numbers alternate with odd numbers, beginning with an odd number, for example, 3 2 7 12.

2. **A.** There are two alternating patterns in this series; in the first pattern the difference between the numbers is 4; in the second pattern the difference is always –2, for example, 92–4=88, 88–2=86, 86–4=82, 82–2=80, and so on.

3. **D.** This series follows the rule +6 +8 +10, and so on, for example, 20+6=26, 26+8=34, 34+10=44,

4. **B.** The numbers in this series increase by 8.

5. **C.** Every other number in this series reverses the digits of the number before it, for example, 12 21 13 31; starting with the first number, the numbers just increase by 1.

6. **B.** The difference between each number in the series is 7, for example, 76–7=69, 69–7=62

7. **A.** The numbers in this series increase by 6, for example, 11+6=17, 17+6=23.

8. **B.** This series follows the rule +6 +8 +10, for example, 25+6=31, 31+8=39.

9. **D.** The numbers in this series increase by 7, for example, 18+7=25, 25+7=32.

10. **C.** The numbers in this series increase by 8, for example, 22+8=30, 30+8=38.

11. **D.** The numbers in this series decrease by 9, for example, 75–9=66, 66–9=57.

12. **A.** The numbers in this series increase by 4, for example, 26+4=30, 30+4=34.

13. **B.** This series follows a pattern of –2 +4, for example, 2–2=0, 0+4=4, 4–2=2, 2+4=6.

14. **D.** There are two alternating series: The first one counts up by 10, for example, 21, 31...; the second series counts up by 1, for example, 3, 4....

15. **A.** The rule followed in this series is –2 –4 –6, and so on.

16. **B.** The first two numbers repeat (7 7) followed by a 3, then increase the first number (8 8) twice again and then decrease the third by one (2); increase twice again and then decrease by one, leaving you with 9 3.

17. **D.** Add 3 to each number, which leaves 46 49.

18. **A.** First number, 6, remains the same throughout. This is followed by a number repeated twice, which starts with 13; then repeat the six and subsequently add one to the number that repeats, which is 15.

19. **D.** Starting with the number 5, add 2 and then add 3, next adding 4, 5, and so on, which eventually has you adding 8 and then 9, resulting in 40 49.

20. **C.** Here the same three numbers are repeated over again 18 20 22.

21. **A.** A repeated number 94 alternates with the result of subtracting increasing even numbers from it, leaving 86 94.

22. **C.** Two numbers, starting with 32 and 9, are increased by 1 over and over, which produces 12 36.

23. **D.** Start with 88 and subtract 3, and then subtract 3 from that number again; repeat the 88 and subtract 4 and then 4 again; finally, repeat 88 and subtract 5 and then 5 again, leaving 83 78.

24. **B.** Here 8 and then 7 are subtracted and then 8 and then 7 again, repeating the subtraction of these two numbers until the final two numbers are 14 and 7.

Bill Roberts Case Study: Number Series Questions Practice Test

Well, I'll be honest with you yet again: I'm a "numbers man." I've always enjoyed mathematics and working with numbers. Back in high school, my best friend was an English whiz. I mean, the guy could read Shakespeare with one eye closed (and read it quickly) and could then turn around and write the most amazing papers, full of great ideas and analysis of what he had read. Me, on the other hand…well, let's just say I struggled with *Cat in the Hat*, and things never got much better. I mean, I like to read, but that was just never my strong suit. On the other hand, the same friend had problems adding two and two. It was funny: Where he was really good with words, I was the same way with numbers.

I've been thinking a lot about that same friend as I've been working through this book, and especially the practice tests where I've been asked to really test my ability with these different question types. I told you earlier that—for me, at least—the memory for addresses is the most difficult. The pressure of having to try to memorize all that information in such a short time is really tough for me. But just like my friend back in high school who was really good with words, I've been talking to a colleague who is also studying for the 460/470 exam, and she seems to think the memory for addresses is the easiest thing she's ever had to prepare for. So I guess it all depends on your specific aptitude and ability.

Still, the point of working through a book like this is to try to bring yourself up to speed on all the different question types, so that no single question type really gives you a case of nerves. The number series are easier for me, but I know that I can't get too confident. The other really important thing I need to keep in mind (and as pointed out by my colleague) is that in an actual testing situation, it's going to be a challenge (and I need to be aware of that challenge) to keep my focus as I move from a section I think is not so difficult (number series) to a set of questions that is going to be tough, such as the memory for addresses.

The more I think about this test, the more I start to think it's all, ultimately, about one thing: keeping your focus on the task at hand. It would be very easy to get distracted with the questions asked on this exam, no matter how easy or difficult you think they might be. Plus, no matter how easy the questions are, I know there is one luxury I won't have when taking this exam, and that luxury is being able to work at my own pace. Having only 20 minutes to answer the number series questions is serious business. But I'm continuing to refer to the general test-taking strategies in this book so that I can, again, keep my focus, which I know is absolutely critical to success on all the different sections of the exam.

Following Oral Instructions Practice Test

You were first introduced to this question type in Chapter 7. If you read through that chapter closely, you realize that

➤ After directions are read to you, they will not be repeated; therefore, your abilities to focus and pay close attention are absolutely critical to your success on this section of the exam.

➤ The only way to really prepare for this section of the exam is to practice with a partner. Although it is possible for you to prepare on your own (read the questions silently to yourself, and have the self-discipline not to read the question more than once), your study time will be much more productive if you can get a friend to serve as the "exam proctor" and read the questions to you.

Take the Oral Instructions Practice Test

To best utilize this practice test (and all Following Oral Instructions practice tests in this book), you should enlist the help of a friend to read the instructions to you; this will more accurately mimic the actual testing environment.

You need to follow some additional rules for this test (note these are the same rules you need to abide by on the actual exam, too):

➤ Questions are read only once.

➤ You are not allowed to ask any questions during this portion of the exam.

➤ When you finish the test, have no more than one space marked for each number. If more than one space is marked for a number, the item will be counted as wrong.

1. Locate a pencil to darken the correct oval on the answer sheet. You can find an answer sheet for this practice test in the back of the book. It is labeled "Chapter 11 Answer Sheet." The following set of questions will be referred to as the worksheet (different from your answer sheet, referenced above):

   1. Monday, Friday, Wednesday, Sunday

   2. 821038746389205672230

   3. 23___, 42___, 37___, 43___

   4. 24496, 32006, 37752, 40021

   5. green + yellow = blue, red + yellow = orange, blue + red = purple

2. Hand the book to your partner, who will be reading the instructions to you.

3. Remember to have your partner read each question only one time.

The intent of this chapter is not so much to present you with a completely realistic simulation of a Following Oral Instructions test; rather, it is to get you used to this type of test: that is, where someone else is reading directions to you. That said, the format of this practice test is somewhat different from the actual exam. For example, some questions will present you with a situation that is false (that is, you will be asked to determine whether a situation is true or equal to a stated value). If it is false, then you will do nothing and not mark anything on your answer sheet, but rather move on to the next question.

TO THE PERSON READING THE INSTRUCTIONS: You should read quickly and clearly. You do not have to read the words in parentheses (note this is the amount of time you should pause before continuing on in reading the question); these have been provided for your guidance in allowing the test taker time to think about/answer each question.

READ THE FOLLOWING TO THE TEST TAKER: You need to mark your answer sheet according to the specific instructions I read to you. I'll pause for a few seconds after each instruction, so you have time to mark your answer sheet.

The test begins now.

1. (Pause 3 seconds.) On line 3, enter letters of the alphabet (A, B, C) in the blanks, starting with the largest number, then the next largest number, and so on. Find the number that has B after it, go to that number on the answer sheet, and darken the letter "D" as in dog. (Pause 5 seconds.)

2. (Pause 3 seconds.) If all the names on line 1 are days of the week, go to number 17 on the answer sheet and darken the letter "A" as in apple. (Pause 5 seconds.)

3. (Pause 3 seconds.) Underline the 3rd and 12th numbers in line 2. Add the two numbers together, find the number on the answer sheet that equals the total, and darken the letter "B" as in boy. (Pause 5 seconds.)

4. (Pause 3 seconds.) On line 5, is one color used each time in all three equations? If no, go to number 23 on the answer sheet and darken the letter "C" as in cat. (Pause 5 seconds.)

5. (Pause 3 seconds.) Add the digits in each ZIP code in line 4. Find the greatest total and go to that number on the answer sheet and darken the letter "D" as in dog. (Pause 5 seconds.)

6. (Pause 3 seconds.) If all the days of the week in line 1 are spelled correctly, go to number 30 on the answer sheet and darken the letter "A" as in apple. If not, go to number 4 on the answer sheet and darken the letter "B" as in boy. (Pause 5 seconds.)

7. (Pause 3 seconds.) Find the 11th number in line 2. Go to that number on the answer sheet and darken the letter "C" as in cat. (Pause 5 seconds.)

8. (Pause 3 seconds.) Add the number 9 to each set of numbers in line 3. When you add each of the three numbers together, are the sums in order from smallest to largest? If yes, go to number 27 on the answer sheet and darken the letter "B" as in boy. (Pause 5 seconds.)

9. (Pause 3 seconds.) On line 2, do each of the numbers 0 through 9 appear at least twice? If yes, go to number 11 on the answer sheet and darken the letter "D" as in dog. (Pause 5 seconds.)

10. (Pause 3 seconds.) Are the ZIP codes on line 4 listed from smallest to largest? If yes, go to number 33 on the answer sheet and darken the letter "A" as in apple. (Pause 5 seconds.)

Evaluating Your Score

Use the following answer key to grade and evaluate how well you did on the practice test. Remember your total score should be the number of questions you answered correctly.

If you answered all the questions correctly, your answer sheet should be be marked as follows:

Question Number	Answer Space Darkened
4	B
8	C
10	B
17	A
23	C
25	D
33	A
42	D

Bill Roberts Case Study: Address Checking Questions Practice Test

Well, the really good news is that, over the course of preparing for this exam, I have—according to my wife—become a much better listener. Apparently, she has not had to tell me more than twice to take out the garbage (a personal record for me), and last Saturday, she told me only once to mow the grass. She is thrilled and amazed at my apparent new attention to detail.

All joking aside, I have found that I am paying closer attention to what people say. Not that I didn't listen closely when people were speaking before, but now—when I am really listening to what someone is saying—I am not just hearing their ideas but making an active, mental note of them. For example, the other day I was working with a client at the bank. She was describing to me a particular situation with her parent's retirement portfolio, and facts and figures were flying out left and right. In the past, I would have listened for only the important details, or more specifically, items I recognized so that I could address those with more detail.

But this time around, I found myself listening to everything the client was saying, from the tone of her voice to the inconsequential details. As it turned out, one of those inconsequential details ended up being very consequential. Over the course of telling me that her parents were moving to Michigan to be closer to grandkids, I realized that a tax law I had just read about would apply differently to their situation after they moved. Again, in the past, I might not have even picked up on that but—and this is probably from studying for this test—I noticed this little detail and as a result was able to give my client more useful, accurate information.

The Following Oral Instructions questions are still giving me some trouble, but I'm finding this not so much because I'm not paying attention (I'm definitely doing that), but that I'm still too anxious to move on to the next question. The problem is that the directions that are read, although not difficult, can be fairly involved: If you don't hear all the details, then it is nearly impossible to answer them with 100% confidence. Worse still, guessing isn't really an option on this portion of the exam: Even though you aren't penalized for guessing, because you have to jump all over your answer sheet darkening answer circles, it would be more like blind luck if you happened to guess correctly.

So, again, I am certainly becoming a better listener, but I still need to work on my general test-taking anxiety. Test day is rapidly approaching, and I know that a case of the nerves will do some serious damage to all the work I've been doing to prepare for the exam. I'm going to review the tips in Chapter 12, and then work through all the chapters (including the practice exams) at least two more times. My wife suggested that as I take the practice exams I treat them as if I was actually taking the test. That is, after I sit down to take the exam, I should imagine I'm in a real exam situation and finish the entire exam before I get up (this would include following the time limits, too, so I get a better sense of what it will be like to take the exams under pressure). It seems at times that I'm putting myself through a lot of trouble, time, and, well, pain in studying for this exam. But I know what a difference a high score will make in my career opportunities with the USPS and I'm ready to move on to this next phase of my professional career.

Preparing for Test Day

Terms You'll Need to Understand

✓ Plan
✓ Prepare
✓ Relax

Concepts/Techniques You'll Need to Master

✓ Finding ways to relax the night before the test.
✓ Gathering all registration materials and test-related items and then placing them in one place.
✓ Watching weather reports and traffic reports as you head to the test site.

If you're reading this chapter in "real time," that means that tomorrow (or perhaps in a few days) is the big day. Perhaps you've been preparing for several months, or maybe you've been getting ready for only a few weeks. Regardless, the day is now upon you and the good news is that you have spent time preparing for the exam. An old saying declares that chance favors the prepared mind; although you shouldn't need to rely a great deal on chance (that is, luck), having good luck never hurt anyone, especially on an exam. But the real focus here should be on the fact you have taken the time to prepare and familiarize yourself with the exam format and the types of questions you'll be asked. By doing so, you are already several steps ahead of other applicants, especially those who will be coming to the exam "cold," with no preparation.

You can look at this short chapter, then, as a final nod of encouragement, a final review of "last minute" preparation, or both. Of course, you might be reading this with several weeks (or more) left before the exam. Indeed, if you are reading the chapters in this book in sequential order, then you have yet to work through the full-length practice exams. If this is your situation, that is okay, too. You might use this chapter as a "real world" case study, and focus on your now-familiar test-taking partner (that is, Bill Roberts).

You should know that postal service entrance exams are used to "rate" your eligibility for employment with the USPS. Specifically, the registers of eligible potential employees are ranked in descending order of exam scores. Don't let this make you nervous: Rather, use it as motivation to concentrate and do your best.

If you are a claimed veteran, additional points can be added to your base score. This is also known as the *claimed veteran's preference*.

A Last-Minute Checklist: Do You Have What You Need?

Don't forget there is nothing wrong with being a little paranoid as test day approaches, especially the night before the exam. As you read in Chapter 3, "General Test-Taking Strategies," a little "nervous anxiety" can be a good thing because it can keep your mind focused as you work through the exam itself.

Of course, you have to keep this anxiety in check, lest it get the better of you. The same thing holds true as you do your last minute preparations, especially the night before the exam. The single most important thing to remember here is that if you've taken the time to prepare, *then you will remain prepared*. Nothing can take that away from you, short of some massive attack of nerves; however, you should be well prepared to deal with even that situation from reading through the tips and techniques presented in this book.

Let's assume for a minute that you are reading this the night before your exam. Let's also assume that you have been preparing for several weeks, and have worked through all the practice material in this book, including the four full-length practice exams. What is the best way, then, for you to prepare for "tomorrow" and what should your last minute checklist consist of? Although the following list is just a recommendation, it's a good recommendation and will be effective for the vast majority of test takers:

1. First, and as we've already mentioned, relax. You are well prepared and will remain so when you wake up the morning of the exam. Perhaps you can go out to a nice dinner, or take a relaxing walk or bike ride. Or maybe you can catch a movie to help clear your mind of test anxiety (although you might want to make it a lighthearted movie and something that won't keep you up all night. Indeed, a four-hour epic can probably wait until tomorrow evening, when you're finished with the exam!)

2. Take just a little time and make sure you've accounted for all the non–exam-related (but still very important) details. In other words, make sure you have all your registration information gathered so that you have all the documentation you will need to get into the test center. A good idea is to gather all this material and put it into a single folder, then—while you're thinking about it—put that folder in your car or somewhere you know you will not forget it (maybe put it under your car keys, as a prompt to remember this material).

3. Take a moment to catch the weather forecast for tomorrow. Are you going to need an umbrella? Is it going to be snowing? By all means, do not let something like the weather make you nervous. Of course, if a blizzard is forecast for your area, that is a different story (and if it is, you probably will want to keep an eye on your local TV stations, to determine whether the test will be cancelled). Just be prepared for any contingency so that it doesn't become an issue the morning of the test. Also, if you live in a large city, keep an ear open for traffic-related problems (accidents, construction) the morning of the exam.

4. At this point in your preparation, it probably won't do you much good to do lots of studying. In fact, trying to cram the night before the exam will probably do more harm than good, as it will distract you and raise your anxiety level. If you aren't prepared by now, you aren't going to be, so use this time to once again relax. One thing you can do, though, as a way of last-minute preparation, is to review the tear-out Cram Sheet found in the front of this book. In fact, you might want to take this with you the morning of the exam, so you can do one last review. Just remember not to have it out during the test (you don't want to be suspected of cheating).

5. Finally, after you've covered items 2–4, then return to the first suggestion on this list...and relax!

A "Real World" Test Preparation Case Study

A special element in many chapters of this book has been the "Bill Roberts" case study, which is intended both to give you a real-world example of how someone might prepare for the test, and to provide you a test-taking partner (that is, a realistic example of someone who is in the same situation as you are).

For this chapter, we'd like to review this case study so that you can use it as another way of doing some last-minute preparations for the exam. As you read through this section, you might want to relate your own situation to that of Bill, and reflect on how he prepares for the test as a reminder of the things you can do at the last minute to prepare (and relax!) as well.

Bill Roberts Case Study: The Night Before the Exam

As you've worked through this book, you've been presented with different aspects of the Bill Roberts case study, and how Bill—as a realistic representation of a test-taker—approached the various elements of preparing for the exam. This final entry of the case study has been written in the first person, in an effort to make it even more realistic. As you read through this, think of your own situation: Are there similarities/comparisons you can draw upon, and can you use Bill's situation as an example of how you can best work through the all-important night before the exam? Also, think of this case study as a last-minute general review, as Bill works through the concepts and techniques presented in this chapter, and those first introduced in Chapter 3.

The Night Before with Bill Roberts

In many ways, I can't believe this is the night before the exam. The last few months have really gone by quickly. I remember first picking up the *Postal Clerk and Carrier Exam Cram* and wondering how I would make my way through all the practice exams. But when I took my time to work through each section, and took time to review my answers to be sure I understood what was being tested, it wasn't that bad. It's a good thing I didn't wait until this evening to begin studying, though, as I had to work through some of the material a few times—especially those math-related questions. I was never that great at math!

I don't want to spend too much time this evening worrying about tomorrow. My family has given me lots of encouragement over the past few months, and I know that I am prepared. Now that I am thinking of it, though, I'm going to put my registration packet in the car so I won't be running around the house tomorrow morning trying to find it. On my way home from work on Tuesday, I drove over to the testing center, just to be sure I know where I'm going and that there isn't any road construction. Plus, I wanted to see about parking and whether I would have to do a lot of walking. I was playing basketball with my son last week, and came down a little hard on my ankle, and it still is a little sore. I definitely don't want to be in pain when I take this test, so if I can avoid walking, then all the better.

It's been cold here lately, and the weather has been very unpredictable. Someone came into the office earlier today and said a heavy snow is expected for the morning. I just checked the weather forecast, and sure enough...the snow is headed our way. The newscast said it wouldn't be hitting until later in the afternoon, but I should probably give myself a little extra time just in case the snow rolls in earlier than expected.

After dinner this evening, I'm going to read through the Cram Sheet once or twice, but I've decided not to work through the practice exams anymore, or spend a lot of time looking at the rest of the practice material. I pretty much figure that if I don't know it now, then I'm not going to know it, and staying up all night in a last-minute cram session is going to do me more harm than good. Before I turn in for the evening, though, I'm going to tear out the Cram Sheet and put it my car, along with my registration packet, so I can maybe read through it one more time after I get to the test center. If I get there early enough (which I plan on doing) I'll read through it in my car, and then leave it there. I don't want to hassle with carrying it (or risk the perception of using it to cheat, which I definitely am not going to do!)

Speaking of tomorrow morning, I think I have everything planned out. My wife is taking off from work to stay at home with the kids, so they are covered. I'm not much of a breakfast person, but I thought it would be good to have a little something in my stomach to help combat the nerves, so I'm going to get up a few minutes early to have time to eat (plus, if we get that bad weather, I'll be giving myself a little extra time to get to the test center). A friend of mine told me I could use the extra time to drink a few extra cups of coffee, but I don't usually have caffeine, so I'll probably skip that and stick to my usual morning glass of orange juice.

As soon as the exam starts, I've made a promise to myself to stay focused and concentrate on the task at hand, which is, of course, getting the highest score I can. If I get through each section early, I'll do some spot-checking of my answers, but I don't plan on doing any major review/making major changes to my initial answers—don't want to risk second-guessing myself too much. I really feel confident that I'm prepared for what is going to be asked of me, so no need to worry. Best of all, I've already made plans to shoot some hoops with my son after the exam, as a way of putting the anxiety of the test behind me. I hope that sore ankle of mine will hold up, but I have a feeling I will be so relieved to be through with the test, it won't be bothering me much!

Full Length Practice Exam I

If practice makes perfect, then perhaps no other test could have that saying applied to it more accurately than the 460/470 exam.

If you've worked your way through the chapters of this book in sequential order, then you know you can apply certain strategies and techniques to help you score higher on the exam. Ultimately, though, there is only so much you can do in "studying" to improve your attention span (a skill you are asked to heavily draw upon for all sections of the test, but especially for the Following Oral Instructions component).

That said, the best way to prepare for this exam is to practice! To help you in this regard, we've included four full-length practice exams, complete with the same number of questions (and presented with the same time limits) you would find on the actual 460/470 exam.

To take best advantage of the practice exams that follow in the next several chapters, you should keep the following in mind:

➤ *Follow all instructions as they are listed*—To make the exams as realistic as possible and to help you best anticipate an actual test environment, you should follow all instructions exactly as they are written. If the instructions ask you to stop before moving on to another section, you should do so. Treat these practice exams as if they were the real thing.

➤ *Do not exceed the time limits for any section of the exam*—Remember that on the actual exam, time limits are strictly enforced. Although it might be tempting on these practice exams to allow yourself a few extra minutes, you should avoid this urge. The time limits have been imposed to test your abilities concerning each of the test sections, so if you give yourself extra time you are really only cheating yourself.

➤ *Put yourself in a "test-taking frame of mind"*—When you sit down to take one of the practice exams, you should imagine you are sitting in an actual test center. And, if you were taking an actual exam, you wouldn't be allowed to take half the exam on one day, and then follow up a few days later with the final sections. In other words, if you want to give yourself an accurate (as possible) testing experience, you should take each practice exam in its entirety, following along with all instructions and time limits. You can certainly go back later and review individual sections of the exam, but to really get the most out of your practice and preparation time, you should complete a practice test in one sitting.

Address Checking

TIME: 6 Minutes, 95 Questions

Directions: For each question, compare the address in the left column with the address in the right column. If the two addresses are exactly alike, mark A on your answer sheet. If they are different in any way, mark D on your answer sheet.

1.	8723 Laughlin Ct	8273 Laughlin Ct
2.	9654 Jennings Ave	9564 Jennings Ave
3.	Bethel, ME 78145	Bethel, ME 78145
4.	63 W Markston	63 E Markston
5.	6474 Valley Road	6474 Valley Road
6.	9958 115th Street	9958 115th Street
7.	1542 Mesopeka Ln	1542 Mesopeka Dr
8.	Fayetteville, WI 44157	Fayetteville, MA 44157
9.	8345 N Senate	8435 N Senate
10.	4527 Tulip Tree Dr	4527 Tulip Tree Dr
11.	250 N Monisseur	250 N Monisseur
12.	6565 Joseph Place	6565 Joseph Palace
13.	4467 Mountain Valley Rd	4467 Mountain Valley Rd
14.	South Bend, IN 45787	South Bend, IN 45778
15.	25532 Oak St	25352 Oak St
16.	6532 Masters Ave	6352 Masters Ave
17.	5557 W 25th Street	5557 W 25th Street
18.	6958 Messing St	6958 Messing St
19.	5448 Dury Lane	54448 Dury Lane
20.	16 E Marywood Dr	16 E Marywood Dr
21.	Georgetown, OH 26045	Georgetown, OH 26405
22.	9494 Staton Rd	9494 Staton Dr
23.	7748 Ferris Ct	7748 Ferris Ct
24.	64025 Pine Street	60425 Pine Street
25.	3533 Seventh Ave	3533 Seventh Ave
26.	994 Jones Dr	994 Jones Dr
27.	9437 Apple Ave	9347 Apple Ave

(continued)

28.	Farmington, WV 33432	Farmington, WV 33342
29.	8847 Buena Vista Ave	8847 Buena Vista Ave
30.	1411 S Thorn St	1411 S Thorn St
31.	6566 Worthington Ave	6656 Worthington Ave
32.	456 Alphabet St	456 Alphabet St
33.	5554 Deacon Dr	5554 Deacon Dr
34.	2001 Forest Hills Ct	2001 Forest Ct
35.	Vernon, OR 70114	Vernon, OR 71044
36.	Miami, FL 22741	Miami, FL 22741
37.	3357 Crestview Dr	3357 Crestway Dr
38.	6854 Washington St	6854 Washington St
39.	5346 Deercreek Rd	5436 Deercreek Rd
40.	9265 N Mullholland	9265 S Mullholland Dr
41.	2541 Lasseter Ct	2451 Lasseter Ct
42.	7746 126th St	7746 126th St
43.	6574 N Blanchard Rd	6574 N Blanchard Rd
44.	Markelville, TN 87554	Markelville, IN 87554
45.	6547 Coney Cape	6547 Coney Cape
46.	1002 National Road	1002 National Road
47.	3202 Poplar Dr	3202 Poplar St
48.	86 Sunset Blvd	86 Sunset Bluff Blvd
49.	Portville, NJ 09554	Portville, NJ 09554
50.	4425 Dickson Dr	4452 Dickson Dr
51.	2626 Commons Rd	2626 Commons Rd
52.	9985 E Lucite Ave	9985 S Lucite Ave
53.	16 Tanner Blvd	166 Tanner Blvd
54.	4515 Devonshire	4515 Devonshire
55.	3536 Taggart Rd	3356 Taggart Rd
56.	645 E Finch Dr	645 E Finch Dr
57.	Strathroy, NY 25882	Strathroy, NY 28852
58.	6595 Lincoln Blvd	9565 Lincoln Blvd
59.	3543 Ivy Hills	3543 Ivy Hills
60.	5572 Chambers Dr	5572 Chambers Dr
61.	873 E Jackson St	873 E Jackson St
62.	3012 W 76th St	3102 W 76th St

(continued)

63.	5518 Thompson Ave	5158 Thompson Ave
64.	3530 5th Street	3350 5th Street
65.	Murphysboro, IL 14260	Murphysboro, IL 14260
66.	42587 Junction Pl	42875 Junction Pl
67.	8154 Parkay Cv	8154 Parkay Ct
68.	2242 Main St	2422 Main St
69.	9956 Mason Ave	9956 Mason Ave
70.	49 Zionsville Rd	49 Zionsville Ln
71.	32757 Knight Blvd	32757 Knight Blvd
72.	847 W Northern Ave	847 E Northern Ave
73.	Fortville, GA 35525	Fortville, GA 35255
74.	8723 Checker St	8723 Checker St
75.	4101 O & M Ave	4101 O & M Ave
76.	2019 Hummingbird Ln	2019 Hummingbird Ln
77.	7875 Myers Rd	7575 Myers Rd
78.	1174 14th Street	1774 14th Street
79.	4598 Cliff Ct	4598 Cliff Ct
80.	865 Jefferson Ln	965 Jefferson Ln
81.	Tempe, AZ 56865	Tempe, AZ 58665
82.	4675 County Line Rd	4675 County Line Rd
83.	5435 Jines St	5433 Jines St
84.	2892 Wall Street	2892 Wall Street
85.	35 W Fourth	35 W Fourth
86.	6455 Diamond Ave	6545 Diamond Ave
87.	1221 Lipton Parkway	1221 Lipton Parkway
88.	Orange, CA 55004	Orange, CA 55004
89.	3643 Temple Blvd	3463 Temple Blvd
90.	15433 Fir St	15433 Fur St
91.	4745 Violet Ln	4575 Violet Ln
92.	565 Needles	565 S Needle
93.	4151 Cardinal St	4115 Cardinal St
94.	Weston, NC 44105	Weston, NC 44105
95.	1005 Ridgeway Dr	1005 Ridgeway Dr

Memory for Addresses

TIME: 5 minutes, 88 questions

Directions: To make this practice exam as realistic as possible allow yourself an additional five minutes to study and memorize this grid. After those five minutes, you should then give yourself an additional five minutes—just as in the actual exam— to answer as many of the 88 questions as you can. On your answer sheet, mark each question A, B, C, D, or E, depending on where the address would be found in the information grid. DO NOT refer back to the grid after your initial five-minute memorization period is up; on the actual exam, you will not be allowed to refer back to the information grid after you complete your practice exercises.

A	B	C	D	E
1000-1499 Oak	1500-2099 Oak	2100-2299 Oak	8300-8499 Oak	4500-4699 Oak
Jennings	Farnsworth	Deering	Fountain	Sirus
2300-2599 Elm	2600-2899 Elm	2900-3099 Elm	6500-6799	4400-4599 Elm
Flint	Maple	Long	Dalbert	Woodlawn
3600-3799 Bethel	3800-4099 Bethel	1200-1499 Bethel	9300-9499 Bethel	5200-5299 Bethel

1. 2900-3099 Elm	31. 1000-1499 Oak	61. 1000-1499 Oak
2. 3800-4099 Bethel	32. 3600-3799 Bethel	62. 1200-1499 Bethel
3. Deering	33. 1200-1499 Bethel	63. Sirus
4. 1000-1499 Oak	34. 8300-8499 Oak	64. Fountain
5. Woodlawn	35. Farnsworth	65. 2600-2899 Elm
6. 4500-4699 Oak	36. Woodlawn	66. 2100-2299 Oak
7. 9300-9499 Bethel	37. 2600-2899 Elm	67. 2300-2599 Elm
8. 1500-2099 Oak	38. Jennings	68. Flint
9. 6500-6799 Elm	39. 2100-2299 Oak	69. 5200-5299 Bethel
10. 3600-3799 Bethel	40. 2900-3099 Elm	70. 9300-9499 Bethel
11. 2600-2899 Elm	41. 4500-4699 Oak	71. 2900-3099 Elm
12. Long	42. 6500-6799 Elm	72. 1500-2099 Oak
13. 8300-8499 Oak	43. Maple	73. 3600-3799 Bethel
14. 1200-1499 Bethel	44. 2900-3099 Elm	74. Woodlawn
15. Flint	45. 3600-3799 Bethel	75. Farnsworth
16. 2600-2899 Elm	46. Dalbert	76. 6500-6799 Elm
17. 5200-5299 Bethel	47. 2100-2299 Oak	77. Dalbert
18. 6500-6799 Elm	48. Sirus	78. 1000-1499 Oak
19. Maple	49. 1500-2099 Oak	79. 2900-3099 Elm
20. 1500-2099 Oak	50. Long	80. 4500-4699 Oak
21. 6500-6799 Elm	51. 6500-6799 Elm	81. Maple
22. Woodlawn	52. 2300-2599 Elm	82. 2300-2599 Elm
23. 1000-1499 Oak	53. 3800-4099 Bethel	83. Long
24. 9300-9499 Bethel	54. Woodlawn	84. 9300-9499 Bethel
25. Maple	55. 2100-2299 Oak	85. 4400-4599 Elm
26. 2100-2299 Oak	56. 1200-1499 Bethel	86. Deering
27. Flint	57. Jennings	87. 1500-2099 Oak
28. 4400-4599 Elm	58. 8300-8499 Oak	88. 3600-3799 Bethel
29. 6500-6799 Elm	59. 4400-4599 Elm	
30. Farnsworth	60. 3800-4099 Bethel	

Number Series

TIME: 20 minutes, 24 questions

Directions: Each number series question consists of a series of numbers that follow some definite, precise order: The numbers progress from left to right, following some determined rule. One lettered pair of numbers (A, B, C, or D) for each question represents the correct answer. That is, only one answer identifies the next numbers that should follow in the series and thus conform to the rule. Choose this correct answer, and mark it on your answer sheet.

1. 14 40 66 92 118 ___ ___
    A. 140 162
    B. 136 152
    C. 144 170
    D. 126 143

2. 978 943 908 873 838 ___ ___
    A. 803 768
    B. 800 765
    C. 815 780
    D. 820 785

3. 18 27 19 26 20 ___ ___
    A. 26 20
    B. 25 20
    C. 25 21
    D. 22 36

4. 33 44 32 45 31 ___ ___
    A. 46 28
    B. 40 50
    C. 42 33
    D. 46 30

5. 373 360 351 342 333 ___ ___
    A. 312 272
    B. 324 315
    C. 320 225
    D. 323 314

6. 14 16 3 18 20 3 22 ___ ___

    A. 24 3

    B. 24 26

    C. 26 28

    D. 26 3

7. 24 19 14 18 13 8 12 ___ ___

    A. 16 20

    B. 7 12

    C. 7 2

    D. 16 11

8. 427 432 437 442 447 ___ ___

    A. 452 459

    B. 454 459

    C. 450 455

    D. 452 457

9. 14 42 126 378 1134 ___ ___

    A. 3402 10206

    B. 3206 9618

    C. 12 48

    D. 20 40

10. 10 5 15 20 10 30 30 ___ ___

    A. 15 45

    B. 520 130

    C. 420 70

    D. 360 40

11. 4 16 64 256 ___ ___

    A. 524 2096

    B. 1024 4096

    C. 924 3696

    D. 1012 4048

12. 18 36 108 432 ___ ___

    A. 1296 5184

    B. 864 1728

    C. 2160 12960

    D. 2060 4120

13. 90 99 108 117 126 ___ ___
    A. 144 153
    B. 135 144
    C. 252 504
    D. 135 945

14. 4 4 8 8 16 16 32 ___ ___
    A. 32 64
    B. 32 66
    C. 32 128
    D. 32 160

15. 6912 divided by 432
    A. 13
    B. 15
    C. 16
    D. 14

16. 127 multiplied by 15
    A. 1905
    B. 1745
    C. 1865
    D. 1645

17. 3×4×5×6
    A. 400
    B. 360
    C. 420
    D. 340

18. 7686 divided by 3
    A. 2822
    B. 2622
    C. 2462
    D. 2562

19. 10 1 20 2 30 3 ___ ___
    A. 50 5
    B. 40 4
    C. 20 4
    D. 30 5

20. 4 16 8 32 16 ___ ___
    A. 64 32
    B. 1727 5181
    C. 2304 6912
    D. 1728 3456

21. 7 8 9 8 7 8 ___ ___
    A. 9 8
    B. 9 10
    C. 7 8
    D. 8 9

22. 55 54 13 55 54 ___ ___
    A. 54 53
    B. 55 54
    C. 13 55
    D. 13 54

23. 10 11 12 12 13 14 ___ ___
    A. 12 13
    B. 15 15
    C. 15 12
    D. 13 12

24. 10 + 9 + 8 + 7 + 6 + 5 + 4 + 3 + 2 + 1
    A. 55
    B. 47
    C. 62
    D. 57

Following Oral Instructions

TIME: 25 minutes

Directions: When you are ready to practice this section of the exam, you'll need to ask a friend to help. First, copy the 10 questions below, exactly as you see them here, onto another piece of paper (your worksheet). Your friend will read you specific instructions as to how to work with and answer each of the questions.

1. 0692385, 5609382, 2098563, 8365049

2. apple, orange, cherry, potatoe

3. 375, 480, 30, 225

4. February, April, June, November

5. 10001, 02135, 32004, 10011

6. 39802716543

7. Bush, Lincoln, Reagan, Kennedy

8. 3 quarters, 5 dimes, 14 nickels, 70 pennies

9. 47C, 39A, 208D, 48B

10. 23___, 50___, 49___, 37___

TO THE PERSON READING THE INSTRUCTIONS: *You should read slowly and clearly. You do not have to read the words in parentheses; these have been provided for your guidance in allowing the test taker time to think about/answer each question.*

READ THE FOLLOWING TO THE TEST TAKER: *You need to mark your answer sheet according to the specific instructions I read to you. I'll pause for a few seconds after each instruction, so you have time to mark your answer sheet.*

The test begins now.

1. (Pause 2–3 seconds.) If all the series of numbers listed on line one have the same numbers, go to number 22 on the answer sheet and darken the letter "A" as in apple. (Pause 5 seconds.)

2. (Pause 2–3 seconds.) Look at the months listed on line four. All the months listed have 30 days or fewer. If this statement is true go to number 40 on the answer sheet and darken the letter "C" as in cat. (Pause 5 seconds)

3. (Pause 2–3 seconds.) On line one, add the third series of numbers. Find the sum on the answer sheet and darken the letter "B" as in boy. (Pause 5 seconds.)

4. (Pause 2–3 seconds.) If all the numbers in line three are divisible by 15, go to number 17 on the answer sheet and darken the letter "D" as in dog. (Pause 5 seconds.)

5. (Pause 2–3 seconds.) Have all the names listed on line seven been names of presidents (past and present)? If yes, go to number 14 on the answer sheet and darken the letter "B" as in boy. (Pause 5 seconds.)

6. (Pause 2–3 seconds.) If the numbers in the ZIP codes on line five are added together, is the total then 35? If the statement is true, go to number 34 on the answer sheet and darken the letter "A" as in apple. If the statement is false, go to number 35 on the answer sheet and darken the letter "C" as in cat. (Pause 5 seconds.)

7. (Pause 2–3 seconds.) All the items on line two are fruits and vegetables. If the statement is true, go to number 20 on the answer sheet and darken the letter "D" as in dog. (Pause 5 seconds.)

8. (Pause 2–3 seconds.) Look at the number on line 6. Are all numbers from 0–9 used only once in this number? If yes, go to number 21 on the answer sheet and darken the letter "B" as in boy. (Pause 5 seconds.)

9. (Pause 2–3 seconds.) On line 8, total each set of coins. The coins are in order of their worth. If this statement is true, go to number 44 on the answer sheet and darken the letter "A" as in apple. (Pause 5 seconds.)

10. (Pause 2–3 seconds.) There are no misspelled words on line two. If this statement is true, go to number 13 on the answer sheet and darken the letter "D" as is dog. If the statement is false, go to number 25 on the answer sheet and darken the letter "B" as in boy. (Pause 5 seconds.)

11. (Pause 2–3 seconds.) On line 9, find the highest number that is followed by "B." Darken the appropriate spot on your answer sheet that corresponds to this letter-number combination (Pause 5 seconds).

12. (Pause 2–3 seconds.) Add the number 5 to the end of each number on line ten. Add each set of numbers. More than one of the sums is greater than 15. If this statement is true, go to number 18 on the answer sheet and darken the letter "A" as in apple. If this statement is false, go to number 19 on the answer sheet and darken the letter "C" as in cat. (Pause 5 seconds.)

13. (Pause 2–3 seconds.) The month of February has 29 days every 5 years. If this statement is true, go to number 26 on the answer sheet and darken the letter "B" as in boy. (Pause 5 seconds.)

14. (Pause 2–3 seconds.) On line 10, add the letters A, B, C, and D to the numbers with A after the highest number, B after the next highest, and so on. Darken the spot on your answer sheet that corresponds with the letter-number combination for the letter C. (Pause 5 seconds.)

15. (Pause 2–3 seconds.) Add up the number of letters in the second word on line two. If the sum is evenly divisible by 3, 4, 5, and 6 then go to number 1 on the answer sheet and darken the letter "D" as in dog. (Pause 5 seconds.)

16. (Pause 2–3 seconds.) On line 1, the number "9" is the third number in two of the series of numbers. If this statement is true, go to number 29 on the answer sheet and darken the letter "A" as in apple. (Pause 5 seconds.)

17. (Pause 2–3 seconds.) One line 6, the fifth and seventh numbers total the number that appears as both the first and last number. If this statement is true, go to number 45 on the answer sheet and darken the letter "B" as in boy. (Pause 5 seconds.)

18. (Pause 2–3 seconds.) On line two, all the correct spellings of the fruits and vegetables have an "e" in them. If this statement is false, go to number 9 on the answer sheet and darken the letter "D" as in dog. (Pause 5 seconds.)

19. (Pause 2-3 seconds) Divide the third number on line 9 by 4. This result is still the largest number listed on line nine. If this statement is true, go to number 12 on the answer sheet and darken the letter "A" as is apple. If this statement is false, go to number 39 on the answer sheet and darken the letter "C" as in cat. (Pause 5 seconds.)

Answer Key: Full Length Practice Exam I

Address Checking Answer Key

1. D	17. A	33. A
2. D	18. A	34. D
3. A	19. D	35. D
4. D	20. A	36. A
5. A	21. D	37. D
6. A	22. D	38. A
7. D	23. A	39. D
8. D	24. D	40. D
9. D	25. A	41. D
10. A	26. A	42. A
11. A	27. D	43. A
12. D	28. D	44. D
13. A	29. A	45. A
14. D	30. A	46. A
15. D	31. D	47. D
16. D	32. A	48. D

49. A	**65.** A	**81.** D
50. D	**66.** D	**82.** A
51. A	**67.** D	**83.** D
52. D	**68.** D	**84.** A
53. D	**69.** A	**85.** A
54. A	**70.** D	**86.** D
55. D	**71.** A	**87.** A
56. A	**72.** D	**88.** A
57. D	**73.** D	**89.** D
58. D	**74.** A	**90.** D
59. A	**75.** A	**91.** D
60. A	**76.** A	**92.** D
61. A	**77.** D	**93.** D
62. D	**78.** D	**94.** A
63. D	**79.** A	**95.** A
64. D	**80.** D	

Memory for Addresses Answer Key

1. C	**12.** C	**23.** A
2. B	**13.** D	**24.** D
3. C	**14.** C	**25.** B
4. A	**15.** A	**26.** C
5. E	**16.** B	**27.** A
6. E	**17.** E	**28.** E
7. D	**18.** D	**29.** D
8. B	**19.** B	**30.** B
9. D	**20.** B	**31.** A
10. A	**21.** D	**32.** A
11. B	**22.** E	**33.** C

34. D	**53.** B	**72.** B
35. B	**54.** E	**73.** A
36. E	**55.** C	**74.** E
37. B	**56.** C	**75.** B
38. A	**57.** A	**76.** D
39. C	**58.** D	**77.** D
40. C	**59.** E	**78.** A
41. E	**60.** B	**79.** C
42. D	**61.** A	**80.** E
43. B	**62.** C	**81.** B
44. C	**63.** E	**82.** A
45. A	**64.** D	**83.** C
46. D	**65.** B	**84.** D
47. C	**66.** C	**85.** E
48. E	**67.** A	**86.** C
49. B	**68.** A	**87.** B
50. C	**69.** E	**88.** A
51. D	**70.** D	
52. A	**71.** C	

Number Series Answer Key

1. C. Each number in the pattern is the result of adding 26 to the previous number; 14+26 = 40, 40+26 = 66, and so on.

2. A. Each number in the pattern is the result of subtracting 35 from the previous number; 978–943=35.

3. C. This pattern alternates between addition and subtraction, based off each specific number in the series, and then continuing in sequential order. The difference between the first two numbers is 9 (addition), the difference between the second and third numbers is 8 (subtraction), the difference between the third and fourth numbers is 7 (addition), and so on.

4. D. This pattern is very similar to that of question 3, as the pattern is in sequential order, with the next number being determined either by addition or subtraction. The difference between the first and second number is 11 (addition), the difference between the second and third number is 12 (subtraction), the difference between the third and fourth number is 13 (addition), and so on.

5. B. Add the digits together for each number and subtract the total from the number itself. For the first number, the total of 3+7+3=13. If you subtract this from the number itself (373), you get 360, which happens to be the next number in the series. If you add the digits of 360 together, you get 9; subtract that from the number itself (360) and you get 351.

6. A. There are two patterns: The number 3 is inserted every third number in the series. The rest of the series follows a +2 pattern; for example, 14+2=16, 16+2=18, and so on.

7. C. This is another pattern that utilizes addition and subtraction. The first pattern is to subtract five from the first two numbers; the second pattern (after the first) is to add 4. So, 24–5=19, 19–5=14, 14 + 4=18, and so on.

8. D. A simple pattern. Simply add five to each number to get the next number in the series.

9. A. Another simple pattern, albeit one that produces large numbers fairly quickly. The pattern is to multiply each number by 3: $14 \times 3 = 42$; $42 \times 3 = 126$, and so on.

10. A. A more extensive pattern is in use here, in that you are asked to both divide and multiply by specific numbers. The pattern is to first divide by two, and then multiply by three. Looking at the pattern, then, we see 10 divided by 2 equals 5, and then 5 multiplied by 3 equals 15. Next we see 20 divided by 2 which equals 10, and then multiplied by 3 equals 30. So the next two numbers in the pattern would be 30 divided by 2 (15), and then 15 multiplied by 3, which equals 45.

11. B. Simply multiply each number by 4 to get the next number in the series.

12. C. This is an addition pattern, in that you need to increment by 1; however, you multiply by the increment in order to get the next number. So, the pattern is to first multiply by 2, then multiply by 3, and then multiply by 4 (so you are adding one as you go, and then multiplying by the number you come up with).

13. B. Add 9 to each number to get the next concurrent number in the series.

14. A. This pattern asks you to repeat each number twice, then multiply by 2. So for the first numbers in the pattern, we see the number 4 repeated, then that number multiplied by 2 ($4 \times 2 = 8$). Then 8 is repeated twice, and then multiplied by 2 ($8 \times 2 = 16$), and so on.

15. C. A simple division problem, although one that asks you to divide a four-digit number. 6912 divided by 432 is 16.

16. A. Similar to question 15, except you are multiplying here. 127 multiplied by 15 is 1905.

17. B. The series represents a sequential number progression (3, 4, 5, 6...); when each number is multiplied by the number that follows, the total sum is 360.

18. D. A simple division problem: 7686 divided by 3 is 2562.

19. B. This question asks you to identify two separate addition patterns. The first pattern is to add 10 to get the next number (10, 20, 30); the second pattern is to add one to get the next sequential order (1, 2, 3). So, the next two sequential numbers in the pattern are 40, 4.

20. A. Similar to number 10 above, this pattern asks you to both divide and multiply by specific numbers. The pattern is to first multiply by 4, and then divide by 2. Looking at the pattern, then, we see 4 multiplied by 4 equals 16, and then divided by 2 equals 8; next, we have 8 multiplied by 4 equaling 32, then divided by 2 equaling 16. So the final two numbers, then, are 64 and 32: 16 multiplied by 4 (64), and then divided by 2 (32).

21. A. With this question, there is no mathematical operation (addition, subtraction, or anything else); you are just asked to identify the two-number pattern. That pattern is 7, 8, then 9, 8, then 7, 8, then 9, 8 and so on.

22. C. The pattern here is to repeat the first two numbers, and then place a 13.

23. B. A pattern based on some simple addition. Here, this series counts up by one, repeating the third number along the way.

24. A. The last question asks you to again identify the sum of adding sequential numbers in the pattern. Each number sequentially added produces 55 as a sum.

Following Oral Instructions Answer Key

These spots should be darkened on your answer sheet when the test is complete:

40. C

33. B

17. D

14. B

34. A

20. D

48. B

19. C

37. C

1. D

29. A

45. B

9. D

12. A

25. B

15

Full Length Practice Exam II

Address Checking

TIME: 6 Minutes, 95 Questions

Directions: For each question, compare the address in the left column with the address in the right column. If the two addresses are exactly alike, mark A on your answer sheet. If they are different in any way, mark D on your answer sheet.

1.	1867 Merryweather Way	1876 Maryweather Way
2.	4107 Kingston Dr	4107 Kingston Dr
3.	Fremont, OH 72604	Fremont, OH 72604
4.	5354 Mining Rd	5453 Mining Rd
5.	Loughton, MI 92580	Loughton, MI 92850
6.	18 Aris Cte	18 Aris Ct
7.	6209 Jennings St	6209 Jennings St
8.	4000 N State	4000 E State
9.	6220 Massy Ave	6220 Massy Ave
10.	Springfield, MS 56801	Springfield, MI 56801
11.	8220 Hummingbird Dr	8220 Hummingbird Dr
12.	Ferry, KS 85770	Ferry, KS 85770
13.	3332 Autumn Ln	3332 Automn Ln
14.	7887 Drury Ave	8778 Drury Ave
15.	Rochester, NY 44414	Rochester, NY 44144
16.	8989 Lincoln Ct	8989 Lincoln Ct
17.	1658 Rogers St	1658 Rogers St
18.	8952 Pine St	8952 Pine Ave
19.	120 Regala Dr	12 Regala Dr
20.	Happenstance, KY 68520	Happenstance, KY 68520
21.	8525 Masters Rd	8225 Masters Rd
22.	866 Lyons Blvd	866 Lions Blvd
23.	14 S Francis	14 N Francis
24.	1998 Rolling Hills	1998 Rolling Hills
25.	Appleville, MD 24687	Appleville, MD 24687
26.	2324 Presidential Way	2423 Presidential Way
27.	321 Foxfire Rd	321 Foxfire Rd
28.	6335 Montpelier Dr	6553 Montpelier Dr
29.	852 Mining St	852 Minning St

(continued)

30.	Indianapolis, IN 46528	Indianapolis, IN 46528
31.	Terrence, CA 66832	Torrence, CA 66832
32.	1542 25th St	1542 25th St
33.	5423 Simmons Ct	5423 Simon Ct
34.	620 Marcus Way	620 Marcus Way
35.	8752 Treemont	8752 Treemont
36.	652 24th St	652 25th St
37.	Ft Harris, TX 96102	Ft Harris, TX 96012
38.	7465 Johnson St	7465 Johnson Rd
39.	4517 Masters Pike	4517 Masters Pike
40.	916 Central Park W	916 Central Park N
41.	Semi Valley, CA 24801	Semi Valley, CA 24801
42.	673 N Crimson Blvd	673 N Crimson Blvd
43.	56838 Crestview Ave	56383 Crestview Ave
44.	8754 Lima Ct	8754 Lima Ct
45.	Nashville, TN 75621	Nashville, IN 75621
46.	938 Johnston Rd	938 Jonston Rd
47.	9366 Harvey Pl	9366 Harvey Pl
48.	3255 5th St	3255 25th St
49.	6566 Nestor Rd	6566 Nestor Rd
50.	Paris, IN 47863	Paris, IN 47683
51.	1142 Cardinal St	1142 Cardinal Ave
52.	856 Masterson Dr	8956 Masterson Dr
53.	4572 Ferris Ct	4572 Feris Ct
54.	9975 River Rd	9975 River Rd
55.	2546 N Finch	2456 N Finch
56.	3475 Conway Ave	3475 Conway Ave
57.	Marion, UT 04587	Marion, UT 04587
58.	Napal, GA 58221	Napal, GA 58221
59.	8454 Foliage Dr	8545 Foliage Dr
60.	8765 Elm St	8765 Elm St
61.	78 West Parkway Pl	78 West Parkway Pl
62.	3658 Washington St	3685 Washington St
63.	Cleveland, OH 64754	Cleveland, OH 65754
64.	847 Caspers Cv	847 Caspers Cv

(continued)

65.	1052 Tunic Dr	1052 Tunic Ave
66.	6525 S Hampton	6525 S Hampton
67.	3327 Morris Ave	3337 Morris Ave
68.	Portland, OR 78875	Portland, OR 78875
69.	5673 115th St	5673 15th St
70.	3545 Fosters St	3454 Fosters St
71.	1007 Graham Rd	107 Graham Rd
72.	2287 MacLaughlin	2287 MacLaughlin
73.	8774 Christmas Tree Ln	8774 Christmas Tree Ln
74.	Detroit, MI 45572	Detroit, MI 44572
75.	241 N Myers	2411 N Myers
76.	8720 Sesame Rd	8720 Sesame Rd
77.	3034 Farnsworth Ave	3034 Fansworth Ave
78.	9686 Taylor Dr	9686 Taylor Dr
79.	Chicago, IL 63532	Chicago, IL 63352
80.	584 W Barns St	584 E Barns St
81.	2440 Farber St	2440 Farber St
82.	3565 Green Acres	3656 Green Acres
83.	8778 Pine Ct	8778 Pine Ct
84.	Annapolis, MD 58842	Annapolis, MD 58842
85.	1425 Heritage Rd	1425 Heritage Rd
86.	25487 Poplar Ave	24587 Poplar Ave
87.	5874 7th St	5874 7th Ave
88.	5472 W Mockingbird Ln	5472 W Mockingbird Ln
89.	332 Zion Dr	3322 Zion Dr
90.	6142 Carrington	6142 Carrington
91.	Tempe, AZ 54725	Tempe, AZ 54275
92.	6470 Apple St	6470 Apple St
93.	2420 Sixth Ave	24220 Sixth Ave
94.	87 E Martinsville	87 W Martinsville
95.	25473 Ridgeway Ave	25473 Ridgeway Ave

Memory for Addresses

TIME: 5 minutes, 88 questions

Directions: To make this practice exam as realistic as possible allow yourself an additional five minutes to study and memorize this grid. After those five minutes, you should then give yourself an additional five minutes—just as in the actual exam— to answer as many of the 88 questions as you can. On your answer sheet, mark each question A, B, C, D, or E, depending on where the address would be found in the information grid. DO NOT refer back to the grid after your initial five-minute memorization period is up; on the actual exam, after your practice exercises, you will not be allowed to refer back to the information grid.

A	B	C	D	E
7700–7799 Hamilton	1250–1299 Hamilton	5600–5750 Hamilton	7100–7500 Hamilton	9200–9500 Hamilton
Ariel	Knightsbridge	Albertson	Arleigh	Redwood
5399–5600 Inwood	2000–2199 Inwood	4300–4900 Inwood	7200–7299 Inwood	8199–8250 Inwood
Dakota	Arbor	Pembroke	Elm	Watermill
1999–2999 Willis	3400–3699 Willis	5500–5999 Willis	9100–9199 Willis	7199–7250 Willis

1. Elm	45. 3400–3699 Willis
2. Watermill	46. 2000–2199 Inwood
3. 9200–9500 Hamilton	47. Knightsbridge
4. 2000–2199 Inwood	48. Redwood
5. Dakota	49. 7199–7250 Willis
6. 3400–3699 Willis	50. 1250–1299 Hamilton
7. Pembroke	51. Dakota
8. 4300–4900 Inwood	52. Arleigh
9. 7100–7500 Hamilton	53. 8199–8250 Inwood
10. Arleigh	54. 5399–5600 Inwood
11. 5399–5600 Inwood	55. Pembroke
12. Albertson	56. 5500–5999 Willis
13. 7100–7500 Hamilton	57. 7200–7299 Inwood
14. 7199–7250 Willis	58. Watermill
15. Elm	59. 9200–9500 Hamilton
16. Redwood	60. 7700–7799 Hamilton
17. 7700–7799 Hamilton	61. Arbor
18. Arbor	62. Redwood
19. Watermill	63. 9100–9199 Willis
20. 2000–2199 Inwood	64. 2000–2199 Inwood
21. 5500–5999 Willis	65. Elm
22. 4300–4900 Inwood	66. Ariel
23. Pembroke	67. 5600–5750 Hamilton
24. Dakota	68. 3400–3699 Willis
25. 1250–1299 Hamilton	69. Knightsbridge
26. 7100–7500 Hamilton	70. 1999–2999 Willis
27. Ariel	71. Albertson
28. Watermill	72. 7200–7299 Inwood
29. 7200–7299 Inwood	73. 9200–9500 Hamilton
30. 7199–7250 Willis	74. Pembroke
31. Arbor	75. Arbor
32. Redwood	76. 2000–2199 Inwood
33. 1999–2999 Willis	77. 9100–9199 Willis
34. 2000–2199 Inwood	78. 5399–5600 Inwood
35. Pembroke	79. Redwood

(continued)

36. Knightsbridge	80. Watermill
37. 4300–4900 Inwood	81. Arleigh
38. 7100–7500 Hamilton	82. 7100–7500 Hamilton
39. Albertson	83. 5500–5999 Willis
40. Dakota	84. Dakota
41. 9100–9199 Willis	85. Knightsbridge
42. 1250–1299 Hamilton	86. 7199–7250 Willis
43. Elm	87. 5600–5750 Hamilton
44. Arbor	88. Elm

Number Series

TIME: 20 minutes, 24 questions

Directions: Each number series question consists of a series of numbers that follow some definite, precise order: The numbers progress from left to right, following some determined rule. One lettered pair of numbers (identified as A, B, C, D, or E) for each question represents the correct answer: that is, the next two numbers that should follow in the order, and thus conform to the rule. Choose the correct answer, and mark it on your answer sheet.

1. 2 6 10 14 18 22 ___ ___
   A. 24 26
   B. 26 30
   C. 24 30
   D. 26 34

2. 45 40 35 30 25 ___ ___
   A. 20 15
   B. 20 10
   C. 15 5
   D. 20 5

3. 98 87 76 65 54 ___ ___
   A. 46 37
   B. 44 34
   C. 43 32
   D. 40 36

4. 12 8 5 3 6 10 ___ ___
   A. 8 12
   B. 12 16
   C. 15 21
   D. 10 16

5. 87 94 101 108 115 ___ ___
   A. 121 127
   B. 122 129
   C. 120 125
   D. 123 130

6. 120 90 110 80 100 70 ___ ___
   A. 90 60
   B. 90 50
   C. 100 80
   D. 80 100

7. 24 20 17 15 14 16 19 ___ ___
   A. 21 25
   B. 23 27
   C. 22 28
   D. 23 28

8. 5 10 15 20 25 ___ ___
   A. 35 40
   B. 30 35
   C. 30 40
   D. 30 45

9. 12 6 24 12 48 ___ ___
   A. 24 96
   B. 24 104
   C. 12 48
   D. 20 40

10. 3 3 6 6 12 12 24 ___ ___
   A. 24 36
   B. 24 48
   C. 24 36
   D. 36 40

11. 20 40 80 160 ___ ___
   A. 320 640
   B. 300 620
   C. 320 630
   D. 320 680

12. 9 18 27 36 45 ___ ___
   A. 54 63
   B. 54 64
   C. 50 64
   D. 52 63

13. 100 200 40 80 ___ ___
   A. 24 48
   B. 32 60
   C. 32 64
   D. 16 32

14. 63 56 49 42 ___ ___
    A. 35 27
    B. 32 28
    C. 28 35
    D. 35 28

15. 2 4 8 16 ___ ___
    A. 32 64
    B. 124 248
    C. 122 244
    D. 120 240

16. 8 16 24 32 ___ ___
    A. 44 52
    B. 40 48
    C. 42 50
    D. 40 46

17. 99 90 81 72 ___ ___
    A. 56 49
    B. 52 43
    C. 45 27
    D. 63 54

18. 44 40 36 32 ___ ___
    A. 28 24
    B. 26 22
    C. 30 26
    D. 28 22

19. 10 1 11 2 12 3 ___ ___
    A. 13 5
    B. 13 4
    C. 11 4
    D. 10 5

20. 2 2 4 4 8 8 ___ ___
    A. 16 16
    B. 10 10
    C. 32 32
    D. 12 12

21. 92 80 68 56 ___ ___
    A. 48 36
    B. 44 32
    C. 40 30
    D. 46 34

22. 1 3 5 7 9 ___ ___
    A. 12 15
    B. 11 13
    C. 11 15
    D. 12 17

23. 2 3 5 8 ___ ___
    A. 12 18
    B. 14 20
    C. 12 17
    D. 15 18

24. +10 −1 +11 −2 +12 −3 ___ ___
    A. +15 −4
    B. +16 −5
    C. +13 −4
    D. +13 −5

Following Oral Instructions

TIME: 25 minutes

Directions: When you are ready to practice this section of the exam, you need to ask a friend to help. Your friend will read you specific instructions as to how to work with and answer each of the questions.

Refer to the following information to work through this section of the exam. The questions will refer to this information as your "worksheet":

1. January, March, May, July, October, December

2. 83795901673, 37619059738

3. 63, 42, 75, 90

4. New York 8:00 a.m., Indiana 7:00 a.m., Illinois 6:00 a.m.

5. 2 + 14, 3 + 15, 4 + 16, 5 + 17

6. 46032, 46140, 46240, 46290

7. 51, 70, 34, 24

8. 835610972

9. Amy, Brad, Charity, Dean, Fred

10. Foot = Sock, Car = Garage, Dog = Flea, Hand = Glove, Head = Hat

TO THE PERSON READING THE INSTRUCTIONS: You should read quickly and clearly. You do not have to read the words in parentheses; these have been provided for your guidance in allowing the test taker time to think about/answer each question.

READ THE FOLLOWING TO THE TEST TAKER: You need to mark your answer sheet according to the specific instructions I read to you. I'll pause for a few seconds after each instruction, so you have time to mark your answer sheet.

The test begins now.

1. (Pause 2–3 seconds.) If the months listed on line 1 all have 31 days, go to number 30 on the answer sheet and darken the letter "B" as in boy. (Pause 5 seconds.)

2. (Pause 2–3 seconds.) If the sixth number from the right of both groups of numbers in line 2 is 9, go to number 4 on the answer sheet and darken the letter "B" as in boy. (Pause 5 seconds.)

3. (Pause 2–3 seconds.) If the numbers on line 2 mirror each other, go to number 12 on the answer sheet and darken the letter "A" as in apple. (Pause 5 seconds.)

4. (Pause 2–3 seconds.) If all the numbers in line 3 are divisible by 7, go to number 2 on the answer sheet and darken the letter "B" as in boy. (Pause 5 seconds.)

5. (Pause 2–3 seconds.) If the months listed on line 1 are all the months of the year with 31 days, go to number 24 on the answer sheet and darken the letter "D" as in dog. (Pause 5 seconds.)

6. (Pause 2–3 seconds.) If the ZIP codes in line 6 are in numerical order, go to number 4 on the answer sheet and darken the letter "C" as in cat. (Pause 5 seconds.)

7. (Pause 2–3 seconds.) All the sums of the equations in line 5 are divisible by 5. If this statement is true, go to number 36 on the answer sheet and darken the letter "A" as in apple. (Pause 5 seconds.)

8. (Pause 2–3 seconds.) In line 7, add the first and last numbers together. If the total is greater than any number listed on line 7, go to number 39 on the answer sheet and darken the letter "B" as in boy. (Pause 5 seconds.)

9. (Pause 2–3 seconds.) If the month in which Labor Day falls is listed on line 1, go to number 33 on the sheet and darken the letter "D" as in dog. (Pause 5 seconds.)

10. (Pause 2–3 seconds.) If any numbers in line 3 are divisible by 5, go to number 26 on the answer sheet and darken "C" as in cat. (Pause 5 seconds.)

11. (Pause 2–3 seconds.) If the sum of the third ZIP code in line 6 is less than 20, go to number 18 on the answer sheet and darken the letter "A" as in apple. (Pause 5 seconds.)

12. (Pause 2–3 seconds.) All the sums of the equations in line 5 equal an even number. If this statement is true, go to number 26 on the answer sheet and darken the letter "B" as in boy. (Pause 5 seconds.)

13. (Pause 2–3 seconds.) Add each of the two digits together in line 7. If the sum of any two equal six (6), go to number 40 on the answer sheet and darken the letter "B" as in boy. (Pause 5 seconds.)

14. (Pause 2–3 seconds.) Using the example in line 4, if John, in New York, needs to call Mary, in Illinois, at 1:00 p.m. Illinois time, John should call Mary at 3:00 p.m. New York time. If this statement is true, go to number 1 on the answer sheet and darken the letter "D" as in dog. (Pause 5 seconds.)

15. (Pause 2–3 seconds.) Underline the seventh number in line 8. Locate this number on your answer sheet and darken the letter "C" as in cat. (Pause 5 seconds.)

16. (Pause 2–3 seconds.) In line 8, if the third number is five, add six, find this number on the answer sheet and darken the letter "A" as in apple. (Pause 5 seconds.)

17. (Pause 2–3 seconds.) If the names in line 9 in are in alphabetical order, go to number 9 on the answer sheet and darken the letter "D" as in dog. (Pause 5 seconds.)

18. (Pause 2–3 seconds.) In line 10, does each saying represent an object being covered? If yes, go to number 23 on the answer sheet and darken the letter "B" as in boy. If no, go to number 37 on the answer sheet and darken the letter "D" as in dog. (Pause 5 seconds.)

19. (Pause 2–3 seconds.) Are all the names in line 9 less than six letters? If yes, go to number 2 on the answer sheet and darken the letter "A" as in apple. If no, go to number 35 on the answer sheet and darken the letter "C" as in cat. (Pause 5 seconds.)

16

Answer Key: Full Length Practice Exam II

Address Checking Answer Key

1. D	17. A	33. D
2. A	18. D	34. A
3. A	19. D	35. A
4. D	20. A	36. D
5. D	21. D	37. D
6. D	22. D	38. D
7. A	23. D	39. A
8. D	24. A	40. D
9. A	25. A	41. A
10. D	26. D	42. A
11. A	27. A	43. D
12. A	28. D	44. A
13. D	29. D	45. D
14. D	30. A	46. D
15. D	31. D	47. A
16. A	32. A	48. D

49. A	**65.** A	**81.** A
50. D	**66.** A	**82.** D
51. D	**67.** D	**83.** A
52. D	**68.** A	**84.** A
53. D	**69.** D	**85.** A
54. A	**70.** D	**86.** D
55. D	**71.** D	**87.** D
56. A	**72.** A	**88.** A
57. A	**73.** A	**89.** D
58. A	**74.** D	**90.** A
59. D	**75.** D	**91.** D
60. A	**76.** A	**92.** A
61. A	**77.** D	**93.** D
62. D	**78.** A	**94.** D
63. D	**79.** D	**95.** A
64. A	**80.** D	

Memory for Addresses Answer Key

1. D	**12.** C	**23.** C
2. E	**13.** D	**24.** A
3. E	**14.** E	**25.** B
4. B	**15.** D	**26.** D
5. A	**16.** E	**27.** A
6. B	**17.** A	**28.** E
7. C	**18.** B	**29.** D
8. C	**19.** E	**30.** E
9. D	**20.** B	**31.** B
10. D	**21.** C	**32.** E
11. A	**22.** C	**33.** A

34. B	**53.** E	**72.** D
35. C	**54.** A	**73.** E
36. B	**55.** C	**74.** C
37. C	**56.** C	**75.** B
38. D	**57.** D	**76.** B
39. C	**58.** E	**77.** D
40. A	**59.** E	**78.** A
41. D	**60.** A	**79.** E
42. B	**61.** B	**80.** E
43. D	**62.** E	**81.** D
44. B	**63.** D	**82.** D
45. B	**64.** B	**83.** C
46. B	**65.** D	**84.** A
47. B	**66.** A	**85.** B
48. E	**67.** C	**86.** E
49. E	**68.** B	**87.** C
50. B	**69.** B	**88.** D
51. A	**70.** A	
52. D	**71.** C	

Number Series Answer Key

1. B. The pattern here is to add 4 to each number to get the next number in the sequence (2+4=6, 6+4=10, and so on.).

2. A. This pattern is very similar to that of #1, except rather than add 4 to get the next number in the sequence, you subtract five (45–5=40, 40–5=35, and so on).

3. C. For this pattern, simply subtract 11 from each number to get the next number in the sequence.

4. C. This pattern takes you down (subtraction) and back up again (addition). Subtract 4 from the first number, 3 from the second number, and 2 from the third number; add 3 to the next number, 4 to the next number, 5 to the next number, and 6 to the next number.

5. B. Simply Add 7 to each number to achieve the pattern in this sequence.

6. A. This pattern is a combination of subtraction and addition, asking you to subtract 30, then add 20. Subtract 30 from first number, add 20 to next number, subtract 30 from next number, and so on.

7. D. This pattern is just like the one described in #4. Subtract 4 from the first number, 3 from the second number, 2 from the third number, and 1 from the fourth number; add 2 to next number, add 3 to next number, and then add 4 and then 5.

8. B. A relatively easy pattern to uncover: Add 5 to each number.

9. A. A division and multiplication pattern is in effect here. Divide the first number by 2, and then multiply the next number by 4 and repeat.

10. B. A multiplication pattern, but one that asks you to repeat a number first. So, as shown in the question, repeat each number and then multiply it by 2.

11. A. Multiply each number by 2 to fulfill the pattern.

12. A. This pattern asks you to recognize that the numbers in the series are all multiples of 9 (that is, they can all be divided evenly by 9).

13. D. This pattern requires that you first multiply and then divide. Multiply the first number by 2, then divide by 5 and repeat.

14. D. Similar to the pattern you saw in #12, except in this case the numbers are all multiples of 7 and rather than increase, the numbers decrease.

15. A. In this pattern, each number is doubled to achieve the next number: 2 doubled is 4; 4 doubled is 8; 8 doubled is 16, and so on.

16. C. The numbers in the series are multiples of 8, and are similar to #12 and #14. In this case, the numbers are increasing.

17. A. More multiplication is utilized here, with the numbers all being multiples of 9. The pattern starts with 9 multiplied by 11 (99), then works backward (9 multiplied by 10 is 90; 9 multiplied by 9 is 81, and so on).

18. D. The numbers in the series are multiples of 4, counted backward.

19. B. For this pattern, all you need to do is add one, but you also need to recognize the starting points (10 and 1) for the pattern. So, there are really two patterns here, both getting the next sequential number, but each starting at a different point (again, 10 and 1).

20. A. This question uses a factor of two to get the next two concurrent numbers in the series. Starting with 2 (or for the pattern 2, 2), each set of concurrent numbers is generated by multiplying by a factor of 2. So, 2 multiplied by 2 is 4 (4, 4); 4 multiplied by 2 is 8 (8, 8); 8 multiplied by 2 is 16 (16, 16), and so on.

21. B. After the more complicated patterns of the previous questions, this is a simpler one. Just subtract 12 from each number to get the next number in the series.

22. B. Starting with 1 add 2 to each number to produce a string of all odd numbers.

23. C. This pattern asks you to count up (starting from one), adding the number in the count to each successive number in the pattern. Begin by adding 1 to the first number, 2 to the second number, and so on.

24. C. For this final question, you are asked to work with positive and negative numbers to find the patterns. This is very similar to #19: The starting positions are 10 and 1, except in this pattern it is positive 10 and negative 1. The first pattern increases by one (10, 11, 12, and so on), whereas the second decreases by negative 1 (-1, -2, -3, and so on).

Following Oral Instructions Answer Key

These spots should be darkened on your answer sheet when the test is complete:

1. D

4. C

9. C

11. A

18. A

26. C

30. B

39. B

40. B

54. D

Full Length Practice Exam III

Address Checking

TIME: 6 Minutes, 95 Questions

Directions: For each question, compare the address in the left column with the address in the right column. If the two addresses are exactly alike, mark A on your answer sheet. If they are different in any way, mark D on your answer sheet.

1. 10501 NE 38th Pl	10501 NE 38th Pl
2. Dallas, TX 75229	Dallas, TX 72559
3. Milwaukie, OR	Milwaukee, WI
4. 823 11th Ave	823 11th St
5. Marlton, NJ	Marlboro, NJ
6. 6450 Roswell Rd NE	6450 Roswell Rd NE
7. Ahoskie, NC	Ashokan, NY
8. 2415 Michigan Ave	2415 Mitchelson Ave
9. 5100 Edina Industrial Blvd Ste 230	5100 Adinan Industrial Blvd Ste 230
10. Phoenix, AZ 85034	Phoenix, AZ 85034
11. 1201 S Beckham	1201 S Barkam
12. Redlake, MN 56671	Redlake, MN 56671
13. 424 E 15th St	424 E 16th St
14. 410 N 44th St Ste 700	410 N 41st St Ste 700
15. East Brunswick, NJ 08816	New Brunswick, NJ 08816
16. 400 Delancey St, Newark, NJ	400 Delancey St., New York, NY
17. 69 County Rd 264	69 Country Rd 264
18. 3215 E Camelback Rd	3215 E Camelback Rd
19. Denver, CO 80237	Denver, CO 80237
20. 1395 Greg St Ste 107	1395 Greg St Ste 107
21. Grand Forks, ND 58201	Grand Forks, ND 58201
22. 701 Carlson Pkwy	701 Carlson St
23. 4034 SE Hammock Pl	4034 SE Hammock Pl
24. 44 Main Street	44 Maine St
25. 1615 Poydras St	1615 Poydros St
26. Kansas City, MO	Kansas City, KA
27. 4305 Frederick Ave	4305 Fredericks Ave
28. 5485 Hixson Pike	5485 Hixson Pl
29. 1665 Lakes Pkwy	1665 Lakes Pkwy

(continued)

30. Sun Valley, CA	Sun Valley, AZ
31. 15 N Robinson Ave	15 N Robeson Ave
32. Hempstead, NY 11050	Hempstead, NY 11050
33. 1850 Atlanta Ave	1850 Atlantic Ave
34. 10280 Greenville Hwy	10280 Greenville Hwy
35. San Antonio, TX 78212	San Antonio, TX 78212
36. 1320 Freeport Blvd	1320 Freeport Rd
37. Salt Lake City, UT 04111	Salt Lake City, UT 84101
38. Rapid City, SD	Rapid City, SD
39. 6001 N 91st St	6001 S 91st St
40. 7961 Shaffer Pkwy	7961 Schaeffer Pkwy
41. Omaha, NE 68124	Omaha, NE 68124
42. 255 W Fleming St	255 W Fleming St
43. New York, NY 10017	New York, NY 10011
44. Lowell, MA	Lowell, MA
45. St. Paul, MN 55144	St. Paul, MN 55114
46. 1 Capital Dr	1 Capitol Rd
47. 4900 Stewart Ave	4900 Steward Ave
48. 920 E State Rd	920 E State Rd
49. Anniston, AL 36202	Anniston, AL 36202
50. Charlotte, NC	Charlottesville, VA
51. 38000 Chester Rd	38000 Cheshire Rd
52. Mill Creek, OK 74856	Mill Creek, OK 74856
53. Patchogue, NY	Cutchogue, NY
54. 30057 Orchard Lake Rd	30057 Orchard Rd
55. 30 Coldenham Rd	30 Goldenham Rd
56. 2317 South Santa Fe Ave	2317 South Santa Fe Ave
57. 7995 Tyler Blvd	7995 Tayler Blvd
58. 2701 Beacon Ave S	2701 Beacon Dr S
59. Livingston, NJ	Livingston, NJ
60. 47 Hillside Ave	47 Hillsdale Ave
61. 916 Finch Ave	916 Finch Rd
62. 126 Hwy 51 S	126 Hwy 51
63. 10421 Ford Rd	1041 Ford Rd
64. 2503 Jackson Bluff Rd	2503 Jackson Bluff Rd

(continued)

65. Cleveland, OH 44115	Cleveland, OH 44115
66. 2175 Southpark Ct	2175 South Park Ct
67. Henderson, NV 89015	Henderson, NV 89015
68. 4665 Hollins Ferry Rd	4665 Holland Ferry Rd
69. Lincolnshire, IL	Lincoln, IL
70. 9685 Scranton Rd	9685 Scrampton Rd
71. 310 E 96th St	312 E 96th St
72. 7301 Pkwy Dr	7301 Pkwy Dr
73. St Louis, MO	Bay St Louis, MS
74. Niles, IL	Nile, IL
75. Merrimack, NH	Mamaroneck, NY
76. Rockville, MD	Rochester, MN
77. Birmingham, AL	Birmingham, AL
78. 600 Montgomery St	600 Montgomery Ave
79. Miami, FL	Miami, OH
80. Jacksonville, FL	Jackson, MS
81. 4615 Murray Pl	4615 Murrey Pl
82. 11100 Belmont Ave	1100 Belmont Ave
83. 5200 Buffington Rd	5200 Buffington Rd
84. 8585 Duke Blvd.	8585 Duke Blvd.
85. 5421 N 59th St	5421 N 58th St
86. 4040 El Dorado Rd	4040 Dorado Rd
87. 171 Weidner Rd	171 Weiden Rd
88. New Orleans, LA 70113	New Orleans, LA 70113
89. 14 Indiana Ave	14 Indian Ave
90. 1 S Wacker Dr	1 S Wacker Dr
91. Compton, CA	Compton, CA
92. 426 Lancaster Ave	436 Lancaster Ave
93. Carlstadt, NJ	Carlsbad, CA
94. 11 Madison Ave	11 Madison Ave
95. 400 Centre St	400 Centre St

Memory for Addresses

TIME: 5 minutes, 88 questions

Directions: On the actual exam, you will have three practice exercises designed to give you an opportunity to memorize more thoroughly the information grid.

To make this practice exam as realistic as possible in this regard, allow yourself an additional five minutes to study and memorize this grid. After those five minutes, you should then give yourself an additional five minutes—just like the actual exam—to answer as many of the 88 questions as you can. On your answer sheet, mark each question A, B, C, D, or E, depending on where the address would be found in the information grid. DO NOT refer back to the grid after your initial five minute memorization is up: On the actual exam, after your practice exercises, you will not be allowed to refer back to the information grid.

A	B	C	D	E
6500–7400 Talbot	3300–3900 Talbot	5400–6100 Talbot	2100–2999 Talbot	7200–8000 Talbot
Marlin	Magnolia	Hillside	Jeanette	Davis
8300–8999 Yale	6100–6999 Yale	1200–1999 Yale	4200–5000 Yale	3500–4000 Yale
Liberty	Roger	Lawrence	Roselle	Charles
9300–9999 Northern	6399–6999 Northern	3300–4000 Northern	1200–2000 Northern	5500–6200 Northern

1. Magnolia	45. Lawrence
2. 6399–6999 Northern	46. 3300–4000 Northern
3. 1200–1999 Northern	47. 7200–8000 Talbot
4. Jeanette	48. Charles
5. 4200–5000 Yale	49. Roger
6. Charles	50. 1200–1999 Yale
7. 7200–8000 Talbot	51. 6500–7400 Talbot
8. 3500–4000 Yale	52. Liberty
9. Davis	53. Roselle
10. 8300–8999 Yale	54. 5400–6100 Talbot
11. Marlin	55. Jeanette
12. 5400–6100 Talbot	56. 2100–2999 Talbot
13. Hillside	57. 8300–8999 Yale
14. 9300–9999 Northern	58. Hillside
15. Liberty	59. Davis
16. 2100–2999 Talbot	60. 6399–6999 Northern
17. Roger	61. 3500–4000 Yale
18. 3300–4000 Northern	62. Magnolia
19. 1200–2000 Northern	63. Marlin
20. Lawrence	64. 5500–6200 Northern
21. 4200–5000 Yale	65. 6100–6999 Yale
22. Roselle	66. Roger
23. Magnolia	67. Lawrence
24. 7200–8000 Talbot	68. 9300–9999 Northern
25. 6399–6999 Northern	69. Roselle
26. Charles	70. Liberty
27. 1200–1999 Northern	71. 3300–4000 Northern
28. 8300–8999 Yale	72. Hillside
29. Jeanette	73. Roger
30. Hillside	74. 7200–8000 Talbot
31. 4200–5000 Yale	75. 1200–1999 Yale
32. 3300–4000 Northern	76. 2100–2999 Talbot
33. 5500–6200 Northern	77. Charles
34. 8300–8999 Yale	78. Jeanette
35. Liberty	79. 6399–6999 Northern

(continued)

36. Marlin	80. Marlin
37. 4200–5000 Yale	81. Davis
38. Davis	82. 8300–8999 Yale
39. Lawrence	83. 3500–4000 Yale
40. 9300–9999 Northern	84. Magnolia
41. 1200–1999 Northern	85. Hillside
42. 4200–5000 Yale	86. 6100–6999 Yale
43. Rogor	87. 6399–6999 Northern
44. Marlin	88. 7200–8000 Talbot

Number Series

TIME: 20 minutes, 24 questions

Directions: Each number series question consists of a series of numbers that follow some definite, precise order: The numbers progress from left to right, following some determined rule. One lettered pair of numbers (A, B, C, D, or E) for each question represents the correct answer; that is, the next series of numbers that should follow in the order, and thus conform to the rule. Choose this correct answer, and mark it on your answer sheet.

1. 19 28 37 46 55 64 73 __ __
   - ❏ A. 82 91
   - ❏ B. 81 91
   - ❏ C. 82 92
   - ❏ D. 81 90

2. 29 35 27 41 47 27 53 __ __
   - ❏ A. 59 65
   - ❏ B. 27 59
   - ❏ C. 59 27
   - ❏ D. 27 27

3. 85 79 73 67 61 55 49 __ __
   - ❏ A. 43 37
   - ❏ B. 37 43
   - ❏ C. 50 51
   - ❏ D. 42 40

4. 26 27 30 35 42 51 62 __ __
   - ❏ A. 70 80
   - ❏ B. 75 90
   - ❏ C. 80 89
   - ❏ D. 77 78

5. 15 23 21 29 27 35 33 __ __
   - ❏ A. 41 39
   - ❏ B. 39 41
   - ❏ C. 43 35
   - ❏ D. 36 44

6. 1 2 4 8 10 20 22 __ __
   - ❏ A. 44 88
   - ❏ B. 24 26
   - ❏ C. 35 45
   - ❏ D. 44 46

7. 14 24 33 41 48 54 59 __ __
   - ❏ A. 60 61
   - ❏ B. 70 84
   - ❏ C. 63 66
   - ❏ D. 61 62

8. 7 14 8 16 10 20 14 __ __
   - ❏ A. 22 28
   - ❏ B. 21 13
   - ❏ C. 28 22
   - ❏ D. 10 14

9. 7 2 10 5 13 8 16 __ __
   - ❏ A. 11 19
   - ❏ B. 6 14
   - ❏ C. 20 15
   - ❏ D. 7 10

10. 93 90 85 78 69 58 45 __ __
    - ❏ A. 30 13
    - ❏ B. 40 36
    - ❏ C. 30 20
    - ❏ D. 42 39

11. 13 10 15 12 17 14 19 __ __
    - ❏ A. 21 16
    - ❏ B. 26 30
    - ❏ C. 16 21
    - ❏ D. 20 21

12. 29 32 40 37 40 40 45 __ __
    - ❏ A. 49 39
    - ❏ B. 40 40
    - ❏ C. 46 52
    - ❏ D. 48 40

13. 15 19 25 33 43 55 69 __ __
- ❑ A. 85 103
- ❑ B. 85 104
- ❑ C. 77 79
- ❑ D. 80 84

14. 59 51 55 46 50 40 44 __ __
- ❑ A. 37 33
- ❑ B. 33 37
- ❑ C. 38 40
- ❑ D. 50 52

15. 6 12 18 24 30 36 42 __ __
- ❑ A. 48 54
- ❑ B. 46 55
- ❑ C. 55 57
- ❑ D. 42 45

16. 92 2 84 4 76 6 68 __ __
- ❑ A. 12 69
- ❑ B. 6 62
- ❑ C. 66 8
- ❑ D. 8 60

17. 25 28 31 34 37 40 43 __
- ❑ A. 45 47
- ❑ B. 46 49
- ❑ C. 47 50
- ❑ D. 44 47

18. 65,536 16,384 4096 1024 256 64 16 __ __
- ❑ A. 11 14
- ❑ B. 4 1
- ❑ C. 8 4
- ❑ D. 8 2

19. 88 81 74 67 60 53 46 __ __
- ❑ A. 44 40
- ❑ B. 39 33
- ❑ C. 38 33
- ❑ D. 39 32

20. 38 43 48 43 38 43 48 __ __
    - ❏ A. 44 43
    - ❏ B. 43 38
    - ❏ C. 50 52
    - ❏ D. 41 44

21. 3 1 9 1 27 1 81 __ __
    - ❏ A. 111 115
    - ❏ B. 1 244
    - ❏ C. 1 243
    - ❏ D. 23 331

22. 201 21 202 22 203 23 204 __ __
    - ❏ A. 205 206
    - ❏ B. 23 205
    - ❏ C. 24 205
    - ❏ D. 206 207

23. –8 +9 +10 –11 +12 +13 –14 __ __
    - ❏ A. +15 +16
    - ❏ B. –15 +16
    - ❏ C. +15 –16
    - ❏ D. –17 –16

24. 419 259 160 99 61 38 23 __ __
    - ❏ A. 15 8
    - ❏ B. 16 7
    - ❏ C. 15 16
    - ❏ D. 20 14

Following Oral Instructions

TIME: 25 minutes

Directions: When you are ready to practice this section of the exam, you'll need to ask a friend to help. First, copy the 12 questions below, exactly as you see them here, onto another piece of paper (your worksheet). Your friend will read you specific instructions as to how to work with and answer each of the questions.

1. October, November, December, January, February

2. 8:32 a.m., 12:35 p.m., 2:30 p.m., 5:45 a.m.

3. 73, 25, 32

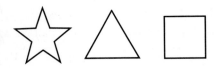

4. 02134, 02146, 02154, 02167

5. _____A, _____P, _____R, _____K

6. 37B, 22E, 123C, 85A, 14C, 27B

7. 25, 25, 30, 73, 50

8. 4583927383

9. 45___, 64___, 52___, 33___

10. ___B, ____C, ____A, ____E

11. C___, A___, E___

12. 41, 78, 57, 70

TO THE PERSON READING THE INSTRUCTIONS: You should read quickly and clearly. You do not have to read the words in parentheses; these have been provided for your guidance in allowing the test taker time to think about/answer each question.

1. Examine Sample 1. (Pause 2–3 seconds) If these months are in order, according to the yearly calendar, go to number 64 on your answer sheet, and darken the letter B, as in boy. (Pause 5 seconds.) If the months are not in order, go to number 23 on your answer sheet, and darken the letter C, as in cat. (Pause 5 seconds.)

2. Examine Sample 1 again. (Pause 2–3 seconds.) If Halloween falls in October, Thanksgiving in November, and Christmas in December, go to number 10 on your answer sheet, and darken the letter A as in apple. (Pause 5 seconds.) If Valentines Day is in February, go to number 9 and darken letter B as in boy. (Pause 5 seconds.)

3. Examine Sample 2. (Pause 2–3 seconds.) If the first two times given are approximate times for the first two meals of the day (breakfast and lunch), then go to number 25 on your answer sheet, and darken the letter D as in dog. (Pause 5 seconds)

4. Examine Sample 2 again. (Pause 2–3 seconds.) If all the times end in the number 5, then go to number 62 on your answer sheet and darken the letter A as in apple. (Pause 5 seconds.) If all of the times do not end in the number 5, go to number 62 anyway, and darken the letter E, as in elephant. (Pause 5 seconds.)

5. Examine Sample 3. (Pause 2–3 seconds.) Select the highest number in this sample. Go to that number on your answer sheet, and darken the letter B as in boy. (Pause 5 seconds.)

6. Examine Sample 3 again. (Pause 2–3 seconds.) If the highest number is less than 50, go to number 50 on your answer sheet, and darken the letter C as in cat. (Pause 5 seconds.) If it is more than 50, go to

number 50 on your answer sheet anyway, and darken the letter A as in apple. (Pause 5 seconds.)

7. Examine Sample 3 again. (Pause 2–3 seconds.) If one of these shapes is a triangle, go to number 75 on your answer sheet, and darken the letter E as in elephant. (Pause 5 seconds.) If the triangle is the first shape, go to #83 on your answer sheet, and darken the letter A as in apple. (Pause 5 seconds.) If it is not the first shape, go to number 85 on your answer sheet and darken the letter C as in cat. (Pause 5 seconds.)

8. Examine Sample 4. (Pause 2–3 seconds.) If these ZIP codes are in numerical order, write the number 22 on the line to the right of the last ZIP code. (Pause 5 seconds.) If the third ZIP code ends in a number 4, add 4 to the number 22. (Pause 5 seconds.) Find the sum of this equation on your answer sheet, and darken the letter B as in boy. (Pause 5 seconds.)

9. Examine Sample 4 again. (Pause 2–3 seconds.) If the sum of the digits in the first ZIP code is ten, go to number 35 on your answer sheet, and darken the letter D as in dog. (Pause 5 seconds.) If the sum of the digits in the first and second zip codes combined, equal less than 25, go to number 34 on your answer sheet and darken the letter A as in apple. (Pause 5 seconds.)

10. Examine Sample 5. (Pause 2–3 seconds.) If you can reverse the first two letters and form a common word, then go to number 59 on your answer sheet and darken the letter B as in boy. (Pause 5 seconds.)

11. Examine Sample 5 again. (Pause 2–3 seconds.) Write numbers 17, 19, 21, and 23 in order in the blanks provided. Take the second number from the right, and go to your answer sheet and darken that space on your answer sheet with the letter E as in elephant. (Pause 5 seconds.)

12. Examine Sample 6. (Pause 2–3 seconds.) Find the highest number that is followed by the letter B; then find that number on your answer sheet, and darken the letter C as in cat. (Pause 5 seconds.)

13. Examine Sample 6 again. (Pause 2–3 seconds.) Look at the second number from the right. Add the two digits together. Darken the appropriate spot on your answer sheet that corresponds to this letter-number combination. (Pause 5 seconds.)

14. Examine Sample 7. (Pause 2–3 seconds.) If the first two numbers added together are equal to the last number, go to number 83 on your answer sheet, and darken the letter A as in apple. (Pause 5 seconds.)

15. Examine Sample 7 again. (Pause 2–3 seconds.) If the third number is greater than the first, but smaller than the last, then go to number 30 on your answer sheet and darken the letter B as in boy. (Pause 5 seconds.)

16. Examine Sample 8. (Pause 2–3 seconds.) Underline the third digit from the left. (Pause 2 seconds) If that number is less than the number 9, find that same number on your answer sheet and darken the letter D as in dog. (Pause 5 seconds) If it is greater than the number 9, find number 9 on your answer sheet and darken the letter C as in cat. (Pause 5 seconds.)

17. Examine Sample 9. (Pause 2–3 seconds.) Write the letters A and C in the first and third blanks. Go to your answer sheet and fill in these letter-number combinations in the appropriate spots. (Pause 5 seconds.)

18. Examine Sample 10. (Pause 2–3 seconds.) Fill in the blanks with the numbers 57, 77, 27, and 47. Take the highest number-letter combination and darken the appropriate spot on your answer sheet. (Pause 5 seconds.)

19. Examine Sample 11. (Pause 2–3 seconds.) On the line beside the third letter, write the highest in this series of numbers: 15, 25, 18, 42, 20, 32 (Pause 2 seconds) On your answer sheet, find and darken the space that corresponds with this letter-number combination. (Pause 5 seconds.)

20. Examine Sample 12. (Pause 2–3 seconds.) Reading from right to left, find the first number that is greater than 50. Locate this number on your answer sheet, and darken the letter E as in elephant. (Pause 5 seconds.)

21. Examine Sample 12 again. (Pause 2–3 seconds.) Find the only number in the line that is less than 50 and draw a box around it. Now, find the number in the box on your answer sheet, and darken the letter B as in boy. (Pause 5 seconds.)

22. Examine Sample 12 again. (Pause 2–3 seconds.) Find the smallest number and add 2. Find this number on your answer sheet and darken the letter C as in cat.

Answer Key: Full Length Practice Exam III

Address Checking Answer Key

1. A	17. D	33. D
2. D	18. A	34. A
3. D	19. A	35. A
4. D	20. A	36. D
5. D	21. A	37. D
6. A	22. D	38. A
7. D	23. A	39. D
8. D	24. D	40. D
9. D	25. D	41. A
10. A	26. D	42. A
11. D	27. D	43. D
12. A	28. D	44. A
13. D	29. A	45. D
14. D	30. D	46. D
15. D	31. D	47. D
16. D	32. A	48. A

49. A	**65.** A	**81.** D
50. D	**66.** D	**82.** D
51. D	**67.** A	**83.** A
52. A	**68.** D	**84.** A
53. D	**69.** D	**85.** D
54. D	**70.** D	**86.** D
55. D	**71.** D	**87.** D
56. A	**72.** A	**88.** A
57. D	**73.** D	**89.** D
58. D	**74.** D	**90.** A
59. A	**75.** D	**91.** A
60. D	**76.** D	**92.** D
61. D	**77.** A	**93.** D
62. D	**78.** D	**94.** A
63. D	**79.** D	**95.** A
64. A	**80.** D	

Memory for Addresses Answer Key

1. B	**12.** C	**23.** B
2. B	**13.** C	**24.** E
3. D	**14.** A	**25.** B
4. D	**15.** A	**26.** E
5. D	**16.** D	**27.** D
6. E	**17.** B	**28.** A
7. E	**18.** C	**29.** D
8. E	**19.** D	**30.** C
9. E	**20.** C	**31.** D
10. A	**21.** D	**32.** C
11. A	**22.** D	**33.** E

34. A	**53.** D	**72.** C
35. A	**54.** C	**73.** B
36. A	**55.** D	**74.** E
37. D	**56.** D	**75.** C
38. E	**57.** A	**76.** D
39. C	**58.** C	**77.** E
40. A	**59.** E	**78.** D
41. D	**60.** B	**79.** B
42. D	**61.** E	**80.** A
43. B	**62.** B	**81.** E
44. A	**63.** A	**82.** A
45. C	**64.** E	**83.** E
46. C	**65.** B	**84.** B
47. E	**66.** B	**85.** C
48. E	**67.** C	**86.** B
49. B	**68.** A	**87.** B
50. C	**69.** D	**88.** E
51. A	**70.** A	
52. A	**71.** C	

Number Series Answer Key

1. A. The numbers in this series increase by 9, for example, 19+9=28, 28+9=37.

2. C. There are two patterns at work: The number 27 is inserted every third number; the rest of the series follows a +6 pattern, for example, 29+6=35, 35+6=41.

3. A. The numbers in the series decrease by 6, for example, 85–6=79, 79–6=73.

4. B. The addends in the series increase by 2, for example, 26+1=27, 27+3=30, 30+5=35.

5. **A.** The pattern in this series is +8 –2 +8 –2, for example, 15+8=23, 23–2=21, 21+8=29, 29–2=27.

6. **D.** Each number in the series is multiplied by 2 to get the next number, for example, 1×2=2, 2×2=4.

7. **C.** This series follows the rule +10 +9 +8..., for example, 14+10=24, 24+9=33, 33+8=41.

8. **C.** This series follows the rule ×2 –6 ×2 –6, for example, 7×2=14, 14–6=8, 8×2=16, 16–6=10.

9. **A.** The pattern followed here is –5 +8 –5 +8, for example, 7–5=2, 2+8=10, 10–5=5, 5+8=13.

10. **A.** The difference between subsequent numbers in this series increases by 2, for example, 93–3=90, 90–5=85, 85–7=78.

11. **C.** This series follows the pattern –3 +5 –3 +5, for example, 13–3=10, 10+5=15, 15–3=12, 12+5=17.

12. **D.** There are two patterns at work in this series: The first pattern follows the rule +3 +5 +3 +5; then every third number is 40, for example, 29+3=32, 32+5=37, 37+3=40.

13. **A.** The addends in this series keep increasing by 2, for example, 15+4=19, 19+6=25, 25+8=33.

14. **B.** There are two patterns in this series: The first has the difference between numbers increasing by 1 and the second adds 4 to every other number, for example, 59–8=51, 51+4=55, 55–9=46, 46+4=50.

15. **A.** This series counts up by sixes, for example, 6+6=12, 12+6=18.

16. **D.** There are two alternating series within this series: The difference between every other number is 8, for example, 92–8=84, 84–8=76; the numbers in the other pattern increase by 2, for example, 2+2=4, 4+2=6.

17. **B.** The numbers in this series increase by 3, for example, 25+3=28, 28+3=31.

18. **B.** Divide each number in the series to get the next number, for example, 65,536÷4=16,384÷4=4096.

19. **D.** The difference between numbers in this series is 7, for example, 88–7=81, 81–7=74.

20. **B.** This series follows a pattern of +5 +5 –5 –5, for example, 38+5=43, 43+5=48, 48–5=43, 43–5=38.

21. **C.** There are two alternating patterns: First, every other number is a 1; the other numbers are multiplied by 3 to get subsequent numbers, for example, 3×3=9, 9×3=27.

22. **C.** Each three-digit number is followed by a two-digit number that uses the same digits without the 0 in the middle, for example, 201 21, 301 31. The three-digit numbers increase by 1, for example, 201+1=202, 202+1=203.

23. **A.** This is a very simple series with two patterns. the numbers count up by 1, for example, 8 9 10, and so on; and the signs form a pattern of – + +, – + +.

24. **A.** In this series, the second number is subtracted from the first number to get the third number; then the fourth number is subtracted from the third number to get the fifth number, and so on, for example, 419–259=160, 160–99=61.

Following Oral Instructions Answer Key

These spots should be darkened on your answer sheet when the test is complete:

5. C	**35.** D	**62.** E
8. D	**37.** C	**64.** B
9. B	**41.** B	**70.** E
10. A	**42.** E	**73.** B
21. E	**43.** C	**75.** E
25. D	**45.** A	**77.** C
26. B	**50.** A	**83.** A
30. B	**52.** C	**85.** C
34. A	**59.** B	

Full Length Practice Exam IV

Address Checking

TIME: 6 Minutes, 95 Questions

Directions: For each question, compare the address in the left column with the address in the right column. If the two addresses are exactly alike, mark A on your answer sheet. If they are different in any way, mark D on your answer sheet.

1. 108 Maple St	180 Maple St
2. 130 S Middle Neck Rd	130 N Middle Neck Rd
3. 1981 Marcus Ave	1981 Marcus Ave
4. 45 North Station Plaza	45 South Station Plaza
5. 1 Bellingham Lane	1 Bellingham Lane East
6. 14 Steven Lane	14 Stephen Lane
7. Brooklyn NY	Brooklyn Alabama
8. 48035 Clinton Township	48035 Clinton Township
9. 48080 Saint Clair Shores	48008 Saint Clair Shores
10. 8 Sycamore Drive	8 Sycamore Drive
11. 41 Farm Lane	14 Farm Lane
12. 182 Grace Ct. N	182 Grace Rd. N
13. 60 Knightsbridge Rd.	60 Knightsbridge Dr.
14. 1979 Tuddington Rd.	1979 Tuddington Rd.
15. 233 East Shore Rd.	233 West Shore Rd.
16. 15 Sutton Place	15 Sutton Street
17. 250 Schenck Ave. SW	250 Schenck Ave. NW
18. 1010 Northern Blvd.	1010 Northern Blvd.
19. Bloomfield Hills, MI 48304	Bloomfield Hills, MI 48303
20. Evergreen, CO 80437	Evergreen, CO 80439
21. 39 School House Lane	39 Schoolhouse Lane
22. 15 Hill Park Street	15 Hillpark Drive
23. 125 Knightsbridge Rd.	125 Kensington Rd.
24. 35 Somer Blvd.	35 Summer Blvd.
25. 1872 Terrace Circle	1872 Terrace Dr.
26. 95 Beech Court	95 Beach Court
27. Point Washington, FL	Port Washington, NY

(continued)

28. Gainesville, FL 32611	Gainesville, FL 32611
29. Steamboat Springs, CO 80487	Steamboat Springs, CO 80487
30. Bethania, NC 27010	Bethania, NC 27010
31. 1983–56 Cambridge Rd.	1983–56 Cambridge Rd.
32. 6 Ascot Rdg	6 Ascot Rd
33. 87 Poplar Court	87 Popular Court
34. 108 Forest Row	108 Forest Road
35. 534 Lakeville Rd. W	534 Lakeville Rd. E
36. 73 Cumberland Lane	73 Cumberland Lane
37. White Plains, NC	White Plains, NY
38. Winston Salem, NC 27117	Winston Salem, NC 27199
39. Lexington, KY	Lexington, NC
40. Limerick, ME	Limington, ME
41. Auburn, ME 04212	Auburn, ME 04212
42. 254–08 West End Dr.	254–08 West End Dr.
43. 61 Jayson Ave.	61 Jason Ave.
44. 5003 Madelyn Place	5003 Madeline Place
45. 2862 Rebecca Road	2862 Rebecca Road
46. 7341 Katie Court	7431 Katie Court
47. Boothbay, ME	East Boothbay, ME
48. Glen Cove, ME	Glen Cove, NY
49. Phoenix, AZ 85034	Phoenix, AZ 85034
50. Superior, AZ 85273	Surprise, AZ 85374
51. 9004 Farm Lane	9004 Farmhouse Lane
52. 38 Cherry Brook Pl.	38 Cherry Brook Rd.
53. 9A Surrey Lane	98 Surrey Lane
54. Alexandria, VA	Alexandria, LA
55. 3167 Beverly Rd.	3167 Beverly Rd.
56. Forest Hill, LA	Forest Hills, NY
57. Allentown, NJ 08501	Allenwood, NJ 08720
58. 251 Fairfield Ave.	251 Fairview Ave.
59. Franklin Park, NJ 08823	Franklin Lakes, NJ 07417
60. Baton Rouge, LA 70896	Baton Rouge, LA 70896
61. 7000 Longfellow Rd.	700 Longfellow Rd.
62. Green Brook, NJ 08812	Green Creek, NJ 08219

(continued)

63. 74A Forest Row	74 Forest Row
64. 576 E 81st St.	576 E 81st St
65. 1082 4th Rd.	1082 4th Dr.
66. 3429 Hickory Drive	3429 Hickory Drive
67. 255–23 West End Dr.	245–23 West End Dr.
68. 8999 Whitman Way	8995 Whitman Way
69. 3800 Hallie Hwy	3800 Hallie Hwy
70. 23 Tamara Tpke.	23 Tamara Pkwy.
71. 4711 Derek Dr	4711 Derek Dr
72. 4604 Ari Avenue	4604 Ari Avenue
73. 7872 Susan St.	7287 Susan St.
74. Hackensack, NJ 07608	Hackettstown, NJ 07840
75. Akron, NY	Akron, OH
76. Midland, PA 15059	Midway, PA 15060
77. Pittsburgh, PA 15226	Pittsburgh, PA 15216
78. 246 Jenna Junction	246 Jenna Junction
79. 9658 Rachel Rd.	9568 Rachel Rd.
80. 4243 Lexi Lane S	4243 Lexi Lane N
81. 151 Shelley St	151 Shelley St
82. 5221 Debbie Drive	5121 Debbie Drive
83. 813 S Sara Rd.	813 S Sara Dr.
84. 812 Ben Franklin Blvd	812 Ben Franklin Blvd
85. 9 Vista Dr.	9 Vista Hill Dr.
86. 44 Stonecutter Rd	44 Stonecutter Rd
87. 17 Jaimie Court	17 Jamie Court
88. 975 Franklin Ave	957 Franklin Ave
89. Lumberton, NJ	Lumberton, NC
90. Sacramento, CA	Sacramento, CA
91. Duluth, IA	Dubuque, IA
92. Macon, GA 31216	Macon, GA 31216
93. 8 N Pine Dr	8 Northpine Dr
94. 69 Duck Pond Rd	69 Duck Pond Rd
95. 29 G Meadow Green Circle	29 C Meadow Green Circle

Memory for Addresses

TIME: 5 minutes, 88 questions

Directions: On the actual exam, you will have three practice exercises designed to give you an opportunity to memorize more thoroughly the information grid.

*To make this practice exam as realistic as possible in this regard, allow yourself an additional five minutes to study and memorize this grid. After those five minutes, you should then give yourself an additional five minutes—just like the actual exam—to answer as many of the 88 questions as you can. On your answer sheet, mark each question A, B, C, D, or E, depending on where the address would be found in the information grid. DO NOT refer back to the grid after your initial five minute memorization is up: On the actual exam, after your practice exercises, you will not be allowed to refer back to the information grid.

A	B	C	D	E
7700–7799 Hamilton	1250–1299 Hamilton	5600–5750 Hamilton	7100–7500 Hamilton	9200–9500 Hamilton
Ariel	Knightsbridge	Albertson	Arleigh	Redwood
5399–5600 Inwood	2000–2199 Inwood	4300–4900 Inwood	7200–7299 Inwood	8199–8250 Inwood
Dakota	Arbor	Pembroke	Elm	Watermill
1999–2999 Willis	3400–3699 Willis	5500–5999 Willis	9100–9199 Willis	7199–7250 Willis

1. Elm	45. 3400–3699 Willis
2. Watermill	46. 2000–2199 Inwood
3. 9200–9500 Hamilton	47. Knightsbridge
4. 2000–2199 Inwood	48. Redwood
5. Dakota	49. 7199–7250 Willis
6. 3400–3699 Willis	50. 1250–1299 Hamilton
7. Pembroke	51. Dakota
8. 4300–4900 Inwood	52. Arleigh
9. 7100–7500 Hamilton	53. 8199–8250 Inwood
10. Arleigh	54. 5399–5600 Inwood
11. 5399–5600 Inwood	55. Pembroke
12. Albertson	56. 5500–5999 Willis
13. 7100–7500 Hamilton	57. 7200–7299 Inwood
14. 7199–7250 Willis	58. Watermill
15. Elm	59. 9200–9500 Hamilton
16. Redwood	60. 7700–7799 Hamilton
17. 7700–7799 Hamilton	61. Arbor
18. Arbor	62. Redwood
19. Watermill	63. 9100–9199 Willis
20. 2000–2199 Inwood	64. 2000–2199 Inwood
21. 5500–5999 Willis	65. Elm
22. 4300–4900 Inwood	66. Ariel
23. Pembroke	67. 5600–5750 Hamilton
24. Dakota	68. 3400–3699 Willis
25. 1250–1299 Hamilton	69. Knightsbridge
26. 7100–7500 Hamilton	70. 1999–2999 Willis
27. Ariel	71. Albertson
28. Watermill	72. 7200–7299 Inwood
29. 7200–7299 Inwood	73. 9200–9500 Hamilton
30. 7199–7250 Willis	74. Pembroke
31. Arbor	75. Arbor
32. Redwood	76. 2000–2199 Inwood
33. 1999–2999 Willis	77. 9100–9199 Willis
34. 2000–2199 Inwood	78. 5399–5600 Inwood
35. Pembroke	79. Redwood

(continued)

36. Knightsbridge	80. Watermill
37. 4300–4900 Inwood	81. Arleigh
38. 7100–7500 Hamilton	82. 7100–7500 Hamilton
39. Albertson	83. 5500–5999 Willis
40. Dakota	84. Dakota
41. 9100–9199 Willis	85. Knightsbridge
42. 1250–1299 Hamilton	86. 7199–7250 Willis
43. Elm	87. 5600 5750 Hamilton
44. Arbor	88. Elm

Number Series

TIME: 20 minutes, 24 questions

Directions: Each number series question consists of a series of numbers that follow some definite, precise order: The numbers progress from left to right, following some determined rule. One lettered pair of numbers (A, B, C, D, or E) for each question represents the correct answer: that is, the next series of numbers that should follow in the order, and thus conform to the rule. Choose this correct answer, and mark it on your answer sheet.

1. 512 256 128 64 32 16 8 __ __
   - A. 6 4
   - B. 4 2
   - C. 4 3
   - D. 6 3

2. 5 8 11 14 17 20 23 __ __
   - A. 30 34
   - B. 25 27
   - C. 26 29
   - D. 24 30

3. 35 31 27 23 19 15 11 __ __
   - A. 10 9
   - B. 8 7
   - C. 9 4
   - D. 7 3

4. 2 3 2 3 2 3 2 __ __
   - A. 3 2
   - B. 2 3
   - C. 3 3
   - D. 2 2

5. 7 14 21 28 35 42 49 __ __
   - A. 52 58
   - B. 53 60
   - C. 55 57
   - D. 56 63

6. 1 1 5 2 2 5 3 __ __
   - A. 3 5
   - B. 5 3
   - C. 5 5
   - D. 3 3

7. 22 33 44 55 66 77 88 __ __
   - A. 98 108
   - B. 111 121
   - C. 99 110
   - D. 99 111

8. 2 4 5 6 8 5 10 __ __
   - A. 11 12
   - B. 5 11
   - C. 12 5
   - D. 12 10

9. 576 578 580 582 584 586 588 __ __
   - A. 591 593
   - B. 592 593
   - C. 589 591
   - D. 590 592

10. 6400 3200 1600 800 400 200 __ __
    - A. 300 200
    - B. 100 50
    - C. 100 40
    - D. 100 10

11. 2 4 12 24 72 144 432 __ __
    - A. 864 2592
    - B. 684 2952
    - C. 1245 2232
    - D. 864   986

12. 11023 11026 11029 11032 11035 11038 11041 _____ _____
    - A. 11043 11047
    - B. 11042 11043
    - C. 11046 11048
    - D. 11044 11047

13. 13 18 23 28 28 33 38 43 __ __
   - A. 44 45
   - B. 45 52
   - C. 48 53
   - D. 47 49

14. 1 2 3 5 6 7 9 __ __
   - A. 11 12
   - B. 10 11
   - C. 11 13
   - D. 10 13

15. 400 398 396 394 392 390 388 ___ ___
   - A. 387 386
   - B. 385 383
   - C. 386 384
   - D. 384 380

16. 15 17 19 21 23 25 27 __ __
   - A. 29 31
   - B. 30 32
   - C. 35 37
   - D. 39 40

17. 95 91 87 83 79 75 71 __ __
   - A. 69 68
   - B. 67 63
   - C. 70 69
   - D. 70 67

18. 66 71 76 81 86 91 96 __ __
   - A. 99 104
   - B. 100 104
   - C. 103 107
   - D. 101 106

19. 3 7 9 13 15 19 21 __ __
   - A. 23 25
   - B. 25 27
   - C. 22 24
   - D. 22 23

20. 3 3 7 4 4 7 5 __ __
    A. 7 7
    B. 5 5
    C. 5 7
    D. 6 7

21. 27 34 41 48 55 62 69 __ __
    A. 76 83
    B. 72 79
    C. 75 79
    D. 80 83

22. 21 26 31 36 41 46 51 __ __
    A. 61 66
    B. 56 61
    C. 53 55
    D. 60 61

23. 7 2 10 5 13 8 16 __ __
    A. 10 9
    B. 17 18
    C. 16 18
    D. 11 19

24. 8 16 24 32 40 48 56 __ __
    A. 74 84
    B. 60 68
    C. 64 72
    D. 59 62

Following Oral Instructions

TIME: 25 minutes

Directions: When you are ready to practice this section of the exam, you'll need to ask a friend to help. First, copy the 12 questions below, exactly as you see them here, onto another piece of paper (your worksheet). Your friend will read you specific instructions as to how to work with and answer each of the questions.

1. 33, 48, 26, 53, 82, 73

2. ____E

3. 20, 30, 50, 60

4. ____A, ____B, ____C, ____D

5.
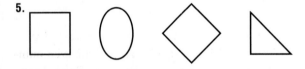

6. 90, 78, 64, 52

7.
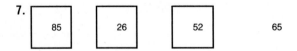

8.

9. 07461, 17461, 27461, 37461, 47461

10. 5:34 p.m., 2:56 a.m., 3:33 p.m., 9:05 a.m., 8:33 p.m.

11. ___K, ___R, ___M

12. 81, 16, 28, 79, 41, 98

TO THE PERSON READING THE INSTRUCTIONS: *You should read quickly and clearly. You do not have to read the words in parentheses; these have been provided for your guidance in allowing the test taker time to think about/answer each question.*

READ THE FOLLOWING TO THE TEST TAKER: *You need to mark your answer sheet according to the specific instructions I read to you. I'll pause for a few seconds after each instruction, so you have time to mark your answer sheet.*

The test begins now.

1. Examine Sample 1. (Pause 2–3 seconds.) Draw circles around all the odd numbers. (Pause 2 seconds.) Draw squares around the even numbers. (Pause 2 seconds.) Select the highest odd number. (Pause 2 seconds.) Find that number on your answer sheet, and darken the letter C as in cat. (Pause 5 seconds.) Find the highest even number on your answer sheet, and darken the letter A as in apple. (Pause 5 seconds.)

2. Examine Sample 2. (Pause 2–3 seconds.) Find the sum of 25+25 and write that number on the line. (Pause 5–7 seconds.) Go to your answer sheet and darken this number-letter combination. (Pause 5 seconds.)

3. Examine Sample 3. (Pause 2–3 seconds.) If the second number multiplied by 2 is equal to the last number, go to number 75 on your answer sheet, and darken the letter E as in elephant. (Pause 5 seconds.) If not, go to number 75 and darken the letter B as in boy. (Pause 5 seconds.)

4. Examine Sample 3. (Pause 2–3 seconds.) If the first number added to the second number is equal to the third number, go to number 15 on your answer sheet, and darken the letter A as in apple. (Pause 5 seconds.)

5. Examine Sample 4. (Pause 2–3 seconds.) Write the numbers 86, 72, 93, and 56 on the lines next to the letters. Select the first and third

number-letter combinations and darken the corresponding spaces on your answer sheet. (Pause 5 seconds.)

6. Examine Sample 4. (Pause 2–3 seconds.) If two of the numbers are even numbers, go to number 37 on your answer sheet, and darken the D as in dog. (Pause 5 seconds.) If more than two are even numbers, go to number 37 anyway, and darken the letter B as in boy. (Pause 5 seconds.)

7. Examine Sample 5. (Pause 2–3 seconds.) Write the number 5 in the oval, (pause 2 seconds) 8 in the square, (pause 2 seconds) 12 in the triangle, (pause 2 seconds) and 25 in the diamond. (Pause 2 seconds.) Add the numbers in the oval and the diamond together. (Pause 2 seconds.) Find this number on your answer sheet, and darken the letter A as in apple. (Pause 5 seconds.)

8. Examine Sample 5. (Pause 2–3 seconds.) Take the number contained in the triangle and subtract 2. (Pause 2 seconds.) Find this number on your answer sheet, and darken the letter D as in dog. (Pause 5 seconds.)

9. Examine Sample 6. (Pause 2–3 seconds.) If the first number is larger than the second number, find this number on your answer sheet, and darken the letter E as in elephant. (Pause 5 seconds.) If not, find number 75 and darken the letter E as in elephant. (Pause 5 seconds.)

10. Examine Sample 6. (Pause 2–3 seconds.) Find the lowest number in this string of numbers. (Pause 2 seconds.) Locate this number on your answer sheet, and darken the letter C as in cat. (Pause 5 seconds.)

11. Examine Sample 7. (Pause 2–3 seconds.) Find the number not enclosed in a geometric shape. (Pause 2 seconds.) Locate this number on your answer sheet and darken the letter B as in boy. (Pause 5 seconds.)

12. Examine Sample 7. (Pause 2–3 seconds.) Find the lowest number enclosed in a square. (Pause 2 seconds.) Find this number on your answer sheet and darken the letter D as in dog. (Pause 5 seconds.)

13. Examine Sample 7. (Pause 2–3 seconds.) Find the highest number enclosed in a square. (Pause 2 seconds.) Find this number on your answer sheet and darken the letter E as in elephant. (Pause 5 seconds.)

14. Examine Sample 8. (Pause 2–3 seconds.) Place an A in the square, a B in the triangle, a C in the diamond and a D beside the number without a shape around it. (Pause 2 seconds.) Take the two highest number-letter combinations and find and darken them on your answer sheet. (Pause 8 seconds.)

15. Examine Sample 9. (Pause 2–3 seconds.) If the last number is greater than the first number, go to number 53 your answer sheet and darken the letter B as in boy. (Pause 5 seconds.)

16. Examine Sample 9. (Pause 2–3 seconds.) If the sum of all the digits in the first ZIP code is over 10, (pause 2 seconds) go to number 24 on your answer sheet, and darken the letter C as in cat. (Pause 5 seconds.) If the number is under 10, go to number 24 and darken the letter A as in apple. (Pause 5 seconds.) If the number is equal to 10, go to number 24 on your answer sheet and darken the letter D as in dog. (Pause 5 seconds.)

17. Examine Sample 10. (Pause 2–3 seconds.) Draw a circle around the first three times. (Pause 2 seconds.) Now, underline the minutes portion of these items. (Pause 2 seconds.) Using one number at a time, for a total of three spaces on your answer sheet, locate the number on your answer sheet that corresponds to the underlined minutes, and darken the letter E as in elephant. (Pause 8 seconds.)

18. Examine Sample 10. (Pause 2–3 seconds.) Add the 3 or 4 digits in each time together, and write that sum above or below the time itself. (Pause 3 seconds.) Two of the sums are equal. Find that number on your answer sheet and darken the letter C as in cat. (Pause 5 seconds.)

19. Examine Sample 11. (Pause 2–3 seconds.) Write the numbers 6, 23, and 19 on the lines next to the letters, K, R, and M. (Pause 3 seconds.) Locate the numbers beside the R and the M on your answer sheet and darken the letter D as in dog. (Pause 8 seconds.)

20. Examine Sample 11. (Pause 2–3 seconds.) Find the number beside the letter K on your answer sheet and darken the letter B as in boy. (Pause 5 seconds.)

21. Examine Sample 12. (Pause 2–3 seconds.) Underline every other number beginning with the first. (Pause 2 seconds.) Put two lines under the remaining numbers. (Pause 2 seconds.) Select all the numbers that are underlined just once. Find the corresponding numbers on your answer sheet, and darken the letter A as in apple in each one. (Pause 8–10 seconds.)

22. Examine Sample 12. (Pause 2–3 seconds.) Select all the numbers that are underlined twice. Find the corresponding numbers on your answer sheet, and darken the letter B as in boy in each one. (Pause 8–10 seconds.)

Answer Key: Full Length Practice Exam IV

Address Checking Answer Key

1. D	17. D	33. D
2. D	18. A	34. D
3. A	19. D	35. D
4. D	20. D	36. A
5. D	21. D	37. D
6. D	22. D	38. D
7. D	23. D	39. D
8. A	24. D	40. D
9. D	25. D	41. A
10. A	26. D	42. A
11. D	27. D	43. D
12. D	28. A	44. D
13. D	29. A	45. A
14. A	30. A	46. D
15. D	31. A	47. D
16. D	32. D	48. D

49. A	65. D	81. A
50. D	66. A	82. D
51. D	67. D	83. D
52. D	68. D	84. A
53. D	69. A	85. D
54. D	70. D	86. A
55. A	71. A	87. D
56. D	72. A	88. D
57. D	73. D	89. D
58. D	74. D	90. A
59. D	75. D	91. D
60. A	76. D	92. A
61. D	77. D	93. D
62. D	78. A	94. A
63. D	79. D	95. D
64. A	80. D	

Memory for Addresses Answer Key

1. D	12. C	23. C
2. E	13. D	24. A
3. E	14. E	25. B
4. B	15. D	26. D
5. A	16. E	27. A
6. B	17. A	28. E
7. C	18. B	29. D
8. C	19. E	30. E
9. D	20. B	31. B
10. D	21. C	32. E
11. A	22. C	33. A

34. B	**53.** E	**72.** D
35. C	**54.** A	**73.** E
36. B	**55.** C	**74.** C
37. C	**56.** C	**75.** B
38. D	**57.** D	**76.** B
39. C	**58.** E	**77.** D
40. A	**59.** E	**78.** A
41. D	**60.** A	**79.** E
42. B	**61.** B	**80.** E
43. D	**62.** E	**81.** D
44. B	**63.** D	**82.** D
45. B	**64.** B	**83.** C
46. B	**65.** D	**84.** A
47. B	**66.** A	**85.** B
48. E	**67.** C	**86.** E
49. E	**68.** B	**87.** C
50. B	**69.** B	**88.** D
51. A	**70.** A	
52. D	**71.** C	

Number Series Answer Key

1. B. In this series each number is divided by 2 to get the next number, for example, $512 \div 2 = 256$, $256 \div 2 = 128$.

2. C. Numbers increase by 3 in this series, for example, $5+3=8$, $8+3=11$.

3. D. 4 is subtracted from each number to get the next number in the series, for example, $35-4=31$, $31-4=27$.

4. A. This simple series follows a pattern of 2 3 2 3.

5. D. This series counts up by sevens, for example, $7+7=14$, $14+7=21$.

6. A. There are two patterns in this series: The first pattern counts up by 1 with that number repeating, for example, 1 1 2 2 3 3; every third number in this series is a 5.

7. C. The numbers in this series increase by 11, for example, 22+11=33, 33+11=44.

8. C. There are two alternating series: The first series consists of numbers that increase by 2, for example, 2+2=4, 4+2=6, 6+2=8; then every third number in this series is a 5.

9. D. The numbers in this series increase by 2, for example, 576+2=578, 578+2=580.

10. B. Each number in this series is divided by 2 to get the subsequent number, for example, 6400÷2=3200, 3200÷2=1600.

11. A. This series follows the rule ×2 ×3 ×2 ×3, for example, 2×2=4, 4×3=12, 12×2=24, 24×3=72.

12. D. The numbers in this series increase by 3, for example, 11023+3=11026, 11026+3=11029.

13. C. The numbers in this series increase by 5, for example, 13+5=18, 18+5=23, 23+5=28.

14. B. This series counts up, skipping every fourth number.

15. C. The difference between each number in this series is 2, for example, 400–2=398, 398–2=396.

16. A. The numbers in this series increase by 2, for example, 15+2=17, 17+2=19.

17. B. The numbers in this series decrease by 4, for example, 95–4=91, 91–4=87.

18. D. The numbers in this series increase by 5, for example, 66+5=71, 71+5=76.

19. B. This series follows the rule +4 +2 +4 +2, for example, 3+4=7, 7+2=9, 9+4=13, 13+2=15.

20. C. There are two patterns in this series: The first pattern counts up by 1 with that number repeating, for example, 3 3 4 4; the second pattern places a 7 between each of those pairs.

21. A. The numbers in this series increase by 7, for example, 27+7=34, 34+7=41.

22. B. The numbers in this series increase by 5, for example, 21+5=26, 26+5=31.

23. D. This series follows a pattern of –5 +8 –5 +8, for example, 7–5=2, 2+8=10, 10–5=5, 5+8=13.

24. C. This series counts up by eights, for example, 8+8=16, 16+8=24.

Following Oral Instructions Answer Key

These spots should be darkened on your answer sheet when the test is complete:

6. B	**33.** E	**73.** C
10. D	**34.** E	**75.** E
14. C	**37.** B	**79.** B
15. A	**41.** A	**81.** A
16. B	**45.** B	**82.** A
19. D	**50.** E	**85.** E
23. D	**52.** C	**86.** A
24. C	**53.** B	**90.** E
26. D	**56.** E	**93.** C
28. A	**58.** D	**98.** B
30. A	**65.** B	

USPS Resources and Career Development

After you successfully pass the exam, your next major area of interest will be finding a job with the USPS.

Fortunately, the process for locating a job is well organized, and you can utilize a variety of resources (many of them web-based) in your job search:

➤ Access the USPS website for current job openings. The website can be found at http://www.usps.com.

➤ Check the federal government online listing of job openings, located at http://www.usajobs.opm.gov, as illustrated in Figure A.1.

  If you click on the New to USAJOBS link (in the lower-right corner of your screen), you are presented with a three-step approach to using the site, as shown in Figure A.2.

 You can also reach USAJOBS at (478) 757-3000, or TDD (478) 744-2299.

➤ Finally, check out an individual state's official website for more information on jobs and job openings in specific cities and/or counties. Table A.1 lists the addresses for each of the 50 states' websites.

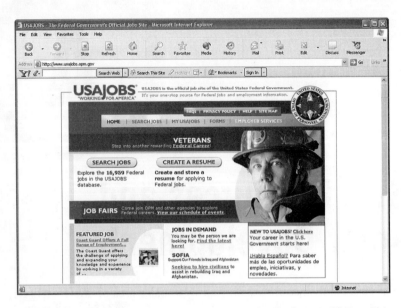

Figure A.1 The USAJOBS website is an excellent, comprehensive "one-stop" listing of job openings and career resource–related information.

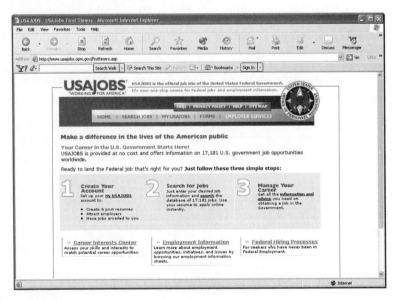

Figure A.2 Take advantage of this free service and utilize it as an easy and powerful way to organize and improve your job search and career development.

Websites have a habit of going down from time to time. If you are trying to access one of these sites and aren't having much luck, try again a bit later, as the site is probably experiencing transient technical difficulties.

Table A.1	Listing of State Websites		
Alabama	www.state.al.us	Montana	www.mt.gov
Alaska	www.state.ak.us	Nebraska	www.state.ne.us
Arizona	www.az.gov	Nevada	www.nv.gov
Arkansas	www.state.ar.us	New Hampshire	www.state.nh.us
California	www.state.ca.us/state/ portal/myca_homepage.jsp	New Jersey	www.state.nj.us
Colorado	www.colorado.gov	New Mexico	www.state.nm.us
Connecticut	www.state.ct.us	New York	www.state.ny.us
Delaware	www.delaware.gov	North Carolina	www.ncgov.com
District of Columbia	www.dc.gov	North Dakota	www.discovernd.com
Florida	www.myflorida.com	Ohio	www.state.oh.us
Georgia	www.georgia.gov	Oklahoma	www.state.ok.us
Hawaii	www.state.hi.us	Oregon	www.oregon.gov
Idaho	www.state.id.us	Pennsylvania	www.state.pa.us
Illinois	www.state.il.us	Rhode Island	www.state.ri.us
Indiana	www.state.in.us	South Carolina	www.myscgov.com
Iowa	www.iowa.gov/state/ main/index.html	South Dakota	www.state.sd.us
Kansas	www.accesskansas.org	Tennessee	www.state.tn.us
Kentucky	www.kentucky.gov	Texas	www.state.tx.us
Louisiana	www.state.la.us	Utah	www.utah.gov
Maine	www.state.me.us	Vermont	www.vermont.gov
Maryland	www.state.md.us	Virginia	www.vipnet.org
Massachusetts	www.mass.gov	Washington	www.access.wa.gov
Michigan	www.michigan.gov	West Virginia	www.wv.gov
Minnesota	www.state.mn.us	Wisconsin	www.wisconsin.gov
Mississippi	www.state.ms.us	Wyoming	www.state.wy.us
Missouri	www.state.mo.us		

Additional Career Resource Information

In addition to the websites listed in Table A.1, you can consult a variety of additional resources to improve your job search and career development.

For general information on the USPS, consult the following sources:

➤ *Postal Facts*—http://www.usps.com/communications/organization/ postalfacts.htm. This site contains interesting facts and figures about the post office.

➤ *USPS Financials*—http://www.usps.com/financials. Here you can view and/or download financial reports.

➤ *Postal Clerks and Mail Carriers (Occupational Outlook Handbook)*— http://www.stats.bls.gov/oco/ocos141.htm. Find descriptions of all jobs, working conditions, and so on.

You might also want to consult the following additional online publications that are USPS-related:

➤ *Federal Daily*—http://www.fendonline.com. Federal news—updated daily—for government employees.

➤ *Postal News from FederalTimes.com*— http://federaltimes.com/index.php?C=570476.php. News for employees of the USPS.

➤ *Postal Association Press*—http://www.apwupostalpress.org.

➤ *Postal Report.com*—http://www.lunewsviews.com.

➤ *Postal Mag.com*—http://postalworkersonline.com.

➤ *Postal News.com*—http://www.postalnews.com.

Specific information on unions that represent USPS employees can be found on their respective websites. To view the most current bargaining agreements, go to the National Association of Letter Carriers (http://www.nrlca.org) or the American Postal Workers Union, APWU (http://www.apwu.org), and search the sites for more information. Also, you may want to access the National Postal Mail Handlers Union (http://www.npmhu.org), as well as the National Rural Letter Carriers Association (http://www.nrlca.org).

Finally, although this is in no way a complete listing, the following links take you to message boards, web rings, and USPS-related blogs that may offer you additional information:

➤ *Mailman "Stuff"*—http://www.rollanet.org/~gary/index.html.

➤ *Branch Directory*—http://www.rollanet.org/~gary/nalc-directory.

➤ *Lu's News and Views*—http://www.quicktopic.com/24/H/DpXxjPtHFGJ. An online discussion forum.

➤ *Post Office Locator*—http://www.mapsonus.com/db/USPS.

➤ *Postal Mag Forums*—http://pub169.ezboard.com/ bpostalmagezforums93124.

➤ *Postal Workers' Web Ring*—http://www.seaknight.com/pwring.

➤ *Topix.net*—http://www.topix.net/business/postal.

➤ *Postalblog*—http://unionblog.blogspot.com.

City, State, and Thoroughfare Abbreviations

Use this handy reference as both a study guide and a quick reference for commonly used abbreviations.

State Abbreviations

Table B.1 is a listing of all state abbreviations.

Table B.1 State Abbreviations, Including District of Columbia

Alabama	AL	Missouri	MO
Alaska	AK	Montana	MT
Arizona	AZ	Nebraska	NE
Arkansas	AR	Nevada	NV
California	CA	New Hampshire	NH
Colorado	CO	New Jersey	NJ
Connecticut	CT	New Mexico	NM
Delaware	DE	New York	NY
District of Columbia	DC	North Carolina	NC
Florida	FL	North Dakota	ND
Georgia	GA	Ohio	OH
Hawaii	HI	Oklahoma	OK
Idaho	IA	Oregon	OR
Illinois	IL	Pennsylvania	PA
Indiana	IN	Rhode Island	RI
Iowa	IA	South Carolina	SC
Kansas	KS	South Dakota	SD
Kentucky	KY	Tennessee	TN
Lousiana	LA	Texas	TX
Maine	ME	Utah	UT
Maryland	MD	Vermont	VT
Massachussetts	MA	Virginia	VA
Michigan	MI	Washington	WA
Minnesota	MN	West Virginia	WV
Mississippi	MS	Wisconsin	WI
		Wyoming	WY

U.S. Possessions Abbreviations

Table B.2 is a listing of abbreviations for all U.S. possessions.

Table B.2	U.S. Possessions Abbreviations
American Samoa	AS
Federated States of Micronesia	FM
Guam	GU
Marshall Islands	MH
Northern Mariana Islands	MP
Palau	PW
Puerto Rico	PR
Virgin Islands	VI

Thoroughfare Abbreviations

Table B.3 is a listing of all thoroughfare abbreviations.

Table B.3	Thoroughfare Abbreviations
Alley	Aly
Annex	Anx
Arcade	Arc
Avenue	Ave
Bayoo	Byu
Beach	Bch
Bend	Bnd
Bluff	Blf
Bottom	Btm
Boulevard	Blvd
Branch	Br
Bridge	Brg
Brook	Brk
Brooks	Brks
Burg	Bg
Burgs	Bgs
Bypass	Byp
Camp	Cp
Canyon	Cyn

(continued)

Table B.3 Thoroughfare Abbreviations *(continued)*

Cape	Cpe
Causeway	Cswy
Center	Ctr
Centers	Ctrs
Circle	Cir
Circles	Cirs
Cliff	Clf
Cliffs	Clfs
Club	Clb
Common	Cmn
Corner	Cor
Corners	Cors
Course	Crse
Court	Ct
Courts	Cts
Cove	Cv
Coves	Cvs
Creek	Crk
Crescent	Cres
Crest	Crst
Crossing	Xing
Crossroad	Xrd
Curve	Curv
Dale	Dl
Dam	Dm
Divide	Dv
Drive	Dr
Drives	Drs
Estate	Est
Estates	Ests
Expressway	Expy
Extension	Ext
Extensions	Exts
Fall	Fall

(continued)

Table B.3	Thoroughfare Abbreviations *(continued)*
Falls	Fls
Ferry	Fry
Field	Fld
Fields	Flds
Flat	Flt
Flats	Flts
Ford	Frd
Fords	Frds
Forest	Frst
Forge	Frg
Forges	Frgs
Fork	Frk
Forks	Frks
Fort	Ft
Freeway	Fwy
Garden	Gdn
Gardens	Gdns
Gateway	Gtwy
Glen	Gln
Glens	Glns
Green	Grn
Greens	Grns
Grove	Grv
Groves	Grvs
Harbor	Hbr
Harbors	Hbrs
Haven	Hvn
Heights	Hts
Highway	Hwy
Hill	Hl
Hills	Hls
Hollow	Holw
Inlet	Inlt
Island	Is

(continued)

Table B.3	Thoroughfare Abbreviations *(continued)*
Islands	Iss
Isle	Isle
Junction	Jct
Junctions	Jcts
Key	Ky
Keys	Kys
Knoll	Knl
Knolls	Knls
Lake	Lk
Lakes	Lks
Land	Land
Landing	Lndg
Lane	Ln
Light	Lgt
Lights	Lgts
Loaf	Lf
Lock	Lck
Locks	Lcks
Lodge	Ldg
Loop	Loop
Mall	Mall
Manor	Mnr
Manors	Mnrs
Meadow	Mdw
Meadows	Mdws
Mews	Mews
Mill	Ml
Mills	Mls
Mission	Msn
Motorway	Mtwy
Mount	Mt
Mountain	Mtn
Mountains	Mtns
Neck	Nck

(continued)

Table B.3	Thoroughfare Abbreviations *(continued)*
Orchard	Orch
Oval	Oval
Overpass	Opas
Park	Park
Parks	Park
Parkway	Pkwy
Parkways	Pkwy
Pass	Pass
Passage	Psge
Path	Path
Pike	Pike
Pine	Pne
Pines	Pnes
Place	Pl
Plain	Pln
Plains	Plns
Plaza	Plz
Point	Pt
Points	Pts
Port	Prt
Ports	Prts
Prairie	Pr
Radial	Radl
Ramp	Ramp
Ranch	Rnch
Rapid	Rpd
Rapids	Rpds
Rest	Rst
Ridge	Rdg
Ridges	Rdgs
River	Riv
Road	Rd
Roads	Rds
Route	Rte

(continued)

Table B.3	Thoroughfare Abbreviations *(continued)*
Row	Row
Rue	Rue
Run	Run
Shoal	Shl
Shoals	Shls
Shore	Shr
Shores	Shrs
Skyway	Skwy
Spring	Spg
Springs	Spgs
Spur	Spur
Spurs	Spur
Square	Sq
Squares	Sqs
Station	Sta
Stravenue	Stra
Stream	Strm
Street	St
Streets	Sts
Summit	Smt
Terrace	Ter
Throughway	Trwy
Trace	Trce
Track	Trak
Trafficway	Trfy
Trail	Trl
Tunnel	Tunl
Turnpike	Tpke
Underpass	Upas
Union	Un
Unions	Uns
Valley	Vly
Valleys	Vlys
Viaduct	Via

(continued)

Table B.3	Thoroughfare Abbreviations *(continued)*
View	Vw
Views	Vws
Village	Vlg
Villages	Vlgs
Ville	Vl
Vista	Vis
Walk	Walk
Walks	Walk
Wall	Wall
Way	Way
Ways	Ways
Well	Wl
Wells	Wls

Source: United States Postal Service

Abbreviations for Secondary Units

Table B.4 is a listing of all secondary units.

Table B.4	Secondary Abbreviations
Apartment	Apt
Basement	Bsmt
Building	Bldg
Department	Dept
Floor	Fl
Front	Frnt
Hangar	Hngr
Lobby	Lobby
Lot	Lot
Lower	Lowr
Office	Ofc
Penthouse	Ph
Pier	Pier

(continued)

Table B.4	Secondary Abbreviations *(continued)*
Rear	Rear
Room	Rm
Side	Side
Slip	Slip
Space	Spc
Stop	Stop
Suite	Ste
Trailer	Trlr
Unit	Unit
Upper	Upp

Need to Know More?

. . . .

Chapter 1

The focus of this book is presenting you with information, strategies, and techniques on how to score the highest on the 470 exam. Still, this chapter presented with you a general overview of the benefits and advantages of working for the USPS and gave you some background into the various positions available.

That said, the best place to go for additional and updated information on all aspects of working for the USPS is the official website, which can be found at www.usps.com/employment/welcome.htm?from=home&page=employment.

Chapter 3

The USPS Test Orientation Guide is an excellent general reference that provides some additional useful information on test-taking strategies (as well as other components of the exam). You can find the guide at http://www.usps.com/cpim/ftp/pubs/pub60a/welcome.htm.

Chapter 4

Doing well on the Address Checking section of the exam comes down to two basic issues: How fast can you work and—most importantly—how efficiently can you work?

Paying close attention to the task before you and focusing in to ensure you stay on track are essential elements to scoring well on Address Checking. Although there is no guaranteed method of improving your attention span, you might want to review the following references in specific regard to this section:

➤ Take special note of the tips presented in Chapters 3 and 12. The information in these chapters talks about how to avoid a case of the nerves on test day, and provides tips for how to best prepare (in general) for taking the exam. Although all this material will impact each section of the exam, you can't, for example, pay close attention to someone when you are tired. Therefore, one of the suggestions presented in these chapters is to make sure you get a good night's sleep before the exam and to avoid caffeine overdose. Bottom line: Keep your mind clear so you can focus well.

➤ Practice, practice, and then practice some more with the sample exams/quizzes presented in this book. The more familiar you are with the question format and what is being asked of you, the more comfortable you will be tackling the questions on exam day.

➤ Finally, you might consider investigating some variation of a relaxation technique to enhance your attention span and focus. Yoga and similar practice often come to mind, but for many people, simply listening to some soothing music also does the trick. Take some time (before exam day!) to experiment with different methods and techniques to find what works best for you.

Chapter 5

Now that you know what memory is, how do you improve it? If you were to go out to a web search engine such as Yahoo! or Google and type in "memory enhancement," you would be presented with a very long list. So, although the following list of websites offering advice on memory enhancement is in no way meant to be comprehensive, it should provide you with a solid starting point:

➤ http://dsc.discovery.com/news/briefs/20030203/memory.html—This link talks about the importance of sleep, and how sleep might be a critical factor in the ability to form strong, lasting memories.

➤ http://www.gate.net/~labooks/xLPmemoryBB.html—Here you can find good strategies such as "chunking"—that is, memorizing small chunks of information, while at the same time focusing on your memorization tasks, taking breaks, and so on.

➤ http://www.familyeducation.com/article/0,1120,23-28418,00.html—This link gives you tips for how to use memory-enhancing tools such as flash cards and visual aids/cues.

➤ http://brain.web-us.com/memory/mnemonic_techniques.htm—This site discusses various mnemonic devices that can be of assistance in building memory.

➤ http://www.cnn.com/2003/HEALTH/10/17/improve.memory/—A link to a CNN article that suggests exercise may boost some types of memory (although not necessarily short-term memory).

Chapter 6

The following websites provide a few examples of additional review/study material that—if nothing else—can allow you to become more familiar with number series/patterns, especially in regard to how they are used in test situations.

http://standards.nctm.org/document/examples/chap4/4.5/

http://www.teachingideas.co.uk/maths/nopattern/general.htm

Chapter 7

Scoring well on the Following Oral Instructions section depends most notably on one thing: how well you can focus and pay attention to verbal directives.

In addition to this chapter, the following are all suggested additional resources for improving your ability to pay attention:

➤ Take special note of the tips presented in Chapters 3 and 12. The information in these chapters talks about how to avoid a case of the nerves on test day as well as tips for how to best prepare (in general) for taking the exam. Although all of this material will impact each section of the exam, you can't, for example, pay close attention to someone when you are tired. Therefore, one of the suggestions presented in these chapters is to make sure you get a good night's sleep before the exam and to avoid caffeine overdose. Bottom line: Keep your mind clear so you can focus well.

➤ Avoid being preoccupied and thus not listening to the instructions being read to you.

➤ Don't get "inside your own head" so much that you begin thinking about your answers (or worse—other issues not related to the exam) and as a result don't hear the instructions being delivered.

➤ Avoid making judgments about the speaker. Although this might seem silly as you read it here, you would be surprised at how quickly your mind can resort to stereotypes or other negative issues that have absolutely nothing to do with the test. Remember, your mission is not to formulate an opinion of the test proctor but rather to listen closely to what he or she has to say so that you can score well!

➤ Avoid jumping to conclusions or making quick judgments. Recall the example I gave at the beginning of the chapter and the test I was given in elementary school on reading all directions first before beginning work. The same principle applies here: You need to listen carefully to everything being said before you start working on an answer.

➤ Finally, if you go to any search engine (Yahoo!, Google, and so on) and type in "Tips for Effective Listening," you will be presented with a long list of Web sites and articles offering general tips and strategies for how to become a better listener.

Glossary

bargaining unit employee
An employee who is covered by a collective bargaining agreement negotiated by a labor union. This term can also be referred to as craft employee.

career appointment
Appointment to a permanent position with the USPS.

casual appointment
Temporary position for which an exam is not required.

COLA
Abbreviation for Cost of Living Adjustment; a pay increase specified in a collective bargaining agreement, based on the Consumer Price Index.

grade
A pay category.

mail processing jobs
USPS jobs that include those in maintenance, operations, and transportation.

night shift differential
A specified rate of pay for hours worked between 6:00 p.m. and 6:00 a.m.

overtime pay
Pay received for work that exceeds 8 hours per day, or 40 hours per workweek, generally calculated at one and a half times the regular hourly rate.

part-time flexible employees
Abbreviated as PTF; employees that work only as many hours as the workflow requires. Most new hires begin their postal careers as part-time flexible employees.

qualifying test score
A score of 70 or above, which an applicant must receive to be considered for employment.

reasonable accommodation

Accommodations made for individuals with disabilities so that they enjoy equal employment opportunities; an applicant may request reasonable accommodation for a post office exam.

register of eligibles

A list of those applicants who have taken a competitive examination for employment with the USPS. Applicants are listed by test scores, in descending order; new hires are taken from this list.

step increase

An increase in pay that occurs within a grade. Step increases are given in accordance with time in service.

tour

Post office lingo for "shift." The 24-hour day is broken into Tour 1, Tour 2, and Tour 3.

vacancy announcement number

A number the USPS assigns to a specific job opening; this number must be included on an application.

veterans' preference

Points that may be added to the test score of U.S. veterans.

Index

cheating, 45
checking addresses
  case study, 58
  overview, 52
  practice test, 91-97
  prep questions, 54-55
  scoring, 53, 56-57
  strategies, 52-53
checking answers, 46
citizenship, city carrier and, 12
city carrier description/qualifications,
  11-12
clerk. *See* postal clerk
COD (cash-on-delivery) fees
  city carrier and, 11
  Rural Carrier Associate and, 15
compensation, 3-4
  earnings grades, 8
competition for positions, 15
complaints from customers, 15
court leave, 6

D–E

driving record, Rural Carrier Associate,
  15
drug screenings, city carrier and, 12

earnings, 3
earnings grades, 8
entrance requirements, 7
Exam 460 (Rural Carrier Associate),
  14-15
Exam 470 requirements, 10

F

Family and Medical Leave Act, 6
Federal Daily Web site, 218
Federal employment, Postal Service
  employees competitive position, 9
federal government Web site, 215
FederalTimes.com Web site, 218
FEGLI (Federal Employees' Group Life
  Insurance Program), 5
FEHB (Federal Employee Health
  Benefits Program), 4

flat sorting machine operator, descrip-
  tion/qualifications, 13
flexible spending accounts, 5
following oral instructions
  case study, 89-90
  prep questions, 86-89
  resources, 233
  scoring, 84-85
  strategies, 83-84
  what is tested, 82

G–H

general job qualifications, 16
GS grades, 8

health insurance, 4
holidays, 6

I

insurance benefits, 4
  health insurance, 4
  life insurance, 5
insured mail
  city carrier and, 11
  Rural Carrier Associate and, 15

J - K - L

job vacancy listings, 7

labor unions, 3
leave benefits, 5
leave sharing, 6
life insurance benefits, 5
listing job vacancies, 7
long-term memory, enhancing, 63

M

mail handler description/qualifications,
  14
mark-up clerk description/qualifications,
  14
marking answers, 45

Chapter 2 Mock Exam Answer Sheet

Address Checking

Directions: Allow yourself two minutes to compare each set of addresses to determine if they are exactly alike or different (in even the slightest way). If they are exactly alike, mark A on your answer sheet. If they are different in any way, mark D for that answer.

1. Ⓐ Ⓓ   8. Ⓐ Ⓓ   15. Ⓐ Ⓓ
2. Ⓐ Ⓓ   9. Ⓐ Ⓓ   16. Ⓐ Ⓓ
3. Ⓐ Ⓓ   10. Ⓐ Ⓓ   17. Ⓐ Ⓓ
4. Ⓐ Ⓓ   11. Ⓐ Ⓓ   18. Ⓐ Ⓓ
5. Ⓐ Ⓓ   12. Ⓐ Ⓓ   19. Ⓐ Ⓓ
6. Ⓐ Ⓓ   13. Ⓐ Ⓓ   20. Ⓐ Ⓓ
7. Ⓐ Ⓓ   14. Ⓐ Ⓓ

Memory for Addresses

Directions: Allow three minutes to memorize the information grid. Then give yourself another three minutes to answer the questions. Each question will present you with a segment of an address that will fit into one of the columns (lettered A-E) in the information grid. Remember, DO NOT refer back to the information grid when answering the questions. Good Luck!

1. Ⓐ Ⓑ Ⓒ Ⓓ Ⓔ   8. Ⓐ Ⓑ Ⓒ Ⓓ Ⓔ   15. Ⓐ Ⓑ Ⓒ Ⓓ Ⓔ
2. Ⓐ Ⓑ Ⓒ Ⓓ Ⓔ   9. Ⓐ Ⓑ Ⓒ Ⓓ Ⓔ   16. Ⓐ Ⓑ Ⓒ Ⓓ Ⓔ
3. Ⓐ Ⓑ Ⓒ Ⓓ Ⓔ   10. Ⓐ Ⓑ Ⓒ Ⓓ Ⓔ   17. Ⓐ Ⓑ Ⓒ Ⓓ Ⓔ
4. Ⓐ Ⓑ Ⓒ Ⓓ Ⓔ   11. Ⓐ Ⓑ Ⓒ Ⓓ Ⓔ   18. Ⓐ Ⓑ Ⓒ Ⓓ Ⓔ
5. Ⓐ Ⓑ Ⓒ Ⓓ Ⓔ   12. Ⓐ Ⓑ Ⓒ Ⓓ Ⓔ   19. Ⓐ Ⓑ Ⓒ Ⓓ Ⓔ
6. Ⓐ Ⓑ Ⓒ Ⓓ Ⓔ   13. Ⓐ Ⓑ Ⓒ Ⓓ Ⓔ   20. Ⓐ Ⓑ Ⓒ Ⓓ Ⓔ
7. Ⓐ Ⓑ Ⓒ Ⓓ Ⓔ   14. Ⓐ Ⓑ Ⓒ Ⓓ Ⓔ

Number Series

Directions: Allow 10 minutes to work through ALL of the questions. For each question, you will be given four answer choices. The correct answer represents the pair of numbers that would follow next in the number series.

1. Ⓐ Ⓑ Ⓒ Ⓓ   5. Ⓐ Ⓑ Ⓒ Ⓓ   9. Ⓐ Ⓑ Ⓒ Ⓓ

2. Ⓐ Ⓑ Ⓒ Ⓓ   6. Ⓐ Ⓑ Ⓒ Ⓓ   10. Ⓐ Ⓑ Ⓒ Ⓓ

3. Ⓐ Ⓑ Ⓒ Ⓓ   7. Ⓐ Ⓑ Ⓒ Ⓓ   11. Ⓐ Ⓑ Ⓒ Ⓓ

4. Ⓐ Ⓑ Ⓒ Ⓓ   8. Ⓐ Ⓑ Ⓒ Ⓓ   12. Ⓐ Ⓑ Ⓒ Ⓓ

Oral Instructions

Directions: Listen carefully to the examiner (in this case, a friend). Use your answer sheet to make any notes you need to find the answer. Then mark your answer in the appropriate circle.

1. Ⓐ Ⓑ Ⓒ Ⓓ   5. Ⓐ Ⓑ Ⓒ Ⓓ   8. Ⓐ Ⓑ Ⓒ Ⓓ

2. Ⓐ Ⓑ Ⓒ Ⓓ   6. Ⓐ Ⓑ Ⓒ Ⓓ   9. Ⓐ Ⓑ Ⓒ Ⓓ

3. Ⓐ Ⓑ Ⓒ Ⓓ   7. Ⓐ Ⓑ Ⓒ Ⓓ   10. Ⓐ Ⓑ Ⓒ Ⓓ

4. Ⓐ Ⓑ Ⓒ Ⓓ

Chapter 4 Answer Sheet

Directions: : Allow four minutes to answer the 50 questions provided. Ask a friend or family member to time you, or use a timer (a stopwatch with an alarm, for example) .

Mark A if the two addresses are *exactly* alike and mark D if you notice *any* difference.

When your time is up, stop work immediately even if you are not done.

1. Ⓐ Ⓓ	18. Ⓐ Ⓓ	35. Ⓐ Ⓓ
2. Ⓐ Ⓓ	19. Ⓐ Ⓓ	36. Ⓐ Ⓓ
3. Ⓐ Ⓓ	20. Ⓐ Ⓓ	37. Ⓐ Ⓓ
4. Ⓐ Ⓓ	21. Ⓐ Ⓓ	38. Ⓐ Ⓓ
5. Ⓐ Ⓓ	22. Ⓐ Ⓓ	39. Ⓐ Ⓓ
6. Ⓐ Ⓓ	23. Ⓐ Ⓓ	40. Ⓐ Ⓓ
7. Ⓐ Ⓓ	24. Ⓐ Ⓓ	41. Ⓐ Ⓓ
8. Ⓐ Ⓓ	25. Ⓐ Ⓓ	42. Ⓐ Ⓓ
9. Ⓐ Ⓓ	26. Ⓐ Ⓓ	43. Ⓐ Ⓓ
10. Ⓐ Ⓓ	27. Ⓐ Ⓓ	44. Ⓐ Ⓓ
11. Ⓐ Ⓓ	28. Ⓐ Ⓓ	45. Ⓐ Ⓓ
12. Ⓐ Ⓓ	29. Ⓐ Ⓓ	46. Ⓐ Ⓓ
13. Ⓐ Ⓓ	30. Ⓐ Ⓓ	47. Ⓐ Ⓓ
14. Ⓐ Ⓓ	31. Ⓐ Ⓓ	48. Ⓐ Ⓓ
15. Ⓐ Ⓓ	32. Ⓐ Ⓓ	49. Ⓐ Ⓓ
16. Ⓐ Ⓓ	33. Ⓐ Ⓓ	50. Ⓐ Ⓓ
17. Ⓐ Ⓓ	34. Ⓐ Ⓓ	

Chapter 5 Answer Sheet

Directions: Allow 1 1/2 minutes for the "memorization period". For each question, mark your answer sheet with either A, B, C, D or E to correspond to the box in which the address would be placed.

Allow three minutes to answer as many of the 25 questions as possible. When your time is up, stop work immediately even if you are not done.

1. Ⓐ Ⓑ Ⓒ Ⓓ Ⓔ   10. Ⓐ Ⓑ Ⓒ Ⓓ Ⓔ   18. Ⓐ Ⓑ Ⓒ Ⓓ Ⓔ

2. Ⓐ Ⓑ Ⓒ Ⓓ Ⓔ   11. Ⓐ Ⓑ Ⓒ Ⓓ Ⓔ   19. Ⓐ Ⓑ Ⓒ Ⓓ Ⓔ

3. Ⓐ Ⓑ Ⓒ Ⓓ Ⓔ   12. Ⓐ Ⓑ Ⓒ Ⓓ Ⓔ   20. Ⓐ Ⓑ Ⓒ Ⓓ Ⓔ

4. Ⓐ Ⓑ Ⓒ Ⓓ Ⓔ   13. Ⓐ Ⓑ Ⓒ Ⓓ Ⓔ   21. Ⓐ Ⓑ Ⓒ Ⓓ Ⓔ

5. Ⓐ Ⓑ Ⓒ Ⓓ Ⓔ   14. Ⓐ Ⓑ Ⓒ Ⓓ Ⓔ   22. Ⓐ Ⓑ Ⓒ Ⓓ Ⓔ

6. Ⓐ Ⓑ Ⓒ Ⓓ Ⓔ   15. Ⓐ Ⓑ Ⓒ Ⓓ Ⓔ   23. Ⓐ Ⓑ Ⓒ Ⓓ Ⓔ

7. Ⓐ Ⓑ Ⓒ Ⓓ Ⓔ   16. Ⓐ Ⓑ Ⓒ Ⓓ Ⓔ   24. Ⓐ Ⓑ Ⓒ Ⓓ Ⓔ

8. Ⓐ Ⓑ Ⓒ Ⓓ Ⓔ   17. Ⓐ Ⓑ Ⓒ Ⓓ Ⓔ   25. Ⓐ Ⓑ Ⓒ Ⓓ Ⓔ

9. Ⓐ Ⓑ Ⓒ Ⓓ Ⓔ

Chapter 6 Answer Sheet

Directions: Allow 20 minutes to answer as many of the following questions as possible. For each question, mark you answer sheet with either A, B, C, or D to correspond to the set of numbers which would follow next in the pattern.

When your time is up, stop work immediately, even if you are not done.

1. Ⓐ Ⓑ Ⓒ Ⓓ   9. Ⓐ Ⓑ Ⓒ Ⓓ   17. Ⓐ Ⓑ Ⓒ Ⓓ

2. Ⓐ Ⓑ Ⓒ Ⓓ   10. Ⓐ Ⓑ Ⓒ Ⓓ   18. Ⓐ Ⓑ Ⓒ Ⓓ

3. Ⓐ Ⓑ Ⓒ Ⓓ   11. Ⓐ Ⓑ Ⓒ Ⓓ   19. Ⓐ Ⓑ Ⓒ Ⓓ

4. Ⓐ Ⓑ Ⓒ Ⓓ   12. Ⓐ Ⓑ Ⓒ Ⓓ   20. Ⓐ Ⓑ Ⓒ Ⓓ

5. Ⓐ Ⓑ Ⓒ Ⓓ   13. Ⓐ Ⓑ Ⓒ Ⓓ   21. Ⓐ Ⓑ Ⓒ Ⓓ

6. Ⓐ Ⓑ Ⓒ Ⓓ   14. Ⓐ Ⓑ Ⓒ Ⓓ   22. Ⓐ Ⓑ Ⓒ Ⓓ

7. Ⓐ Ⓑ Ⓒ Ⓓ   15. Ⓐ Ⓑ Ⓒ Ⓓ   23. Ⓐ Ⓑ Ⓒ Ⓓ

8. Ⓐ Ⓑ Ⓒ Ⓓ   16. Ⓐ Ⓑ Ⓒ Ⓓ   24. Ⓐ Ⓑ Ⓒ Ⓓ

Chapter 7 Answer Sheet

Directions: Listen carefully to the examiner (in this case, a friend) as each question is read to you. The question will be read only once. Make any notes on your answer sheet needed in order to find the correct answer. You are allowed only a few seconds to answer each question.

1. Ⓐ Ⓑ Ⓒ Ⓓ Ⓔ   5. Ⓐ Ⓑ Ⓒ Ⓓ Ⓔ   8. Ⓐ Ⓑ Ⓒ Ⓓ Ⓔ

2. Ⓐ Ⓑ Ⓒ Ⓓ Ⓔ   6. Ⓐ Ⓑ Ⓒ Ⓓ Ⓔ   9. Ⓐ Ⓑ Ⓒ Ⓓ Ⓔ

3. Ⓐ Ⓑ Ⓒ Ⓓ Ⓔ   7. Ⓐ Ⓑ Ⓒ Ⓓ Ⓔ   10. Ⓐ Ⓑ Ⓒ Ⓓ Ⓔ

4. Ⓐ Ⓑ Ⓒ Ⓓ Ⓔ

Chapter 8 Answer Sheet

Directions: Allow six minutes to answer all 50 questions. Use an alarm clock or timer or ask a friend or family member to time you.

Mark A if the addresses are *exactly* alike and mark D if you notice *any* difference.

When your time is up, stop work immediately even if you are not done.

1. Ⓐ Ⓓ   13. Ⓐ Ⓓ   25. Ⓐ Ⓓ

2. Ⓐ Ⓓ   14. Ⓐ Ⓓ   26. Ⓐ Ⓓ

3. Ⓐ Ⓓ   15. Ⓐ Ⓓ   27. Ⓐ Ⓓ

4. Ⓐ Ⓓ   16. Ⓐ Ⓓ   28. Ⓐ Ⓓ

5. Ⓐ Ⓓ   17. Ⓐ Ⓓ   29. Ⓐ Ⓓ

6. Ⓐ Ⓓ   18. Ⓐ Ⓓ   30. Ⓐ Ⓓ

7. Ⓐ Ⓓ   19. Ⓐ Ⓓ   31. Ⓐ Ⓓ

8. Ⓐ Ⓓ   20. Ⓐ Ⓓ   32. Ⓐ Ⓓ

9. Ⓐ Ⓓ   21. Ⓐ Ⓓ   33. Ⓐ Ⓓ

10. Ⓐ Ⓓ   22. Ⓐ Ⓓ   34. Ⓐ Ⓓ

11. Ⓐ Ⓓ   23. Ⓐ Ⓓ   35. Ⓐ Ⓓ

12. Ⓐ Ⓓ   24. Ⓐ Ⓓ   36. Ⓐ Ⓓ

37. Ⓐ Ⓓ   57. Ⓐ Ⓓ   77. Ⓐ Ⓓ
38. Ⓐ Ⓓ   58. Ⓐ Ⓓ   78. Ⓐ Ⓓ
39. Ⓐ Ⓓ   59. Ⓐ Ⓓ   79. Ⓐ Ⓓ
40. Ⓐ Ⓓ   60. Ⓐ Ⓓ   80. Ⓐ Ⓓ
41. Ⓐ Ⓓ   61. Ⓐ Ⓓ   81. Ⓐ Ⓓ
42. Ⓐ Ⓓ   62. Ⓐ Ⓓ   82. Ⓐ Ⓓ
43. Ⓐ Ⓓ   63. Ⓐ Ⓓ   83. Ⓐ Ⓓ
44. Ⓐ Ⓓ   64. Ⓐ Ⓓ   84. Ⓐ Ⓓ
45. Ⓐ Ⓓ   65. Ⓐ Ⓓ   85. Ⓐ Ⓓ
46. Ⓐ Ⓓ   66. Ⓐ Ⓓ   86. Ⓐ Ⓓ
47. Ⓐ Ⓓ   67. Ⓐ Ⓓ   87. Ⓐ Ⓓ
48. Ⓐ Ⓓ   68. Ⓐ Ⓓ   88. Ⓐ Ⓓ
49. Ⓐ Ⓓ   69. Ⓐ Ⓓ   89. Ⓐ Ⓓ
50. Ⓐ Ⓓ   70. Ⓐ Ⓓ   90. Ⓐ Ⓓ
51. Ⓐ Ⓓ   71. Ⓐ Ⓓ   91. Ⓐ Ⓓ
52. Ⓐ Ⓓ   72. Ⓐ Ⓓ   92. Ⓐ Ⓓ
53. Ⓐ Ⓓ   73. Ⓐ Ⓓ   93. Ⓐ Ⓓ
53. Ⓐ Ⓓ   74. Ⓐ Ⓓ   94. Ⓐ Ⓓ
55. Ⓐ Ⓓ   75. Ⓐ Ⓓ   95. Ⓐ Ⓓ
56. Ⓐ Ⓓ   76. Ⓐ Ⓓ   96. Ⓐ Ⓓ

Chapter 9 Answer Sheet

Directions: Allow five minutes for the "memorization period". Use a timer or clock to time yourself, or ask a friend to time you.

You have five minutes to answer as many of the 88 questions as possible. Mark your answer sheet with either A, B, C, D or E to correspond to the box in which the address would be placed.

When your time is up, stop work immediately even if you are not done.

1. Ⓐ Ⓑ Ⓒ Ⓓ Ⓔ	22. Ⓐ Ⓑ Ⓒ Ⓓ Ⓔ	43. Ⓐ Ⓑ Ⓒ Ⓓ Ⓔ
2. Ⓐ Ⓑ Ⓒ Ⓓ Ⓔ	23. Ⓐ Ⓑ Ⓒ Ⓓ Ⓔ	44. Ⓐ Ⓑ Ⓒ Ⓓ Ⓔ
3. Ⓐ Ⓑ Ⓒ Ⓓ Ⓔ	24. Ⓐ Ⓑ Ⓒ Ⓓ Ⓔ	45. Ⓐ Ⓑ Ⓒ Ⓓ Ⓔ
4. Ⓐ Ⓑ Ⓒ Ⓓ Ⓔ	25. Ⓐ Ⓑ Ⓒ Ⓓ Ⓔ	46. Ⓐ Ⓑ Ⓒ Ⓓ Ⓔ
5. Ⓐ Ⓑ Ⓒ Ⓓ Ⓔ	26. Ⓐ Ⓑ Ⓒ Ⓓ Ⓔ	47. Ⓐ Ⓑ Ⓒ Ⓓ Ⓔ
6. Ⓐ Ⓑ Ⓒ Ⓓ Ⓔ	27. Ⓐ Ⓑ Ⓒ Ⓓ Ⓔ	48. Ⓐ Ⓑ Ⓒ Ⓓ Ⓔ
7. Ⓐ Ⓑ Ⓒ Ⓓ Ⓔ	28. Ⓐ Ⓑ Ⓒ Ⓓ Ⓔ	49. Ⓐ Ⓑ Ⓒ Ⓓ Ⓔ
8. Ⓐ Ⓑ Ⓒ Ⓓ Ⓔ	29. Ⓐ Ⓑ Ⓒ Ⓓ Ⓔ	50. Ⓐ Ⓑ Ⓒ Ⓓ Ⓔ
9. Ⓐ Ⓑ Ⓒ Ⓓ Ⓔ	30. Ⓐ Ⓑ Ⓒ Ⓓ Ⓔ	51. Ⓐ Ⓑ Ⓒ Ⓓ Ⓔ
10. Ⓐ Ⓑ Ⓒ Ⓓ Ⓔ	31. Ⓐ Ⓑ Ⓒ Ⓓ Ⓔ	52. Ⓐ Ⓑ Ⓒ Ⓓ Ⓔ
11. Ⓐ Ⓑ Ⓒ Ⓓ Ⓔ	32. Ⓐ Ⓑ Ⓒ Ⓓ Ⓔ	53. Ⓐ Ⓑ Ⓒ Ⓓ Ⓔ
12. Ⓐ Ⓑ Ⓒ Ⓓ Ⓔ	33. Ⓐ Ⓑ Ⓒ Ⓓ Ⓔ	54. Ⓐ Ⓑ Ⓒ Ⓓ Ⓔ
13. Ⓐ Ⓑ Ⓒ Ⓓ Ⓔ	34. Ⓐ Ⓑ Ⓒ Ⓓ Ⓔ	55. Ⓐ Ⓑ Ⓒ Ⓓ Ⓔ
14. Ⓐ Ⓑ Ⓒ Ⓓ Ⓔ	35. Ⓐ Ⓑ Ⓒ Ⓓ Ⓔ	56. Ⓐ Ⓑ Ⓒ Ⓓ Ⓔ
15. Ⓐ Ⓑ Ⓒ Ⓓ Ⓔ	36. Ⓐ Ⓑ Ⓒ Ⓓ Ⓔ	57. Ⓐ Ⓑ Ⓒ Ⓓ Ⓔ
16. Ⓐ Ⓑ Ⓒ Ⓓ Ⓔ	37. Ⓐ Ⓑ Ⓒ Ⓓ Ⓔ	58. Ⓐ Ⓑ Ⓒ Ⓓ Ⓔ
17. Ⓐ Ⓑ Ⓒ Ⓓ Ⓔ	38. Ⓐ Ⓑ Ⓒ Ⓓ Ⓔ	59. Ⓐ Ⓑ Ⓒ Ⓓ Ⓔ
18. Ⓐ Ⓑ Ⓒ Ⓓ Ⓔ	39. Ⓐ Ⓑ Ⓒ Ⓓ Ⓔ	60. Ⓐ Ⓑ Ⓒ Ⓓ Ⓔ
19. Ⓐ Ⓑ Ⓒ Ⓓ Ⓔ	40. Ⓐ Ⓑ Ⓒ Ⓓ Ⓔ	61. Ⓐ Ⓑ Ⓒ Ⓓ Ⓔ
20. Ⓐ Ⓑ Ⓒ Ⓓ Ⓔ	41. Ⓐ Ⓑ Ⓒ Ⓓ Ⓔ	62. Ⓐ Ⓑ Ⓒ Ⓓ Ⓔ
21. Ⓐ Ⓑ Ⓒ Ⓓ Ⓔ	42. Ⓐ Ⓑ Ⓒ Ⓓ Ⓔ	63. Ⓐ Ⓑ Ⓒ Ⓓ Ⓔ

64. Ⓐ Ⓑ Ⓒ Ⓓ Ⓔ   73. Ⓐ Ⓑ Ⓒ Ⓓ Ⓔ   81. Ⓐ Ⓑ Ⓒ Ⓓ Ⓔ

65. Ⓐ Ⓑ Ⓒ Ⓓ Ⓔ   74. Ⓐ Ⓑ Ⓒ Ⓓ Ⓔ   82. Ⓐ Ⓑ Ⓒ Ⓓ Ⓔ

66. Ⓐ Ⓑ Ⓒ Ⓓ Ⓔ   75. Ⓐ Ⓑ Ⓒ Ⓓ Ⓔ   83. Ⓐ Ⓑ Ⓒ Ⓓ Ⓔ

67. Ⓐ Ⓑ Ⓒ Ⓓ Ⓔ   76. Ⓐ Ⓑ Ⓒ Ⓓ Ⓔ   84. Ⓐ Ⓑ Ⓒ Ⓓ Ⓔ

68. Ⓐ Ⓑ Ⓒ Ⓓ Ⓔ   77. Ⓐ Ⓑ Ⓒ Ⓓ Ⓔ   85. Ⓐ Ⓑ Ⓒ Ⓓ Ⓔ

69. Ⓐ Ⓑ Ⓒ Ⓓ Ⓔ   78. Ⓐ Ⓑ Ⓒ Ⓓ Ⓔ   86. Ⓐ Ⓑ Ⓒ Ⓓ Ⓔ

70. Ⓐ Ⓑ Ⓒ Ⓓ Ⓔ   79. Ⓐ Ⓑ Ⓒ Ⓓ Ⓔ   87. Ⓐ Ⓑ Ⓒ Ⓓ Ⓔ

71. Ⓐ Ⓑ Ⓒ Ⓓ Ⓔ   80. Ⓐ Ⓑ Ⓒ Ⓓ Ⓔ   88. Ⓐ Ⓑ Ⓒ Ⓓ Ⓔ

72. Ⓐ Ⓑ Ⓒ Ⓓ Ⓔ

Chapter 10 Answer Sheet

Directions: Allow 20 minutes to answer as many of the following questions as possible. For each question, mark you answer sheet with either A, B, C, D or E to correspond to the set of numbers which would follow next in the pattern.

When your time is up, stop work immediately even if you are not done.

1. Ⓐ Ⓑ Ⓒ Ⓓ Ⓔ   9. Ⓐ Ⓑ Ⓒ Ⓓ Ⓔ   17. Ⓐ Ⓑ Ⓒ Ⓓ Ⓔ

2. Ⓐ Ⓑ Ⓒ Ⓓ Ⓔ   10. Ⓐ Ⓑ Ⓒ Ⓓ Ⓔ   18. Ⓐ Ⓑ Ⓒ Ⓓ Ⓔ

3. Ⓐ Ⓑ Ⓒ Ⓓ Ⓔ   11. Ⓐ Ⓑ Ⓒ Ⓓ Ⓔ   29. Ⓐ Ⓑ Ⓒ Ⓓ Ⓔ

4. Ⓐ Ⓑ Ⓒ Ⓓ Ⓔ   12. Ⓐ Ⓑ Ⓒ Ⓓ Ⓔ   20. Ⓐ Ⓑ Ⓒ Ⓓ Ⓔ

5. Ⓐ Ⓑ Ⓒ Ⓓ Ⓔ   13. Ⓐ Ⓑ Ⓒ Ⓓ Ⓔ   21. Ⓐ Ⓑ Ⓒ Ⓓ Ⓔ

6. Ⓐ Ⓑ Ⓒ Ⓓ Ⓔ   14. Ⓐ Ⓑ Ⓒ Ⓓ Ⓔ   22. Ⓐ Ⓑ Ⓒ Ⓓ Ⓔ

7. Ⓐ Ⓑ Ⓒ Ⓓ Ⓔ   15. Ⓐ Ⓑ Ⓒ Ⓓ Ⓔ   23. Ⓐ Ⓑ Ⓒ Ⓓ Ⓔ

8. Ⓐ Ⓑ Ⓒ Ⓓ Ⓔ   16. Ⓐ Ⓑ Ⓒ Ⓓ Ⓔ   24. Ⓐ Ⓑ Ⓒ Ⓓ Ⓔ

Chapter 11 Answer Sheet

Oral Instructions Exam

Directions: When you are ready to practice this section of the exam, ask a friend to help. Your friend will read you the specific instructions for answering each question, or if you have no one to read them to you, then read them yourself, one example at a time. The examples are numbered 1 through 10 and referenced in the directions.

1. Ⓐ Ⓑ Ⓒ Ⓓ Ⓔ　　16. Ⓐ Ⓑ Ⓒ Ⓓ Ⓔ　　31. Ⓐ Ⓑ Ⓒ Ⓓ Ⓔ

2. Ⓐ Ⓑ Ⓒ Ⓓ Ⓔ　　17. Ⓐ Ⓑ Ⓒ Ⓓ Ⓔ　　32. Ⓐ Ⓑ Ⓒ Ⓓ Ⓔ

3. Ⓐ Ⓑ Ⓒ Ⓓ Ⓔ　　18. Ⓐ Ⓑ Ⓒ Ⓓ Ⓔ　　33. Ⓐ Ⓑ Ⓒ Ⓓ Ⓔ

4. Ⓐ Ⓑ Ⓒ Ⓓ Ⓔ　　19. Ⓐ Ⓑ Ⓒ Ⓓ Ⓔ　　34. Ⓐ Ⓑ Ⓒ Ⓓ Ⓔ

5. Ⓐ Ⓑ Ⓒ Ⓓ Ⓔ　　20. Ⓐ Ⓑ Ⓒ Ⓓ Ⓔ　　35. Ⓐ Ⓑ Ⓒ Ⓓ Ⓔ

6. Ⓐ Ⓑ Ⓒ Ⓓ Ⓔ　　21. Ⓐ Ⓑ Ⓒ Ⓓ Ⓔ　　36. Ⓐ Ⓑ Ⓒ Ⓓ Ⓔ

7. Ⓐ Ⓑ Ⓒ Ⓓ Ⓔ　　22. Ⓐ Ⓑ Ⓒ Ⓓ Ⓔ　　37. Ⓐ Ⓑ Ⓒ Ⓓ Ⓔ

8. Ⓐ Ⓑ Ⓒ Ⓓ Ⓔ　　23. Ⓐ Ⓑ Ⓒ Ⓓ Ⓔ　　38. Ⓐ Ⓑ Ⓒ Ⓓ Ⓔ

9. Ⓐ Ⓑ Ⓒ Ⓓ Ⓔ　　24. Ⓐ Ⓑ Ⓒ Ⓓ Ⓔ　　39. Ⓐ Ⓑ Ⓒ Ⓓ Ⓔ

10. Ⓐ Ⓑ Ⓒ Ⓓ Ⓔ　　25. Ⓐ Ⓑ Ⓒ Ⓓ Ⓔ　　40. Ⓐ Ⓑ Ⓒ Ⓓ Ⓔ

11. Ⓐ Ⓑ Ⓒ Ⓓ Ⓔ　　26. Ⓐ Ⓑ Ⓒ Ⓓ Ⓔ　　41. Ⓐ Ⓑ Ⓒ Ⓓ Ⓔ

12. Ⓐ Ⓑ Ⓒ Ⓓ Ⓔ　　27. Ⓐ Ⓑ Ⓒ Ⓓ Ⓔ　　42. Ⓐ Ⓑ Ⓒ Ⓓ Ⓔ

13. Ⓐ Ⓑ Ⓒ Ⓓ Ⓔ　　28. Ⓐ Ⓑ Ⓒ Ⓓ Ⓔ　　43. Ⓐ Ⓑ Ⓒ Ⓓ Ⓔ

14. Ⓐ Ⓑ Ⓒ Ⓓ Ⓔ　　29. Ⓐ Ⓑ Ⓒ Ⓓ Ⓔ　　44. Ⓐ Ⓑ Ⓒ Ⓓ Ⓔ

15. Ⓐ Ⓑ Ⓒ Ⓓ Ⓔ　　30. Ⓐ Ⓑ Ⓒ Ⓓ Ⓔ　　45. Ⓐ Ⓑ Ⓒ Ⓓ Ⓔ

Practice Exam 1 Answer Sheet

If you would like more answer sheets to use for these practice exams, check out this book's website at www.examcram2.com. You can download more answer sheets from the site. We want to offer these to you so you can print as many as you need for practice.

Address Checking

Directions: For each question, compare the address in the left column with the address in the right column. If the two addresses are exactly alike, mark A on your answer sheet. If they are different in any way, mark D on your answer sheet.

1. Ⓐ Ⓓ
2. Ⓐ Ⓓ
3. Ⓐ Ⓓ
4. Ⓐ Ⓓ
5. Ⓐ Ⓓ
6. Ⓐ Ⓓ
7. Ⓐ Ⓓ
8. Ⓐ Ⓓ
9. Ⓐ Ⓓ
10. Ⓐ Ⓓ
11. Ⓐ Ⓓ
12. Ⓐ Ⓓ
13. Ⓐ Ⓓ
14. Ⓐ Ⓓ
15. Ⓐ Ⓓ
16. Ⓐ Ⓓ
17. Ⓐ Ⓓ
18. Ⓐ Ⓓ
19. Ⓐ Ⓓ

20. Ⓐ Ⓓ
21. Ⓐ Ⓓ
22. Ⓐ Ⓓ
23. Ⓐ Ⓓ
24. Ⓐ Ⓓ
25. Ⓐ Ⓓ
26. Ⓐ Ⓓ
27. Ⓐ Ⓓ
28. Ⓐ Ⓓ
29. Ⓐ Ⓓ
30. Ⓐ Ⓓ
31. Ⓐ Ⓓ
32. Ⓐ Ⓓ
33. Ⓐ Ⓓ
34. Ⓐ Ⓓ
35. Ⓐ Ⓓ
36. Ⓐ Ⓓ
37. Ⓐ Ⓓ
38. Ⓐ Ⓓ

39. Ⓐ Ⓓ
40. Ⓐ Ⓓ
41. Ⓐ Ⓓ
42. Ⓐ Ⓓ
43. Ⓐ Ⓓ
44. Ⓐ Ⓓ
45. Ⓐ Ⓓ
46. Ⓐ Ⓓ
47. Ⓐ Ⓓ
48. Ⓐ Ⓓ
49. Ⓐ Ⓓ
50. Ⓐ Ⓓ
51. Ⓐ Ⓓ
52. Ⓐ Ⓓ
53. Ⓐ Ⓓ
54. Ⓐ Ⓓ
55. Ⓐ Ⓓ
56. Ⓐ Ⓓ
57. Ⓐ Ⓓ

58. (A) (D)   71. (A) (D)   84. (A) (D)

59. (A) (D)   72. (A) (D)   85. (A) (D)

60. (A) (D)   73. (A) (D)   86. (A) (D)

61. (A) (D)   74. (A) (D)   87. (A) (D)

62. (A) (D)   75. (A) (D)   88. (A) (D)

63. (A) (D)   76. (A) (D)   89. (A) (D)

64. (A) (D)   77. (A) (D)   90. (A) (D)

65. (A) (D)   78. (A) (D)   91. (A) (D)

66. (A) (D)   79. (A) (D)   92. (A) (D)

67. (A) (D)   80. (A) (D)   93. (A) (D)

68. (A) (D)   81. (A) (D)   94. (A) (D)

69. (A) (D)   82. (A) (D)   95. (A) (D)

70. (A) (D)   83. (A) (D)

Memory for Addresses

Directions: Allow yourself five minutes to study and memorize this grid. Then give yourself five minutes to answer as many of the 88 questions that follow. On your answer sheet, mark each question either A, B, C, D or E. DO NOT refer back to the grid once your initial five minute memorization time is up.

1. (A) (B) (C) (D) (E)   12. (A) (B) (C) (D) (E)   23. (A) (B) (C) (D) (E)

2. (A) (B) (C) (D) (E)   13. (A) (B) (C) (D) (E)   24. (A) (B) (C) (D) (E)

3. (A) (B) (C) (D) (E)   14. (A) (B) (C) (D) (E)   25. (A) (B) (C) (D) (E)

4. (A) (B) (C) (D) (E)   15. (A) (B) (C) (D) (E)   26. (A) (B) (C) (D) (E)

5. (A) (B) (C) (D) (E)   16. (A) (B) (C) (D) (E)   27. (A) (B) (C) (D) (E)

6. (A) (B) (C) (D) (E)   17. (A) (B) (C) (D) (E)   28. (A) (B) (C) (D) (E)

7. (A) (B) (C) (D) (E)   18. (A) (B) (C) (D) (E)   29. (A) (B) (C) (D) (E)

8. (A) (B) (C) (D) (E)   19. (A) (B) (C) (D) (E)   30. (A) (B) (C) (D) (E)

9. (A) (B) (C) (D) (E)   20. (A) (B) (C) (D) (E)   31. (A) (B) (C) (D) (E)

10. (A) (B) (C) (D) (E)   21. (A) (B) (C) (D) (E)   32. (A) (B) (C) (D) (E)

11. (A) (B) (C) (D) (E)   22. (A) (B) (C) (D) (E)   33. (A) (B) (C) (D) (E)

34. Ⓐ Ⓑ Ⓒ Ⓓ Ⓔ   53. Ⓐ Ⓑ Ⓒ Ⓓ Ⓔ   71. Ⓐ Ⓑ Ⓒ Ⓓ Ⓔ

35. Ⓐ Ⓑ Ⓒ Ⓓ Ⓔ   54. Ⓐ Ⓑ Ⓒ Ⓓ Ⓔ   72. Ⓐ Ⓑ Ⓒ Ⓓ Ⓔ

36. Ⓐ Ⓑ Ⓒ Ⓓ Ⓔ   55. Ⓐ Ⓑ Ⓒ Ⓓ Ⓔ   73. Ⓐ Ⓑ Ⓒ Ⓓ Ⓔ

37. Ⓐ Ⓑ Ⓒ Ⓓ Ⓔ   56. Ⓐ Ⓑ Ⓒ Ⓓ Ⓔ   74. Ⓐ Ⓑ Ⓒ Ⓓ Ⓔ

38. Ⓐ Ⓑ Ⓒ Ⓓ Ⓔ   57. Ⓐ Ⓑ Ⓒ Ⓓ Ⓔ   75. Ⓐ Ⓑ Ⓒ Ⓓ Ⓔ

39. Ⓐ Ⓑ Ⓒ Ⓓ Ⓔ   58. Ⓐ Ⓑ Ⓒ Ⓓ Ⓔ   76. Ⓐ Ⓑ Ⓒ Ⓓ Ⓔ

40. Ⓐ Ⓑ Ⓒ Ⓓ Ⓔ   59. Ⓐ Ⓑ Ⓒ Ⓓ Ⓔ   77. Ⓐ Ⓑ Ⓒ Ⓓ Ⓔ

41. Ⓐ Ⓑ Ⓒ Ⓓ Ⓔ   60. Ⓐ Ⓑ Ⓒ Ⓓ Ⓔ   78. Ⓐ Ⓑ Ⓒ Ⓓ Ⓔ

42. Ⓐ Ⓑ Ⓒ Ⓓ Ⓔ   61. Ⓐ Ⓑ Ⓒ Ⓓ Ⓔ   79. Ⓐ Ⓑ Ⓒ Ⓓ Ⓔ

43. Ⓐ Ⓑ Ⓒ Ⓓ Ⓔ   62. Ⓐ Ⓑ Ⓒ Ⓓ Ⓔ   80. Ⓐ Ⓑ Ⓒ Ⓓ Ⓔ

44. Ⓐ Ⓑ Ⓒ Ⓓ Ⓔ   63. Ⓐ Ⓑ Ⓒ Ⓓ Ⓔ   81. Ⓐ Ⓑ Ⓒ Ⓓ Ⓔ

45. Ⓐ Ⓑ Ⓒ Ⓓ Ⓔ   64. Ⓐ Ⓑ Ⓒ Ⓓ Ⓔ   82. Ⓐ Ⓑ Ⓒ Ⓓ Ⓔ

46. Ⓐ Ⓑ Ⓒ Ⓓ Ⓔ   65. Ⓐ Ⓑ Ⓒ Ⓓ Ⓔ   83. Ⓐ Ⓑ Ⓒ Ⓓ Ⓔ

47. Ⓐ Ⓑ Ⓒ Ⓓ Ⓔ   66. Ⓐ Ⓑ Ⓒ Ⓓ Ⓔ   84. Ⓐ Ⓑ Ⓒ Ⓓ Ⓔ

48. Ⓐ Ⓑ Ⓒ Ⓓ Ⓔ   67. Ⓐ Ⓑ Ⓒ Ⓓ Ⓔ   85. Ⓐ Ⓑ Ⓒ Ⓓ Ⓔ

49. Ⓐ Ⓑ Ⓒ Ⓓ Ⓔ   68. Ⓐ Ⓑ Ⓒ Ⓓ Ⓔ   86. Ⓐ Ⓑ Ⓒ Ⓓ Ⓔ

50. Ⓐ Ⓑ Ⓒ Ⓓ Ⓔ   69. Ⓐ Ⓑ Ⓒ Ⓓ Ⓔ   87. Ⓐ Ⓑ Ⓒ Ⓓ Ⓔ

51. Ⓐ Ⓑ Ⓒ Ⓓ Ⓔ   70. Ⓐ Ⓑ Ⓒ Ⓓ Ⓔ   88. Ⓐ Ⓑ Ⓒ Ⓓ Ⓔ

52. Ⓐ Ⓑ Ⓒ Ⓓ Ⓔ

Number Series

TIME: 20 minutes, 24 questions

Directions: Each number series question consists of a series of numbers that follow some definite, precise order: the numbers progress from left to right, following some deterined rule. One lettered pair of numbers (A, B, C, or D) for each question represents the correct answer: that is, the next series of numbers that should follow in the order, and thus conform to the rule. Choose this correct answer, and mark it on your answer sheet.

1. Ⓐ Ⓑ Ⓒ Ⓓ   4. Ⓐ Ⓑ Ⓒ Ⓓ   7. Ⓐ Ⓑ Ⓒ Ⓓ

2. Ⓐ Ⓑ Ⓒ Ⓓ   5. Ⓐ Ⓑ Ⓒ Ⓓ   8. Ⓐ Ⓑ Ⓒ Ⓓ

3. Ⓐ Ⓑ Ⓒ Ⓓ   6. Ⓐ Ⓑ Ⓒ Ⓓ   9. Ⓐ Ⓑ Ⓒ Ⓓ

10. Ⓐ Ⓑ Ⓒ Ⓓ   15. Ⓐ Ⓑ Ⓒ Ⓓ   20. Ⓐ Ⓑ Ⓒ Ⓓ

11. Ⓐ Ⓑ Ⓒ Ⓓ   16. Ⓐ Ⓑ Ⓒ Ⓓ   21. Ⓐ Ⓑ Ⓒ Ⓓ

12. Ⓐ Ⓑ Ⓒ Ⓓ   17. Ⓐ Ⓑ Ⓒ Ⓓ   22. Ⓐ Ⓑ Ⓒ Ⓓ

13. Ⓐ Ⓑ Ⓒ Ⓓ   18. Ⓐ Ⓑ Ⓒ Ⓓ   23. Ⓐ Ⓑ Ⓒ Ⓓ

14. Ⓐ Ⓑ Ⓒ Ⓓ   19. Ⓐ Ⓑ Ⓒ Ⓓ   24. Ⓐ Ⓑ Ⓒ Ⓓ

Oral Instructions Exam

Directions: When you are ready to practice this section of the exam, ask a friend to help. Your friend will read you the specific instructions for answering each question, or if you have no one to read them to you, then read them yourself, one example at a time. The examples are numbered 1 through 10 and referenced in the directions.

1. Ⓐ Ⓑ Ⓒ Ⓓ Ⓔ   18. Ⓐ Ⓑ Ⓒ Ⓓ Ⓔ   35. Ⓐ Ⓑ Ⓒ Ⓓ Ⓔ

2. Ⓐ Ⓑ Ⓒ Ⓓ Ⓔ   19. Ⓐ Ⓑ Ⓒ Ⓓ Ⓔ   36. Ⓐ Ⓑ Ⓒ Ⓓ Ⓔ

3. Ⓐ Ⓑ Ⓒ Ⓓ Ⓔ   20. Ⓐ Ⓑ Ⓒ Ⓓ Ⓔ   37. Ⓐ Ⓑ Ⓒ Ⓓ Ⓔ

4. Ⓐ Ⓑ Ⓒ Ⓓ Ⓔ   21. Ⓐ Ⓑ Ⓒ Ⓓ Ⓔ   38. Ⓐ Ⓑ Ⓒ Ⓓ Ⓔ

5. Ⓐ Ⓑ Ⓒ Ⓓ Ⓔ   22. Ⓐ Ⓑ Ⓒ Ⓓ Ⓔ   39. Ⓐ Ⓑ Ⓒ Ⓓ Ⓔ

6. Ⓐ Ⓑ Ⓒ Ⓓ Ⓔ   23. Ⓐ Ⓑ Ⓒ Ⓓ Ⓔ   40. Ⓐ Ⓑ Ⓒ Ⓓ Ⓔ

7. Ⓐ Ⓑ Ⓒ Ⓓ Ⓔ   24. Ⓐ Ⓑ Ⓒ Ⓓ Ⓔ   41. Ⓐ Ⓑ Ⓒ Ⓓ Ⓔ

8. Ⓐ Ⓑ Ⓒ Ⓓ Ⓔ   25. Ⓐ Ⓑ Ⓒ Ⓓ Ⓔ   42. Ⓐ Ⓑ Ⓒ Ⓓ Ⓔ

9. Ⓐ Ⓑ Ⓒ Ⓓ Ⓔ   26. Ⓐ Ⓑ Ⓒ Ⓓ Ⓔ   43. Ⓐ Ⓑ Ⓒ Ⓓ Ⓔ

10. Ⓐ Ⓑ Ⓒ Ⓓ Ⓔ   27. Ⓐ Ⓑ Ⓒ Ⓓ Ⓔ   44. Ⓐ Ⓑ Ⓒ Ⓓ Ⓔ

11. Ⓐ Ⓑ Ⓒ Ⓓ Ⓔ   28. Ⓐ Ⓑ Ⓒ Ⓓ Ⓔ   45. Ⓐ Ⓑ Ⓒ Ⓓ Ⓔ

12. Ⓐ Ⓑ Ⓒ Ⓓ Ⓔ   29. Ⓐ Ⓑ Ⓒ Ⓓ Ⓔ   46. Ⓐ Ⓑ Ⓒ Ⓓ Ⓔ

13. Ⓐ Ⓑ Ⓒ Ⓓ Ⓔ   30. Ⓐ Ⓑ Ⓒ Ⓓ Ⓔ   47. Ⓐ Ⓑ Ⓒ Ⓓ Ⓔ

14. Ⓐ Ⓑ Ⓒ Ⓓ Ⓔ   31. Ⓐ Ⓑ Ⓒ Ⓓ Ⓔ   48. Ⓐ Ⓑ Ⓒ Ⓓ Ⓔ

15. Ⓐ Ⓑ Ⓒ Ⓓ Ⓔ   32. Ⓐ Ⓑ Ⓒ Ⓓ Ⓔ   49. Ⓐ Ⓑ Ⓒ Ⓓ Ⓔ

16. Ⓐ Ⓑ Ⓒ Ⓓ Ⓔ   33. Ⓐ Ⓑ Ⓒ Ⓓ Ⓔ   50. Ⓐ Ⓑ Ⓒ Ⓓ Ⓔ

17. Ⓐ Ⓑ Ⓒ Ⓓ Ⓔ   34. Ⓐ Ⓑ Ⓒ Ⓓ Ⓔ

Practice Exam 2 Answer Sheet

Address Checking

Directions: For each question, compare the address in the left column with the address in the right column. If the two addresses are exactly alike, mark A on your answer sheet. If they are different in any way, mark D on your answer sheet.

1. Ⓐ Ⓓ	23. Ⓐ Ⓓ	45. Ⓐ Ⓓ
2. Ⓐ Ⓓ	24. Ⓐ Ⓓ	46. Ⓐ Ⓓ
3. Ⓐ Ⓓ	25. Ⓐ Ⓓ	47. Ⓐ Ⓓ
4. Ⓐ Ⓓ	26. Ⓐ Ⓓ	48. Ⓐ Ⓓ
5. Ⓐ Ⓓ	27. Ⓐ Ⓓ	49. Ⓐ Ⓓ
6. Ⓐ Ⓓ	28. Ⓐ Ⓓ	50. Ⓐ Ⓓ
7. Ⓐ Ⓓ	29. Ⓐ Ⓓ	51. Ⓐ Ⓓ
8. Ⓐ Ⓓ	30. Ⓐ Ⓓ	52. Ⓐ Ⓓ
9. Ⓐ Ⓓ	31. Ⓐ Ⓓ	53. Ⓐ Ⓓ
10. Ⓐ Ⓓ	32. Ⓐ Ⓓ	54. Ⓐ Ⓓ
11. Ⓐ Ⓓ	33. Ⓐ Ⓓ	55. Ⓐ Ⓓ
12. Ⓐ Ⓓ	34. Ⓐ Ⓓ	56. Ⓐ Ⓓ
13. Ⓐ Ⓓ	35. Ⓐ Ⓓ	57. Ⓐ Ⓓ
14. Ⓐ Ⓓ	36. Ⓐ Ⓓ	58. Ⓐ Ⓓ
15. Ⓐ Ⓓ	37. Ⓐ Ⓓ	59. Ⓐ Ⓓ
16. Ⓐ Ⓓ	38. Ⓐ Ⓓ	60. Ⓐ Ⓓ
17. Ⓐ Ⓓ	39. Ⓐ Ⓓ	61. Ⓐ Ⓓ
18. Ⓐ Ⓓ	40. Ⓐ Ⓓ	62. Ⓐ Ⓓ
19. Ⓐ Ⓓ	41. Ⓐ Ⓓ	63. Ⓐ Ⓓ
20. Ⓐ Ⓓ	42. Ⓐ Ⓓ	64. Ⓐ Ⓓ
21. Ⓐ Ⓓ	43. Ⓐ Ⓓ	65. Ⓐ Ⓓ
22. Ⓐ Ⓓ	44. Ⓐ Ⓓ	66. Ⓐ Ⓓ

67. Ⓐ Ⓓ   77. Ⓐ Ⓓ   87. Ⓐ Ⓓ

68. Ⓐ Ⓓ   78. Ⓐ Ⓓ   88. Ⓐ Ⓓ

69. Ⓐ Ⓓ   79. Ⓐ Ⓓ   89. Ⓐ Ⓓ

70. Ⓐ Ⓓ   80. Ⓐ Ⓓ   90. Ⓐ Ⓓ

71. Ⓐ Ⓓ   81. Ⓐ Ⓓ   91. Ⓐ Ⓓ

72. Ⓐ Ⓓ   82. Ⓐ Ⓓ   92. Ⓐ Ⓓ

73. Ⓐ Ⓓ   83. Ⓐ Ⓓ   93. Ⓐ Ⓤ

74. Ⓐ Ⓓ   84. Ⓐ Ⓓ   94. Ⓐ Ⓓ

75. Ⓐ Ⓓ   85. Ⓐ Ⓓ   95. Ⓐ Ⓓ

76. Ⓐ Ⓓ   86. Ⓐ Ⓓ

Memory for Addresses

Directions: Allow yourself five minutes to study and memorize this grid. Then give yourself five minutes to answer as many of the 88 questions that follow. On your answer sheet, mark each question either A, B, C, D or E. DO NOT refer back to the grid once your initial five minute memorization time is up.

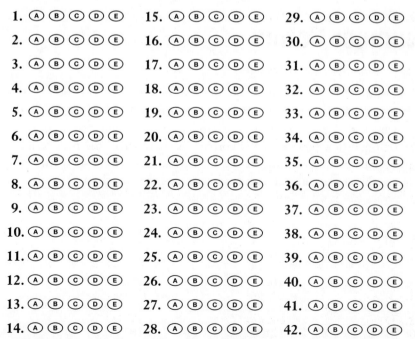

1. Ⓐ Ⓑ Ⓒ Ⓓ Ⓔ   15. Ⓐ Ⓑ Ⓒ Ⓓ Ⓔ   29. Ⓐ Ⓑ Ⓒ Ⓓ Ⓔ

2. Ⓐ Ⓑ Ⓒ Ⓓ Ⓔ   16. Ⓐ Ⓑ Ⓒ Ⓓ Ⓔ   30. Ⓐ Ⓑ Ⓒ Ⓓ Ⓔ

3. Ⓐ Ⓑ Ⓒ Ⓓ Ⓔ   17. Ⓐ Ⓑ Ⓒ Ⓓ Ⓔ   31. Ⓐ Ⓑ Ⓒ Ⓓ Ⓔ

4. Ⓐ Ⓑ Ⓒ Ⓓ Ⓔ   18. Ⓐ Ⓑ Ⓒ Ⓓ Ⓔ   32. Ⓐ Ⓑ Ⓒ Ⓓ Ⓔ

5. Ⓐ Ⓑ Ⓒ Ⓓ Ⓔ   19. Ⓐ Ⓑ Ⓒ Ⓓ Ⓔ   33. Ⓐ Ⓑ Ⓒ Ⓓ Ⓔ

6. Ⓐ Ⓑ Ⓒ Ⓓ Ⓔ   20. Ⓐ Ⓑ Ⓒ Ⓓ Ⓔ   34. Ⓐ Ⓑ Ⓒ Ⓓ Ⓔ

7. Ⓐ Ⓑ Ⓒ Ⓓ Ⓔ   21. Ⓐ Ⓑ Ⓒ Ⓓ Ⓔ   35. Ⓐ Ⓑ Ⓒ Ⓓ Ⓔ

8. Ⓐ Ⓑ Ⓒ Ⓓ Ⓔ   22. Ⓐ Ⓑ Ⓒ Ⓓ Ⓔ   36. Ⓐ Ⓑ Ⓒ Ⓓ Ⓔ

9. Ⓐ Ⓑ Ⓒ Ⓓ Ⓔ   23. Ⓐ Ⓑ Ⓒ Ⓓ Ⓔ   37. Ⓐ Ⓑ Ⓒ Ⓓ Ⓔ

10. Ⓐ Ⓑ Ⓒ Ⓓ Ⓔ   24. Ⓐ Ⓑ Ⓒ Ⓓ Ⓔ   38. Ⓐ Ⓑ Ⓒ Ⓓ Ⓔ

11. Ⓐ Ⓑ Ⓒ Ⓓ Ⓔ   25. Ⓐ Ⓑ Ⓒ Ⓓ Ⓔ   39. Ⓐ Ⓑ Ⓒ Ⓓ Ⓔ

12. Ⓐ Ⓑ Ⓒ Ⓓ Ⓔ   26. Ⓐ Ⓑ Ⓒ Ⓓ Ⓔ   40. Ⓐ Ⓑ Ⓒ Ⓓ Ⓔ

13. Ⓐ Ⓑ Ⓒ Ⓓ Ⓔ   27. Ⓐ Ⓑ Ⓒ Ⓓ Ⓔ   41. Ⓐ Ⓑ Ⓒ Ⓓ Ⓔ

14. Ⓐ Ⓑ Ⓒ Ⓓ Ⓔ   28. Ⓐ Ⓑ Ⓒ Ⓓ Ⓔ   42. Ⓐ Ⓑ Ⓒ Ⓓ Ⓔ

43. Ⓐ Ⓑ Ⓒ Ⓓ Ⓔ   59. Ⓐ Ⓑ Ⓒ Ⓓ Ⓔ   74. Ⓐ Ⓑ Ⓒ Ⓓ Ⓔ
44. Ⓐ Ⓑ Ⓒ Ⓓ Ⓔ   60. Ⓐ Ⓑ Ⓒ Ⓓ Ⓔ   75. Ⓐ Ⓑ Ⓒ Ⓓ Ⓔ
45. Ⓐ Ⓑ Ⓒ Ⓓ Ⓔ   61. Ⓐ Ⓑ Ⓒ Ⓓ Ⓔ   76. Ⓐ Ⓑ Ⓒ Ⓓ Ⓔ
46. Ⓐ Ⓑ Ⓒ Ⓓ Ⓔ   62. Ⓐ Ⓑ Ⓒ Ⓓ Ⓔ   77. Ⓐ Ⓑ Ⓒ Ⓓ Ⓔ
47. Ⓐ Ⓑ Ⓒ Ⓓ Ⓔ   63. Ⓐ Ⓑ Ⓒ Ⓓ Ⓔ   78. Ⓐ Ⓑ Ⓒ Ⓓ Ⓔ
48. Ⓐ Ⓑ Ⓒ Ⓓ Ⓔ   64. Ⓐ Ⓑ Ⓒ Ⓓ Ⓔ   79. Ⓐ Ⓑ Ⓒ Ⓓ Ⓔ
49. Ⓐ Ⓑ Ⓒ Ⓓ Ⓔ   65. Ⓐ Ⓑ Ⓒ Ⓓ Ⓔ   80. Ⓐ Ⓑ Ⓒ Ⓓ Ⓔ
50. Ⓐ Ⓑ Ⓒ Ⓓ Ⓔ   66. Ⓐ Ⓑ Ⓒ Ⓓ Ⓔ   81. Ⓐ Ⓑ Ⓒ Ⓓ Ⓔ
51. Ⓐ Ⓑ Ⓒ Ⓓ Ⓔ   67. Ⓐ Ⓑ Ⓒ Ⓓ Ⓔ   82. Ⓐ Ⓑ Ⓒ Ⓓ Ⓔ
52. Ⓐ Ⓑ Ⓒ Ⓓ Ⓔ   68. Ⓐ Ⓑ Ⓒ Ⓓ Ⓔ   83. Ⓐ Ⓑ Ⓒ Ⓓ Ⓔ
53. Ⓐ Ⓑ Ⓒ Ⓓ Ⓔ   69. Ⓐ Ⓑ Ⓒ Ⓓ Ⓔ   84. Ⓐ Ⓑ Ⓒ Ⓓ Ⓔ
54. Ⓐ Ⓑ Ⓒ Ⓓ Ⓔ   70. Ⓐ Ⓑ Ⓒ Ⓓ Ⓔ   85. Ⓐ Ⓑ Ⓒ Ⓓ Ⓔ
55. Ⓐ Ⓑ Ⓒ Ⓓ Ⓔ   71. Ⓐ Ⓑ Ⓒ Ⓓ Ⓔ   86. Ⓐ Ⓑ Ⓒ Ⓓ Ⓔ
56. Ⓐ Ⓑ Ⓒ Ⓓ Ⓔ   72. Ⓐ Ⓑ Ⓒ Ⓓ Ⓔ   87. Ⓐ Ⓑ Ⓒ Ⓓ Ⓔ
57. Ⓐ Ⓑ Ⓒ Ⓓ Ⓔ   73. Ⓐ Ⓑ Ⓒ Ⓓ Ⓔ   88. Ⓐ Ⓑ Ⓒ Ⓓ Ⓔ
58. Ⓐ Ⓑ Ⓒ Ⓓ Ⓔ

Number Series

TIME: 20 minutes, 24 questions

Directions: Each number series question consists of a series of numbers that follow some definite, precise order: the numbers progress from left to right, following some determed rule. One lettered pair of numbers (A, B, C, or D) for each question represents the correct answer: that is, the next series of numbers that should follow in the order, and thus conform to the rule. Choose this correct answer, and mark it on your answer sheet.

1. Ⓐ Ⓑ Ⓒ Ⓓ   7. Ⓐ Ⓑ Ⓒ Ⓓ   13. Ⓐ Ⓑ Ⓒ Ⓓ
2. Ⓐ Ⓑ Ⓒ Ⓓ   8. Ⓐ Ⓑ Ⓒ Ⓓ   14. Ⓐ Ⓑ Ⓒ Ⓓ
3. Ⓐ Ⓑ Ⓒ Ⓓ   9. Ⓐ Ⓑ Ⓒ Ⓓ   15. Ⓐ Ⓑ Ⓒ Ⓓ
4. Ⓐ Ⓑ Ⓒ Ⓓ   10. Ⓐ Ⓑ Ⓒ Ⓓ   16. Ⓐ Ⓑ Ⓒ Ⓓ
5. Ⓐ Ⓑ Ⓒ Ⓓ   11. Ⓐ Ⓑ Ⓒ Ⓓ   17. Ⓐ Ⓑ Ⓒ Ⓓ
6. Ⓐ Ⓑ Ⓒ Ⓓ   12. Ⓐ Ⓑ Ⓒ Ⓓ   18. Ⓐ Ⓑ Ⓒ Ⓓ

19. Ⓐ Ⓑ Ⓒ Ⓓ 22. Ⓐ Ⓑ Ⓒ Ⓓ 24. Ⓐ Ⓑ Ⓒ Ⓓ

20. Ⓐ Ⓑ Ⓒ Ⓓ 23. Ⓐ Ⓑ Ⓒ Ⓓ 25. Ⓐ Ⓑ Ⓒ Ⓓ

21. Ⓐ Ⓑ Ⓒ Ⓓ

Oral Instructions Exam

Directions: When you are ready to practice this section of the exam, ask a friend to help. Your friend will read you the specific instructions for answering each question, or if you have no one to read them to you, then read them yourself, one example at a time. The examples are numbered 1 through 12 and referenced in the directions.

1. Ⓐ Ⓑ Ⓒ Ⓓ Ⓔ   21. Ⓐ Ⓑ Ⓒ Ⓓ Ⓔ   41. Ⓐ Ⓑ Ⓒ Ⓓ Ⓔ

2. Ⓐ Ⓑ Ⓒ Ⓓ Ⓔ   22. Ⓐ Ⓑ Ⓒ Ⓓ Ⓔ   42. Ⓐ Ⓑ Ⓒ Ⓓ Ⓔ

3. Ⓐ Ⓑ Ⓒ Ⓓ Ⓔ   23. Ⓐ Ⓑ Ⓒ Ⓓ Ⓔ   43. Ⓐ Ⓑ Ⓒ Ⓓ Ⓔ

4. Ⓐ Ⓑ Ⓒ Ⓓ Ⓔ   24. Ⓐ Ⓑ Ⓒ Ⓓ Ⓔ   44. Ⓐ Ⓑ Ⓒ Ⓓ Ⓔ

5. Ⓐ Ⓑ Ⓒ Ⓓ Ⓔ   25. Ⓐ Ⓑ Ⓒ Ⓓ Ⓔ   45. Ⓐ Ⓑ Ⓒ Ⓓ Ⓔ

6. Ⓐ Ⓑ Ⓒ Ⓓ Ⓔ   26. Ⓐ Ⓑ Ⓒ Ⓓ Ⓔ   46. Ⓐ Ⓑ Ⓒ Ⓓ Ⓔ

7. Ⓐ Ⓑ Ⓒ Ⓓ Ⓔ   27. Ⓐ Ⓑ Ⓒ Ⓓ Ⓔ   47. Ⓐ Ⓑ Ⓒ Ⓓ Ⓔ

8. Ⓐ Ⓑ Ⓒ Ⓓ Ⓔ   28. Ⓐ Ⓑ Ⓒ Ⓓ Ⓔ   48. Ⓐ Ⓑ Ⓒ Ⓓ Ⓔ

9. Ⓐ Ⓑ Ⓒ Ⓓ Ⓔ   29. Ⓐ Ⓑ Ⓒ Ⓓ Ⓔ   49. Ⓐ Ⓑ Ⓒ Ⓓ Ⓔ

10. Ⓐ Ⓑ Ⓒ Ⓓ Ⓔ   30. Ⓐ Ⓑ Ⓒ Ⓓ Ⓔ   50. Ⓐ Ⓑ Ⓒ Ⓓ Ⓔ

11. Ⓐ Ⓑ Ⓒ Ⓓ Ⓔ   31. Ⓐ Ⓑ Ⓒ Ⓓ Ⓔ   51. Ⓐ Ⓑ Ⓒ Ⓓ Ⓔ

12. Ⓐ Ⓑ Ⓒ Ⓓ Ⓔ   32. Ⓐ Ⓑ Ⓒ Ⓓ Ⓔ   52. Ⓐ Ⓑ Ⓒ Ⓓ Ⓔ

13. Ⓐ Ⓑ Ⓒ Ⓓ Ⓔ   33. Ⓐ Ⓑ Ⓒ Ⓓ Ⓔ   53. Ⓐ Ⓑ Ⓒ Ⓓ Ⓔ

14. Ⓐ Ⓑ Ⓒ Ⓓ Ⓔ   34. Ⓐ Ⓑ Ⓒ Ⓓ Ⓔ   54. Ⓐ Ⓑ Ⓒ Ⓓ Ⓔ

15. Ⓐ Ⓑ Ⓒ Ⓓ Ⓔ   35. Ⓐ Ⓑ Ⓒ Ⓓ Ⓔ   55. Ⓐ Ⓑ Ⓒ Ⓓ Ⓔ

16. Ⓐ Ⓑ Ⓒ Ⓓ Ⓔ   36. Ⓐ Ⓑ Ⓒ Ⓓ Ⓔ   56. Ⓐ Ⓑ Ⓒ Ⓓ Ⓔ

17. Ⓐ Ⓑ Ⓒ Ⓓ Ⓔ   37. Ⓐ Ⓑ Ⓒ Ⓓ Ⓔ   57. Ⓐ Ⓑ Ⓒ Ⓓ Ⓔ

18. Ⓐ Ⓑ Ⓒ Ⓓ Ⓔ   38. Ⓐ Ⓑ Ⓒ Ⓓ Ⓔ   58. Ⓐ Ⓑ Ⓒ Ⓓ Ⓔ

19. Ⓐ Ⓑ Ⓒ Ⓓ Ⓔ   39. Ⓐ Ⓑ Ⓒ Ⓓ Ⓔ   59. Ⓐ Ⓑ Ⓒ Ⓓ Ⓔ

20. Ⓐ Ⓑ Ⓒ Ⓓ Ⓔ   40. Ⓐ Ⓑ Ⓒ Ⓓ Ⓔ   60. Ⓐ Ⓑ Ⓒ Ⓓ Ⓔ

Practice Exam 3 Answer Sheet

Address Checking

Directions: For each question, compare the address in the left column with the address in the right column. If the two addresses are exactly alike, mark A on your answer sheet. If they are different in any way, mark D on your answer sheet.

1. Ⓐ Ⓓ	23. Ⓐ Ⓓ	45. Ⓐ Ⓓ
2. Ⓐ Ⓓ	24. Ⓐ Ⓓ	46. Ⓐ Ⓓ
3. Ⓐ Ⓓ	25. Ⓐ Ⓓ	47. Ⓐ Ⓓ
4. Ⓐ Ⓓ	26. Ⓐ Ⓓ	48. Ⓐ Ⓓ
5. Ⓐ Ⓓ	27. Ⓐ Ⓓ	49. Ⓐ Ⓓ
6. Ⓐ Ⓓ	28. Ⓐ Ⓓ	50. Ⓐ Ⓓ
7. Ⓐ Ⓓ	29. Ⓐ Ⓓ	51. Ⓐ Ⓓ
8. Ⓐ Ⓓ	30. Ⓐ Ⓓ	52. Ⓐ Ⓓ
9. Ⓐ Ⓓ	31. Ⓐ Ⓓ	53. Ⓐ Ⓓ
10. Ⓐ Ⓓ	32. Ⓐ Ⓓ	54. Ⓐ Ⓓ
11. Ⓐ Ⓓ	33. Ⓐ Ⓓ	55. Ⓐ Ⓓ
12. Ⓐ Ⓓ	34. Ⓐ Ⓓ	56. Ⓐ Ⓓ
13. Ⓐ Ⓓ	35. Ⓐ Ⓓ	57. Ⓐ Ⓓ
14. Ⓐ Ⓓ	36. Ⓐ Ⓓ	58. Ⓐ Ⓓ
15. Ⓐ Ⓓ	37. Ⓐ Ⓓ	59. Ⓐ Ⓓ
16. Ⓐ Ⓓ	38. Ⓐ Ⓓ	60. Ⓐ Ⓓ
17. Ⓐ Ⓓ	39. Ⓐ Ⓓ	61. Ⓐ Ⓓ
18. Ⓐ Ⓓ	40. Ⓐ Ⓓ	62. Ⓐ Ⓓ
19. Ⓐ Ⓓ	41. Ⓐ Ⓓ	63. Ⓐ Ⓓ
20. Ⓐ Ⓓ	42. Ⓐ Ⓓ	64. Ⓐ Ⓓ
21. Ⓐ Ⓓ	43. Ⓐ Ⓓ	65. Ⓐ Ⓓ
22. Ⓐ Ⓓ	44. Ⓐ Ⓓ	66. Ⓐ Ⓓ

67. Ⓐ Ⓓ   77. Ⓐ Ⓓ   87. Ⓐ Ⓓ

68. Ⓐ Ⓓ   78. Ⓐ Ⓓ   88. Ⓐ Ⓓ

69. Ⓐ Ⓓ   79. Ⓐ Ⓓ   89. Ⓐ Ⓓ

70. Ⓐ Ⓓ   80. Ⓐ Ⓓ   90. Ⓐ Ⓓ

71. Ⓐ Ⓓ   81. Ⓐ Ⓓ   91. Ⓐ Ⓓ

72. Ⓐ Ⓓ   82. Ⓐ Ⓓ   92. Ⓐ Ⓓ

73. Ⓐ Ⓓ   83. Ⓐ Ⓓ   93. Ⓐ Ⓓ

74. Ⓐ Ⓓ   84. Ⓐ Ⓓ   94. Ⓐ Ⓓ

75. Ⓐ Ⓓ   85. Ⓐ Ⓓ   94. Ⓐ Ⓓ

76. Ⓐ Ⓓ   86. Ⓐ Ⓓ   95. Ⓐ Ⓓ

Memory for Addresses

Directions: Allow yourself five minutes to study and memorize this grid. Then give yourself five minutes to answer as many of the 88 questions that follow. On your answer sheet, mark each question either A, B, C, D or E. DO NOT refer back to the grid once your initial five minute memorization time is up.

1. Ⓐ Ⓑ Ⓒ Ⓓ Ⓔ   15. Ⓐ Ⓑ Ⓒ Ⓓ Ⓔ   29. Ⓐ Ⓑ Ⓒ Ⓓ Ⓔ

2. Ⓐ Ⓑ Ⓒ Ⓓ Ⓔ   16. Ⓐ Ⓑ Ⓒ Ⓓ Ⓔ   30. Ⓐ Ⓑ Ⓒ Ⓓ Ⓔ

3. Ⓐ Ⓑ Ⓒ Ⓓ Ⓔ   17. Ⓐ Ⓑ Ⓒ Ⓓ Ⓔ   31. Ⓐ Ⓑ Ⓒ Ⓓ Ⓔ

4. Ⓐ Ⓑ Ⓒ Ⓓ Ⓔ   18. Ⓐ Ⓑ Ⓒ Ⓓ Ⓔ   32. Ⓐ Ⓑ Ⓒ Ⓓ Ⓔ

5. Ⓐ Ⓑ Ⓒ Ⓓ Ⓔ   19. Ⓐ Ⓑ Ⓒ Ⓓ Ⓔ   33. Ⓐ Ⓑ Ⓒ Ⓓ Ⓔ

6. Ⓐ Ⓑ Ⓒ Ⓓ Ⓔ   20. Ⓐ Ⓑ Ⓒ Ⓓ Ⓔ   34. Ⓐ Ⓑ Ⓒ Ⓓ Ⓔ

7. Ⓐ Ⓑ Ⓒ Ⓓ Ⓔ   21. Ⓐ Ⓑ Ⓒ Ⓓ Ⓔ   35. Ⓐ Ⓑ Ⓒ Ⓓ Ⓔ

8. Ⓐ Ⓑ Ⓒ Ⓓ Ⓔ   22. Ⓐ Ⓑ Ⓒ Ⓓ Ⓔ   36. Ⓐ Ⓑ Ⓒ Ⓓ Ⓔ

9. Ⓐ Ⓑ Ⓒ Ⓓ Ⓔ   23. Ⓐ Ⓑ Ⓒ Ⓓ Ⓔ   37. Ⓐ Ⓑ Ⓒ Ⓓ Ⓔ

10. Ⓐ Ⓑ Ⓒ Ⓓ Ⓔ   24. Ⓐ Ⓑ Ⓒ Ⓓ Ⓔ   38. Ⓐ Ⓑ Ⓒ Ⓓ Ⓔ

11. Ⓐ Ⓑ Ⓒ Ⓓ Ⓔ   25. Ⓐ Ⓑ Ⓒ Ⓓ Ⓔ   39. Ⓐ Ⓑ Ⓒ Ⓓ Ⓔ

12. Ⓐ Ⓑ Ⓒ Ⓓ Ⓔ   26. Ⓐ Ⓑ Ⓒ Ⓓ Ⓔ   40. Ⓐ Ⓑ Ⓒ Ⓓ Ⓔ

13. Ⓐ Ⓑ Ⓒ Ⓓ Ⓔ   27. Ⓐ Ⓑ Ⓒ Ⓓ Ⓔ   41. Ⓐ Ⓑ Ⓒ Ⓓ Ⓔ

14. Ⓐ Ⓑ Ⓒ Ⓓ Ⓔ   28. Ⓐ Ⓑ Ⓒ Ⓓ Ⓔ   42. Ⓐ Ⓑ Ⓒ Ⓓ Ⓔ

43. Ⓐ Ⓑ Ⓒ Ⓓ Ⓔ　　59. Ⓐ Ⓑ Ⓒ Ⓓ Ⓔ　　74. Ⓐ Ⓑ Ⓒ Ⓓ Ⓔ
44. Ⓐ Ⓑ Ⓒ Ⓓ Ⓔ　　60. Ⓐ Ⓑ Ⓒ Ⓓ Ⓔ　　75. Ⓐ Ⓑ Ⓒ Ⓓ Ⓔ
45. Ⓐ Ⓑ Ⓒ Ⓓ Ⓔ　　61. Ⓐ Ⓑ Ⓒ Ⓓ Ⓔ　　76. Ⓐ Ⓑ Ⓒ Ⓓ Ⓔ
46. Ⓐ Ⓑ Ⓒ Ⓓ Ⓔ　　62. Ⓐ Ⓑ Ⓒ Ⓓ Ⓔ　　77. Ⓐ Ⓑ Ⓒ Ⓓ Ⓔ
47. Ⓐ Ⓑ Ⓒ Ⓓ Ⓔ　　63. Ⓐ Ⓑ Ⓒ Ⓓ Ⓔ　　78. Ⓐ Ⓑ Ⓒ Ⓓ Ⓔ
48. Ⓐ Ⓑ Ⓒ Ⓓ Ⓔ　　64. Ⓐ Ⓑ Ⓒ Ⓓ Ⓔ　　79. Ⓐ Ⓑ Ⓒ Ⓓ Ⓔ
49. Ⓐ Ⓑ Ⓒ Ⓓ Ⓔ　　65. Ⓐ Ⓑ Ⓒ Ⓓ Ⓔ　　80. Ⓐ Ⓑ Ⓒ Ⓓ Ⓔ
50. Ⓐ Ⓑ Ⓒ Ⓓ Ⓔ　　66. Ⓐ Ⓑ Ⓒ Ⓓ Ⓔ　　81. Ⓐ Ⓑ Ⓒ Ⓓ Ⓔ
51. Ⓐ Ⓑ Ⓒ Ⓓ Ⓔ　　67. Ⓐ Ⓑ Ⓒ Ⓓ Ⓔ　　82. Ⓐ Ⓑ Ⓒ Ⓓ Ⓔ
52. Ⓐ Ⓑ Ⓒ Ⓓ Ⓔ　　68. Ⓐ Ⓑ Ⓒ Ⓓ Ⓔ　　83. Ⓐ Ⓑ Ⓒ Ⓓ Ⓔ
53. Ⓐ Ⓑ Ⓒ Ⓓ Ⓔ　　69. Ⓐ Ⓑ Ⓒ Ⓓ Ⓔ　　84. Ⓐ Ⓑ Ⓒ Ⓓ Ⓔ
54. Ⓐ Ⓑ Ⓒ Ⓓ Ⓔ　　70. Ⓐ Ⓑ Ⓒ Ⓓ Ⓔ　　85. Ⓐ Ⓑ Ⓒ Ⓓ Ⓔ
55. Ⓐ Ⓑ Ⓒ Ⓓ Ⓔ　　71. Ⓐ Ⓑ Ⓒ Ⓓ Ⓔ　　86. Ⓐ Ⓑ Ⓒ Ⓓ Ⓔ
56. Ⓐ Ⓑ Ⓒ Ⓓ Ⓔ　　72. Ⓐ Ⓑ Ⓒ Ⓓ Ⓔ　　87. Ⓐ Ⓑ Ⓒ Ⓓ Ⓔ
57. Ⓐ Ⓑ Ⓒ Ⓓ Ⓔ　　73. Ⓐ Ⓑ Ⓒ Ⓓ Ⓔ　　88. Ⓐ Ⓑ Ⓒ Ⓓ Ⓔ
58. Ⓐ Ⓑ Ⓒ Ⓓ Ⓔ

Number Series

TIME: 20 minutes, 24 questions

Directions: Each number series question consists of a series of numbers that follow some definite, precise order: the numbers progress from left to right, following some deterimed rule. One lettered pair of numbers (A, B, C, or D) for each question represents the correct answer: that is, the next series of numbers that should follow in the order, and thus conform to the rule. Choose this correct answer, and mark it on your answer sheet.

1. Ⓐ Ⓑ Ⓒ Ⓓ　　7. Ⓐ Ⓑ Ⓒ Ⓓ　　13. Ⓐ Ⓑ Ⓒ Ⓓ
2. Ⓐ Ⓑ Ⓒ Ⓓ　　8. Ⓐ Ⓑ Ⓒ Ⓓ　　14. Ⓐ Ⓑ Ⓒ Ⓓ
3. Ⓐ Ⓑ Ⓒ Ⓓ　　9. Ⓐ Ⓑ Ⓒ Ⓓ　　15. Ⓐ Ⓑ Ⓒ Ⓓ
4. Ⓐ Ⓑ Ⓒ Ⓓ　　10. Ⓐ Ⓑ Ⓒ Ⓓ　　16. Ⓐ Ⓑ Ⓒ Ⓓ
5. Ⓐ Ⓑ Ⓒ Ⓓ　　11. Ⓐ Ⓑ Ⓒ Ⓓ　　17. Ⓐ Ⓑ Ⓒ Ⓓ
6. Ⓐ Ⓑ Ⓒ Ⓓ　　12. Ⓐ Ⓑ Ⓒ Ⓓ　　18. Ⓐ Ⓑ Ⓒ Ⓓ

19. Ⓐ Ⓑ Ⓒ Ⓓ   21. Ⓐ Ⓑ Ⓒ Ⓓ   23. Ⓐ Ⓑ Ⓒ Ⓓ
20. Ⓐ Ⓑ Ⓒ Ⓓ   22. Ⓐ Ⓑ Ⓒ Ⓓ   24. Ⓐ Ⓑ Ⓒ Ⓓ

Oral Instructions Exam

Directions: When you are ready to practice this section of the exam, ask a friend to help. Your friend will read you the specific instructions for answering each question, or if you have no one to read them to you, then read them yourself, one example at a time. The examples are numbered 1 through 12 and referenced in the directions.

1. Ⓐ Ⓑ Ⓒ Ⓓ Ⓔ   20. Ⓐ Ⓑ Ⓒ Ⓓ Ⓔ   39. Ⓐ Ⓑ Ⓒ Ⓓ Ⓔ
2. Ⓐ Ⓑ Ⓒ Ⓓ Ⓔ   21. Ⓐ Ⓑ Ⓒ Ⓓ Ⓔ   40. Ⓐ Ⓑ Ⓒ Ⓓ Ⓔ
3. Ⓐ Ⓑ Ⓒ Ⓓ Ⓔ   22. Ⓐ Ⓑ Ⓒ Ⓓ Ⓔ   41. Ⓐ Ⓑ Ⓒ Ⓓ Ⓔ
4. Ⓐ Ⓑ Ⓒ Ⓓ Ⓔ   23. Ⓐ Ⓑ Ⓒ Ⓓ Ⓔ   42. Ⓐ Ⓑ Ⓒ Ⓓ Ⓔ
5. Ⓐ Ⓑ Ⓒ Ⓓ Ⓔ   24. Ⓐ Ⓑ Ⓒ Ⓓ Ⓔ   43. Ⓐ Ⓑ Ⓒ Ⓓ Ⓔ
6. Ⓐ Ⓑ Ⓒ Ⓓ Ⓔ   25. Ⓐ Ⓑ Ⓒ Ⓓ Ⓔ   44. Ⓐ Ⓑ Ⓒ Ⓓ Ⓔ
7. Ⓐ Ⓑ Ⓒ Ⓓ Ⓔ   26. Ⓐ Ⓑ Ⓒ Ⓓ Ⓔ   45. Ⓐ Ⓑ Ⓒ Ⓓ Ⓔ
8. Ⓐ Ⓑ Ⓒ Ⓓ Ⓔ   27. Ⓐ Ⓑ Ⓒ Ⓓ Ⓔ   46. Ⓐ Ⓑ Ⓒ Ⓓ Ⓔ
9. Ⓐ Ⓑ Ⓒ Ⓓ Ⓔ   28. Ⓐ Ⓑ Ⓒ Ⓓ Ⓔ   47. Ⓐ Ⓑ Ⓒ Ⓓ Ⓔ
10. Ⓐ Ⓑ Ⓒ Ⓓ Ⓔ   29. Ⓐ Ⓑ Ⓒ Ⓓ Ⓔ   48. Ⓐ Ⓑ Ⓒ Ⓓ Ⓔ
11. Ⓐ Ⓑ Ⓒ Ⓓ Ⓔ   30. Ⓐ Ⓑ Ⓒ Ⓓ Ⓔ   49. Ⓐ Ⓑ Ⓒ Ⓓ Ⓔ
12. Ⓐ Ⓑ Ⓒ Ⓓ Ⓔ   31. Ⓐ Ⓑ Ⓒ Ⓓ Ⓔ   50. Ⓐ Ⓑ Ⓒ Ⓓ Ⓔ
13. Ⓐ Ⓑ Ⓒ Ⓓ Ⓔ   32. Ⓐ Ⓑ Ⓒ Ⓓ Ⓔ   51. Ⓐ Ⓑ Ⓒ Ⓓ Ⓔ
14. Ⓐ Ⓑ Ⓒ Ⓓ Ⓔ   33. Ⓐ Ⓑ Ⓒ Ⓓ Ⓔ   52. Ⓐ Ⓑ Ⓒ Ⓓ Ⓔ
15. Ⓐ Ⓑ Ⓒ Ⓓ Ⓔ   34. Ⓐ Ⓑ Ⓒ Ⓓ Ⓔ   53. Ⓐ Ⓑ Ⓒ Ⓓ Ⓔ
16. Ⓐ Ⓑ Ⓒ Ⓓ Ⓔ   35. Ⓐ Ⓑ Ⓒ Ⓓ Ⓔ   54. Ⓐ Ⓑ Ⓒ Ⓓ Ⓔ
17. Ⓐ Ⓑ Ⓒ Ⓓ Ⓔ   36. Ⓐ Ⓑ Ⓒ Ⓓ Ⓔ   55. Ⓐ Ⓑ Ⓒ Ⓓ Ⓔ
18. Ⓐ Ⓑ Ⓒ Ⓓ Ⓔ   37. Ⓐ Ⓑ Ⓒ Ⓓ Ⓔ   56. Ⓐ Ⓑ Ⓒ Ⓓ Ⓔ
19. Ⓐ Ⓑ Ⓒ Ⓓ Ⓔ   38. Ⓐ Ⓑ Ⓒ Ⓓ Ⓔ   57. Ⓐ Ⓑ Ⓒ Ⓓ Ⓔ

58. Ⓐ Ⓑ Ⓒ Ⓓ Ⓔ
59. Ⓐ Ⓑ Ⓒ Ⓓ Ⓔ
60. Ⓐ Ⓑ Ⓒ Ⓓ Ⓔ
61. Ⓐ Ⓑ Ⓒ Ⓓ Ⓔ
62. Ⓐ Ⓑ Ⓒ Ⓓ Ⓔ
63. Ⓐ Ⓑ Ⓒ Ⓓ Ⓔ
64. Ⓐ Ⓑ Ⓒ Ⓓ Ⓔ
65. Ⓐ Ⓑ Ⓒ Ⓓ Ⓔ
66. Ⓐ Ⓑ Ⓒ Ⓓ Ⓔ
67. Ⓐ Ⓑ Ⓒ Ⓓ Ⓔ
68. Ⓐ Ⓑ Ⓒ Ⓓ Ⓔ
69. Ⓐ Ⓑ Ⓒ Ⓓ Ⓔ
70. Ⓐ Ⓑ Ⓒ Ⓓ Ⓔ
71. Ⓐ Ⓑ Ⓒ Ⓓ Ⓔ
72. Ⓐ Ⓑ Ⓒ Ⓓ Ⓔ

73. Ⓐ Ⓑ Ⓒ Ⓓ Ⓔ
74. Ⓐ Ⓑ Ⓒ Ⓓ Ⓔ
75. Ⓐ Ⓑ Ⓒ Ⓓ Ⓔ
76. Ⓐ Ⓑ Ⓒ Ⓓ Ⓔ
77. Ⓐ Ⓑ Ⓒ Ⓓ Ⓔ
78. Ⓐ Ⓑ Ⓒ Ⓓ Ⓔ
79. Ⓐ Ⓑ Ⓒ Ⓓ Ⓔ
80. Ⓐ Ⓑ Ⓒ Ⓓ Ⓔ
81. Ⓐ Ⓑ Ⓒ Ⓓ Ⓔ
82. Ⓐ Ⓑ Ⓒ Ⓓ Ⓔ
83. Ⓐ Ⓑ Ⓒ Ⓓ Ⓔ
84. Ⓐ Ⓑ Ⓒ Ⓓ Ⓔ
85. Ⓐ Ⓑ Ⓒ Ⓓ Ⓔ
86. Ⓐ Ⓑ Ⓒ Ⓓ Ⓔ

87. Ⓐ Ⓑ Ⓒ Ⓓ Ⓔ
88. Ⓐ Ⓑ Ⓒ Ⓓ Ⓔ
89. Ⓐ Ⓑ Ⓒ Ⓓ Ⓔ
90. Ⓐ Ⓑ Ⓒ Ⓓ Ⓔ
91. Ⓐ Ⓑ Ⓒ Ⓓ Ⓔ
92. Ⓐ Ⓑ Ⓒ Ⓓ Ⓔ
93. Ⓐ Ⓑ Ⓒ Ⓓ Ⓔ
94. Ⓐ Ⓑ Ⓒ Ⓓ Ⓔ
95. Ⓐ Ⓑ Ⓒ Ⓓ Ⓔ
96. Ⓐ Ⓑ Ⓒ Ⓓ Ⓔ
97. Ⓐ Ⓑ Ⓒ Ⓓ Ⓔ
98. Ⓐ Ⓑ Ⓒ Ⓓ Ⓔ
99. Ⓐ Ⓑ Ⓒ Ⓓ Ⓔ
100. Ⓐ Ⓑ Ⓒ Ⓓ Ⓔ

Practice Exam 4 Answer Sheet

Address Checking

Directions: For each question, compare the address in the left column with the address in the right column. If the two addresses are exactly alike, mark A on your answer sheet. If they are different in any way, mark D on your answer sheet.

1. Ⓐ Ⓓ	23. Ⓐ Ⓓ	45. Ⓐ Ⓓ
2. Ⓐ Ⓓ	24. Ⓐ Ⓓ	46. Ⓐ Ⓓ
3. Ⓐ Ⓓ	25. Ⓐ Ⓓ	47. Ⓐ Ⓓ
4. Ⓐ Ⓓ	26. Ⓐ Ⓓ	48. Ⓐ Ⓓ
5. Ⓐ Ⓓ	27. Ⓐ Ⓓ	49. Ⓐ Ⓓ
6. Ⓐ Ⓓ	28. Ⓐ Ⓓ	50. Ⓐ Ⓓ
7. Ⓐ Ⓓ	29. Ⓐ Ⓓ	51. Ⓐ Ⓓ
8. Ⓐ Ⓓ	30. Ⓐ Ⓓ	52. Ⓐ Ⓓ
9. Ⓐ Ⓓ	31. Ⓐ Ⓓ	53. Ⓐ Ⓓ
10. Ⓐ Ⓓ	32. Ⓐ Ⓓ	54. Ⓐ Ⓓ
11. Ⓐ Ⓓ	33. Ⓐ Ⓓ	55. Ⓐ Ⓓ
12. Ⓐ Ⓓ	34. Ⓐ Ⓓ	56. Ⓐ Ⓓ
13. Ⓐ Ⓓ	35. Ⓐ Ⓓ	57. Ⓐ Ⓓ
14. Ⓐ Ⓓ	36. Ⓐ Ⓓ	58. Ⓐ Ⓓ
15. Ⓐ Ⓓ	37. Ⓐ Ⓓ	59. Ⓐ Ⓓ
16. Ⓐ Ⓓ	38. Ⓐ Ⓓ	60. Ⓐ Ⓓ
17. Ⓐ Ⓓ	39. Ⓐ Ⓓ	61. Ⓐ Ⓓ
18. Ⓐ Ⓓ	40. Ⓐ Ⓓ	62. Ⓐ Ⓓ
19. Ⓐ Ⓓ	41. Ⓐ Ⓓ	63. Ⓐ Ⓓ
20. Ⓐ Ⓓ	42. Ⓐ Ⓓ	64. Ⓐ Ⓓ
21. Ⓐ Ⓓ	43. Ⓐ Ⓓ	65. Ⓐ Ⓓ
22. Ⓐ Ⓓ	44. Ⓐ Ⓓ	66. Ⓐ Ⓓ

67. Ⓐ Ⓓ   77. Ⓐ Ⓓ   87. Ⓐ Ⓓ

68. Ⓐ Ⓓ   78. Ⓐ Ⓓ   88. Ⓐ Ⓓ

69. Ⓐ Ⓓ   79. Ⓐ Ⓓ   89. Ⓐ Ⓓ

70. Ⓐ Ⓓ   80. Ⓐ Ⓓ   90. Ⓐ Ⓓ

71. Ⓐ Ⓓ   81. Ⓐ Ⓓ   91. Ⓐ Ⓓ

72. Ⓐ Ⓓ   82. Ⓐ Ⓓ   92. Ⓐ Ⓓ

73. Ⓐ Ⓓ   83. Ⓐ Ⓓ   93. Ⓐ Ⓓ

74. Ⓐ Ⓓ   84. Ⓐ Ⓓ   94. Ⓐ Ⓓ

75. Ⓐ Ⓓ   85. Ⓐ Ⓓ   95. Ⓐ Ⓓ

76. Ⓐ Ⓓ   86. Ⓐ Ⓓ

Memory for Addresses

Directions: Allow yourself five minutes to study and memorize this grid. Then give yourself five minutes to answer as many of the 88 questions that follow. On your answer sheet, mark each question either A, B, C, D or E. DO NOT refer back to the grid once your initial five minute memorization time is up.

1. Ⓐ Ⓑ Ⓒ Ⓓ Ⓔ   15. Ⓐ Ⓑ Ⓒ Ⓓ Ⓔ   29. Ⓐ Ⓑ Ⓒ Ⓓ Ⓔ

2. Ⓐ Ⓑ Ⓒ Ⓓ Ⓔ   16. Ⓐ Ⓑ Ⓒ Ⓓ Ⓔ   30. Ⓐ Ⓑ Ⓒ Ⓓ Ⓔ

3. Ⓐ Ⓑ Ⓒ Ⓓ Ⓔ   17. Ⓐ Ⓑ Ⓒ Ⓓ Ⓔ   31. Ⓐ Ⓑ Ⓒ Ⓓ Ⓔ

4. Ⓐ Ⓑ Ⓒ Ⓓ Ⓔ   18. Ⓐ Ⓑ Ⓒ Ⓓ Ⓔ   32. Ⓐ Ⓑ Ⓒ Ⓓ Ⓔ

5. Ⓐ Ⓑ Ⓒ Ⓓ Ⓔ   19. Ⓐ Ⓑ Ⓒ Ⓓ Ⓔ   33. Ⓐ Ⓑ Ⓒ Ⓓ Ⓔ

6. Ⓐ Ⓑ Ⓒ Ⓓ Ⓔ   20. Ⓐ Ⓑ Ⓒ Ⓓ Ⓔ   34. Ⓐ Ⓑ Ⓒ Ⓓ Ⓔ

7. Ⓐ Ⓑ Ⓒ Ⓓ Ⓔ   21. Ⓐ Ⓑ Ⓒ Ⓓ Ⓔ   35. Ⓐ Ⓑ Ⓒ Ⓓ Ⓔ

8. Ⓐ Ⓑ Ⓒ Ⓓ Ⓔ   22. Ⓐ Ⓑ Ⓒ Ⓓ Ⓔ   36. Ⓐ Ⓑ Ⓒ Ⓓ Ⓔ

9. Ⓐ Ⓑ Ⓒ Ⓓ Ⓔ   23. Ⓐ Ⓑ Ⓒ Ⓓ Ⓔ   37. Ⓐ Ⓑ Ⓒ Ⓓ Ⓔ

10. Ⓐ Ⓑ Ⓒ Ⓓ Ⓔ   24. Ⓐ Ⓑ Ⓒ Ⓓ Ⓔ   38. Ⓐ Ⓑ Ⓒ Ⓓ Ⓔ

11. Ⓐ Ⓑ Ⓒ Ⓓ Ⓔ   25. Ⓐ Ⓑ Ⓒ Ⓓ Ⓔ   39. Ⓐ Ⓑ Ⓒ Ⓓ Ⓔ

12. Ⓐ Ⓑ Ⓒ Ⓓ Ⓔ   26. Ⓐ Ⓑ Ⓒ Ⓓ Ⓔ   40. Ⓐ Ⓑ Ⓒ Ⓓ Ⓔ

13. Ⓐ Ⓑ Ⓒ Ⓓ Ⓔ   27. Ⓐ Ⓑ Ⓒ Ⓓ Ⓔ   41. Ⓐ Ⓑ Ⓒ Ⓓ Ⓔ

14. Ⓐ Ⓑ Ⓒ Ⓓ Ⓔ   28. Ⓐ Ⓑ Ⓒ Ⓓ Ⓔ   42. Ⓐ Ⓑ Ⓒ Ⓓ Ⓔ

43. Ⓐ Ⓑ Ⓒ Ⓓ Ⓔ   59. Ⓐ Ⓑ Ⓒ Ⓓ Ⓔ   74. Ⓐ Ⓑ Ⓒ Ⓓ Ⓔ
44. Ⓐ Ⓑ Ⓒ Ⓓ Ⓔ   60. Ⓐ Ⓑ Ⓒ Ⓓ Ⓔ   75. Ⓐ Ⓑ Ⓒ Ⓓ Ⓔ
45. Ⓐ Ⓑ Ⓒ Ⓓ Ⓔ   61. Ⓐ Ⓑ Ⓒ Ⓓ Ⓔ   76. Ⓐ Ⓑ Ⓒ Ⓓ Ⓔ
46. Ⓐ Ⓑ Ⓒ Ⓓ Ⓔ   62. Ⓐ Ⓑ Ⓒ Ⓓ Ⓔ   77. Ⓐ Ⓑ Ⓒ Ⓓ Ⓔ
47. Ⓐ Ⓑ Ⓒ Ⓓ Ⓔ   63. Ⓐ Ⓑ Ⓒ Ⓓ Ⓔ   78. Ⓐ Ⓑ Ⓒ Ⓓ Ⓔ
48. Ⓐ Ⓑ Ⓒ Ⓓ Ⓔ   64. Ⓐ Ⓑ Ⓒ Ⓓ Ⓔ   79. Ⓐ Ⓑ Ⓒ Ⓓ Ⓔ
49. Ⓐ Ⓑ Ⓒ Ⓓ Ⓔ   65. Ⓐ Ⓑ Ⓒ Ⓓ Ⓔ   80. Ⓐ Ⓑ Ⓒ Ⓓ Ⓔ
50. Ⓐ Ⓑ Ⓒ Ⓓ Ⓔ   66. Ⓐ Ⓑ Ⓒ Ⓓ Ⓔ   81. Ⓐ Ⓑ Ⓒ Ⓓ Ⓔ
51. Ⓐ Ⓑ Ⓒ Ⓓ Ⓔ   67. Ⓐ Ⓑ Ⓒ Ⓓ Ⓔ   82. Ⓐ Ⓑ Ⓒ Ⓓ Ⓔ
52. Ⓐ Ⓑ Ⓒ Ⓓ Ⓔ   68. Ⓐ Ⓑ Ⓒ Ⓓ Ⓔ   83. Ⓐ Ⓑ Ⓒ Ⓓ Ⓔ
53. Ⓐ Ⓑ Ⓒ Ⓓ Ⓔ   69. Ⓐ Ⓑ Ⓒ Ⓓ Ⓔ   84. Ⓐ Ⓑ Ⓒ Ⓓ Ⓔ
54. Ⓐ Ⓑ Ⓒ Ⓓ Ⓔ   70. Ⓐ Ⓑ Ⓒ Ⓓ Ⓔ   85. Ⓐ Ⓑ Ⓒ Ⓓ Ⓔ
55. Ⓐ Ⓑ Ⓒ Ⓓ Ⓔ   71. Ⓐ Ⓑ Ⓒ Ⓓ Ⓔ   86. Ⓐ Ⓑ Ⓒ Ⓓ Ⓔ
56. Ⓐ Ⓑ Ⓒ Ⓓ Ⓔ   72. Ⓐ Ⓑ Ⓒ Ⓓ Ⓔ   87. Ⓐ Ⓑ Ⓒ Ⓓ Ⓔ
57. Ⓐ Ⓑ Ⓒ Ⓓ Ⓔ   73. Ⓐ Ⓑ Ⓒ Ⓓ Ⓔ   88. Ⓐ Ⓑ Ⓒ Ⓓ Ⓔ
58. Ⓐ Ⓑ Ⓒ Ⓓ Ⓔ

Number Series

TIME: 20 minutes, 24 questions

Directions: Each number series question consists of a series of numbers that follow some definite, precise order: the numbers progress from left to right, following some determined rule. One lettered pair of numbers (A, B, C, or D) for each question represents the correct answer: that is, the next series of numbers that should follow in the order, and thus conform to the rule. Choose this correct answer, and mark it on your answer sheet.

1. Ⓐ Ⓑ Ⓒ Ⓓ   7. Ⓐ Ⓑ Ⓒ Ⓓ   13. Ⓐ Ⓑ Ⓒ Ⓓ
2. Ⓐ Ⓑ Ⓒ Ⓓ   8. Ⓐ Ⓑ Ⓒ Ⓓ   14. Ⓐ Ⓑ Ⓒ Ⓓ
3. Ⓐ Ⓑ Ⓒ Ⓓ   9. Ⓐ Ⓑ Ⓒ Ⓓ   15. Ⓐ Ⓑ Ⓒ Ⓓ
4. Ⓐ Ⓑ Ⓒ Ⓓ   10. Ⓐ Ⓑ Ⓒ Ⓓ   16. Ⓐ Ⓑ Ⓒ Ⓓ
5. Ⓐ Ⓑ Ⓒ Ⓓ   11. Ⓐ Ⓑ Ⓒ Ⓓ   17. Ⓐ Ⓑ Ⓒ Ⓓ
6. Ⓐ Ⓑ Ⓒ Ⓓ   12. Ⓐ Ⓑ Ⓒ Ⓓ   18. Ⓐ Ⓑ Ⓒ Ⓓ

19. Ⓐ Ⓑ Ⓒ Ⓓ 21. Ⓐ Ⓑ Ⓒ Ⓓ 23. Ⓐ Ⓑ Ⓒ Ⓓ
20. Ⓐ Ⓑ Ⓒ Ⓓ 22. Ⓐ Ⓑ Ⓒ Ⓓ 24. Ⓐ Ⓑ Ⓒ Ⓓ

Oral Instructions Exam

Directions: When you are ready to practice this section of the exam, ask a friend to help. Your friend will read you the specific instructions for answering each question, or if you have no one to read them to you, then read them yourself, one example at a time. The examples are numbered 1 through 12 and referenced in the directions.

1. Ⓐ Ⓑ Ⓒ Ⓓ Ⓔ 20. Ⓐ Ⓑ Ⓒ Ⓓ Ⓔ 39. Ⓐ Ⓑ Ⓒ Ⓓ Ⓔ
2. Ⓐ Ⓑ Ⓒ Ⓓ Ⓔ 21. Ⓐ Ⓑ Ⓒ Ⓓ Ⓔ 40. Ⓐ Ⓑ Ⓒ Ⓓ Ⓔ
3. Ⓐ Ⓑ Ⓒ Ⓓ Ⓔ 22. Ⓐ Ⓑ Ⓒ Ⓓ Ⓔ 41. Ⓐ Ⓑ Ⓒ Ⓓ Ⓔ
4. Ⓐ Ⓑ Ⓒ Ⓓ Ⓔ 23. Ⓐ Ⓑ Ⓒ Ⓓ Ⓔ 42. Ⓐ Ⓑ Ⓒ Ⓓ Ⓔ
5. Ⓐ Ⓑ Ⓒ Ⓓ Ⓔ 24. Ⓐ Ⓑ Ⓒ Ⓓ Ⓔ 43. Ⓐ Ⓑ Ⓒ Ⓓ Ⓔ
6. Ⓐ Ⓑ Ⓒ Ⓓ Ⓔ 25. Ⓐ Ⓑ Ⓒ Ⓓ Ⓔ 44. Ⓐ Ⓑ Ⓒ Ⓓ Ⓔ
7. Ⓐ Ⓑ Ⓒ Ⓓ Ⓔ 26. Ⓐ Ⓑ Ⓒ Ⓓ Ⓔ 45. Ⓐ Ⓑ Ⓒ Ⓓ Ⓔ
8. Ⓐ Ⓑ Ⓒ Ⓓ Ⓔ 27. Ⓐ Ⓑ Ⓒ Ⓓ Ⓔ 46. Ⓐ Ⓑ Ⓒ Ⓓ Ⓔ
9. Ⓐ Ⓑ Ⓒ Ⓓ Ⓔ 28. Ⓐ Ⓑ Ⓒ Ⓓ Ⓔ 47. Ⓐ Ⓑ Ⓒ Ⓓ Ⓔ
10. Ⓐ Ⓑ Ⓒ Ⓓ Ⓔ 29. Ⓐ Ⓑ Ⓒ Ⓓ Ⓔ 48. Ⓐ Ⓑ Ⓒ Ⓓ Ⓔ
11. Ⓐ Ⓑ Ⓒ Ⓓ Ⓔ 30. Ⓐ Ⓑ Ⓒ Ⓓ Ⓔ 49. Ⓐ Ⓑ Ⓒ Ⓓ Ⓔ
12. Ⓐ Ⓑ Ⓒ Ⓓ Ⓔ 31. Ⓐ Ⓑ Ⓒ Ⓓ Ⓔ 50. Ⓐ Ⓑ Ⓒ Ⓓ Ⓔ
13. Ⓐ Ⓑ Ⓒ Ⓓ Ⓔ 32. Ⓐ Ⓑ Ⓒ Ⓓ Ⓔ 51. Ⓐ Ⓑ Ⓒ Ⓓ Ⓔ
14. Ⓐ Ⓑ Ⓒ Ⓓ Ⓔ 33. Ⓐ Ⓑ Ⓒ Ⓓ Ⓔ 52. Ⓐ Ⓑ Ⓒ Ⓓ Ⓔ
15. Ⓐ Ⓑ Ⓒ Ⓓ Ⓔ 34. Ⓐ Ⓑ Ⓒ Ⓓ Ⓔ 53. Ⓐ Ⓑ Ⓒ Ⓓ Ⓔ
16. Ⓐ Ⓑ Ⓒ Ⓓ Ⓔ 35. Ⓐ Ⓑ Ⓒ Ⓓ Ⓔ 54. Ⓐ Ⓑ Ⓒ Ⓓ Ⓔ
17. Ⓐ Ⓑ Ⓒ Ⓓ Ⓔ 36. Ⓐ Ⓑ Ⓒ Ⓓ Ⓔ 55. Ⓐ Ⓑ Ⓒ Ⓓ Ⓔ
18. Ⓐ Ⓑ Ⓒ Ⓓ Ⓔ 37. Ⓐ Ⓑ Ⓒ Ⓓ Ⓔ 56. Ⓐ Ⓑ Ⓒ Ⓓ Ⓔ
19. Ⓐ Ⓑ Ⓒ Ⓓ Ⓔ 38. Ⓐ Ⓑ Ⓒ Ⓓ Ⓔ 57. Ⓐ Ⓑ Ⓒ Ⓓ Ⓔ

58. Ⓐ Ⓑ Ⓒ Ⓓ Ⓔ   73. Ⓐ Ⓑ Ⓒ Ⓓ Ⓔ   87. Ⓐ Ⓑ Ⓒ Ⓓ Ⓔ
59. Ⓐ Ⓑ Ⓒ Ⓓ Ⓔ   74. Ⓐ Ⓑ Ⓒ Ⓓ Ⓔ   88. Ⓐ Ⓑ Ⓒ Ⓓ Ⓔ
60. Ⓐ Ⓑ Ⓒ Ⓓ Ⓔ   75. Ⓐ Ⓑ Ⓒ Ⓓ Ⓔ   89. Ⓐ Ⓑ Ⓒ Ⓓ Ⓔ
61. Ⓐ Ⓑ Ⓒ Ⓓ Ⓔ   76. Ⓐ Ⓑ Ⓒ Ⓓ Ⓔ   90. Ⓐ Ⓑ Ⓒ Ⓓ Ⓔ
62. Ⓐ Ⓑ Ⓒ Ⓓ Ⓔ   77. Ⓐ Ⓑ Ⓒ Ⓓ Ⓔ   91. Ⓐ Ⓑ Ⓒ Ⓓ Ⓔ
63. Ⓐ Ⓑ Ⓒ Ⓓ Ⓔ   78. Ⓐ Ⓑ Ⓒ Ⓓ Ⓔ   92. Ⓐ Ⓑ Ⓒ Ⓓ Ⓔ
64. Ⓐ Ⓑ Ⓒ Ⓓ Ⓔ   79. Ⓐ Ⓑ Ⓒ Ⓓ Ⓔ   93. Ⓐ Ⓑ Ⓒ Ⓓ Ⓔ
65. Ⓐ Ⓑ Ⓒ Ⓓ Ⓔ   80. Ⓐ Ⓑ Ⓒ Ⓓ Ⓔ   94. Ⓐ Ⓑ Ⓒ Ⓓ Ⓔ
66. Ⓐ Ⓑ Ⓒ Ⓓ Ⓔ   81. Ⓐ Ⓑ Ⓒ Ⓓ Ⓔ   95. Ⓐ Ⓑ Ⓒ Ⓓ Ⓔ
67. Ⓐ Ⓑ Ⓒ Ⓓ Ⓔ   82. Ⓐ Ⓑ Ⓒ Ⓓ Ⓔ   96. Ⓐ Ⓑ Ⓒ Ⓓ Ⓔ
68. Ⓐ Ⓑ Ⓒ Ⓓ Ⓔ   83. Ⓐ Ⓑ Ⓒ Ⓓ Ⓔ   97. Ⓐ Ⓑ Ⓒ Ⓓ Ⓔ
69. Ⓐ Ⓑ Ⓒ Ⓓ Ⓔ   84. Ⓐ Ⓑ Ⓒ Ⓓ Ⓔ   98. Ⓐ Ⓑ Ⓒ Ⓓ Ⓔ
70. Ⓐ Ⓑ Ⓒ Ⓓ Ⓔ   85. Ⓐ Ⓑ Ⓒ Ⓓ Ⓔ   99. Ⓐ Ⓑ Ⓒ Ⓓ Ⓔ
71. Ⓐ Ⓑ Ⓒ Ⓓ Ⓔ   86. Ⓐ Ⓑ Ⓒ Ⓓ Ⓔ   100. Ⓐ Ⓑ Ⓒ Ⓓ Ⓔ
72. Ⓐ Ⓑ Ⓒ Ⓓ Ⓔ

Practice Exam 1 Answer Sheet

If you would like more answer sheets to use for these practice exams, check out this book's website at www.examcram2.com. You can download more answer sheets from the site. We want to offer these to you so you can print as many as you need for practice.

Address Checking

Directions: For each question, compare the address in the left column with the address in the right column. If the two addresses are exactly alike, mark A on your answer sheet. If they are different in any way, mark D on your answer sheet.

1. Ⓐ Ⓓ	20. Ⓐ Ⓓ	39. Ⓐ Ⓓ
2. Ⓐ Ⓓ	21. Ⓐ Ⓓ	40. Ⓐ Ⓓ
3. Ⓐ Ⓓ	22. Ⓐ Ⓓ	41. Ⓐ Ⓓ
4. Ⓐ Ⓓ	23. Ⓐ Ⓓ	42. Ⓐ Ⓓ
5. Ⓐ Ⓓ	24. Ⓐ Ⓓ	43. Ⓐ Ⓓ
6. Ⓐ Ⓓ	25. Ⓐ Ⓓ	44. Ⓐ Ⓓ
7. Ⓐ Ⓓ	26. Ⓐ Ⓓ	45. Ⓐ Ⓓ
8. Ⓐ Ⓓ	27. Ⓐ Ⓓ	46. Ⓐ Ⓓ
9. Ⓐ Ⓓ	28. Ⓐ Ⓓ	47. Ⓐ Ⓓ
10. Ⓐ Ⓓ	29. Ⓐ Ⓓ	48. Ⓐ Ⓓ
11. Ⓐ Ⓓ	30. Ⓐ Ⓓ	49. Ⓐ Ⓓ
12. Ⓐ Ⓓ	31. Ⓐ Ⓓ	50. Ⓐ Ⓓ
13. Ⓐ Ⓓ	32. Ⓐ Ⓓ	51. Ⓐ Ⓓ
14. Ⓐ Ⓓ	33. Ⓐ Ⓓ	52. Ⓐ Ⓓ
15. Ⓐ Ⓓ	34. Ⓐ Ⓓ	53. Ⓐ Ⓓ
16. Ⓐ Ⓓ	35. Ⓐ Ⓓ	54. Ⓐ Ⓓ
17. Ⓐ Ⓓ	36. Ⓐ Ⓓ	55. Ⓐ Ⓓ
18. Ⓐ Ⓓ	37. Ⓐ Ⓓ	56. Ⓐ Ⓓ
19. Ⓐ Ⓓ	38. Ⓐ Ⓓ	57. Ⓐ Ⓓ

58. (A) (D) 71. (A) (D) 84. (A) (D)

59. (A) (D) 72. (A) (D) 85. (A) (D)

60. (A) (D) 73. (A) (D) 86. (A) (D)

61. (A) (D) 74. (A) (D) 87. (A) (D)

62. (A) (D) 75. (A) (D) 88. (A) (D)

63. (A) (D) 76. (A) (D) 89. (A) (D)

64. (A) (D) 77. (A) (D) 90. (A) (D)

65. (A) (D) 78. (A) (D) 91. (A) (D)

66. (A) (D) 79. (A) (D) 92. (A) (D)

67. (A) (D) 80. (A) (D) 93. (A) (D)

68. (A) (D) 81. (A) (D) 94. (A) (D)

69. (A) (D) 82. (A) (D) 95. (A) (D)

70. (A) (D) 83. (A) (D)

Memory for Addresses

Directions: Allow yourself five minutes to study and memorize this grid. Then give yourself five minutes to answer as many of the 88 questions that follow. On your answer sheet, mark each question either A, B, C, D or E. DO NOT refer back to the grid once your initial five minute memorization time is up.

1. (A) (B) (C) (D) (E)   12. (A) (B) (C) (D) (E)   23. (A) (B) (C) (D) (E)

2. (A) (B) (C) (D) (E)   13. (A) (B) (C) (D) (E)   24. (A) (B) (C) (D) (E)

3. (A) (B) (C) (D) (E)   14. (A) (B) (C) (D) (E)   25. (A) (B) (C) (D) (E)

4. (A) (B) (C) (D) (E)   15. (A) (B) (C) (D) (E)   26. (A) (B) (C) (D) (E)

5. (A) (B) (C) (D) (E)   16. (A) (B) (C) (D) (E)   27. (A) (B) (C) (D) (E)

6. (A) (B) (C) (D) (E)   17. (A) (B) (C) (D) (E)   28. (A) (B) (C) (D) (E)

7. (A) (B) (C) (D) (E)   18. (A) (B) (C) (D) (E)   29. (A) (B) (C) (D) (E)

8. (A) (B) (C) (D) (E)   19. (A) (B) (C) (D) (E)   30. (A) (B) (C) (D) (E)

9. (A) (B) (C) (D) (E)   20. (A) (B) (C) (D) (E)   31. (A) (B) (C) (D) (E)

10. (A) (B) (C) (D) (E)   21. (A) (B) (C) (D) (E)   32. (A) (B) (C) (D) (E)

11. (A) (B) (C) (D) (E)   22. (A) (B) (C) (D) (E)   33. (A) (B) (C) (D) (E)

34. Ⓐ Ⓑ Ⓒ Ⓓ Ⓔ   53. Ⓐ Ⓑ Ⓒ Ⓓ Ⓔ   71. Ⓐ Ⓑ Ⓒ Ⓓ Ⓔ

35. Ⓐ Ⓑ Ⓒ Ⓓ Ⓔ   54. Ⓐ Ⓑ Ⓒ Ⓓ Ⓔ   72. Ⓐ Ⓑ Ⓒ Ⓓ Ⓔ

36. Ⓐ Ⓑ Ⓒ Ⓓ Ⓔ   55. Ⓐ Ⓑ Ⓒ Ⓓ Ⓔ   73. Ⓐ Ⓑ Ⓒ Ⓓ Ⓔ

37. Ⓐ Ⓑ Ⓒ Ⓓ Ⓔ   56. Ⓐ Ⓑ Ⓒ Ⓓ Ⓔ   74. Ⓐ Ⓑ Ⓒ Ⓓ Ⓔ

38. Ⓐ Ⓑ Ⓒ Ⓓ Ⓔ   57. Ⓐ Ⓑ Ⓒ Ⓓ Ⓔ   75. Ⓐ Ⓑ Ⓒ Ⓓ Ⓔ

39. Ⓐ Ⓑ Ⓒ Ⓓ Ⓔ   58. Ⓐ Ⓑ Ⓒ Ⓓ Ⓔ   76. Ⓐ Ⓑ Ⓒ Ⓓ Ⓔ

40. Ⓐ Ⓑ Ⓒ Ⓓ Ⓔ   59. Ⓐ Ⓑ Ⓒ Ⓓ Ⓔ   77. Ⓐ Ⓑ Ⓒ Ⓓ Ⓔ

41. Ⓐ Ⓑ Ⓒ Ⓓ Ⓔ   60. Ⓐ Ⓑ Ⓒ Ⓓ Ⓔ   78. Ⓐ Ⓑ Ⓒ Ⓓ Ⓔ

42. Ⓐ Ⓑ Ⓒ Ⓓ Ⓔ   61. Ⓐ Ⓑ Ⓒ Ⓓ Ⓔ   79. Ⓐ Ⓑ Ⓒ Ⓓ Ⓔ

43. Ⓐ Ⓑ Ⓒ Ⓓ Ⓔ   62. Ⓐ Ⓑ Ⓒ Ⓓ Ⓔ   80. Ⓐ Ⓑ Ⓒ Ⓓ Ⓔ

44. Ⓐ Ⓑ Ⓒ Ⓓ Ⓔ   63. Ⓐ Ⓑ Ⓒ Ⓓ Ⓔ   81. Ⓐ Ⓑ Ⓒ Ⓓ Ⓔ

45. Ⓐ Ⓑ Ⓒ Ⓓ Ⓔ   64. Ⓐ Ⓑ Ⓒ Ⓓ Ⓔ   82. Ⓐ Ⓑ Ⓒ Ⓓ Ⓔ

46. Ⓐ Ⓑ Ⓒ Ⓓ Ⓔ   65. Ⓐ Ⓑ Ⓒ Ⓓ Ⓔ   83. Ⓐ Ⓑ Ⓒ Ⓓ Ⓔ

47. Ⓐ Ⓑ Ⓒ Ⓓ Ⓔ   66. Ⓐ Ⓑ Ⓒ Ⓓ Ⓔ   84. Ⓐ Ⓑ Ⓒ Ⓓ Ⓔ

48. Ⓐ Ⓑ Ⓒ Ⓓ Ⓔ   67. Ⓐ Ⓑ Ⓒ Ⓓ Ⓔ   85. Ⓐ Ⓑ Ⓒ Ⓓ Ⓔ

49. Ⓐ Ⓑ Ⓒ Ⓓ Ⓔ   68. Ⓐ Ⓑ Ⓒ Ⓓ Ⓔ   86. Ⓐ Ⓑ Ⓒ Ⓓ Ⓔ

50. Ⓐ Ⓑ Ⓒ Ⓓ Ⓔ   69. Ⓐ Ⓑ Ⓒ Ⓓ Ⓔ   87. Ⓐ Ⓑ Ⓒ Ⓓ Ⓔ

51. Ⓐ Ⓑ Ⓒ Ⓓ Ⓔ   70. Ⓐ Ⓑ Ⓒ Ⓓ Ⓔ   88. Ⓐ Ⓑ Ⓒ Ⓓ Ⓔ

52. Ⓐ Ⓑ Ⓒ Ⓓ Ⓔ

Number Series

TIME: 20 minutes, 24 questions

Directions: Each number series question consists of a series of numbers that follow some definite, precise order: the numbers progress from left to right, following some deterined rule. One lettered pair of numbers (A, B, C, or D) for each question represents the correct answer: that is, the next series of numbers that should follow in the order, and thus conform to the rule. Choose this correct answer, and mark It on your answer sheet.

1. Ⓐ Ⓑ Ⓒ Ⓓ   4. Ⓐ Ⓑ Ⓒ Ⓓ   7. Ⓐ Ⓑ Ⓒ Ⓓ

2. Ⓐ Ⓑ Ⓒ Ⓓ   5. Ⓐ Ⓑ Ⓒ Ⓓ   8. Ⓐ Ⓑ Ⓒ Ⓓ

3. Ⓐ Ⓑ Ⓒ Ⓓ   6. Ⓐ Ⓑ Ⓒ Ⓓ   9. Ⓐ Ⓑ Ⓒ Ⓓ

10. Ⓐ Ⓑ Ⓒ Ⓓ   15. Ⓐ Ⓑ Ⓒ Ⓓ   20. Ⓐ Ⓑ Ⓒ Ⓓ

11. Ⓐ Ⓑ Ⓒ Ⓓ   16. Ⓐ Ⓑ Ⓒ Ⓓ   21. Ⓐ Ⓑ Ⓒ Ⓓ

12. Ⓐ Ⓑ Ⓒ Ⓓ   17. Ⓐ Ⓑ Ⓒ Ⓓ   22. Ⓐ Ⓑ Ⓒ Ⓓ

13. Ⓐ Ⓑ Ⓒ Ⓓ   18. Ⓐ Ⓑ Ⓒ Ⓓ   23. Ⓐ Ⓑ Ⓒ Ⓓ

14. Ⓐ Ⓑ Ⓒ Ⓓ   19. Ⓐ Ⓑ Ⓒ Ⓓ   24. Ⓐ Ⓑ Ⓒ Ⓓ

Oral Instructions Exam

Directions: When you are ready to practice this section of the exam, ask a friend to help. Your friend will read you the specific instructions for answering each question, or if you have no one to read them to you, then read them yourself, one example at a time. The examples are numbered 1 through 10 and referenced in the directions.

1. Ⓐ Ⓑ Ⓒ Ⓓ Ⓔ   18. Ⓐ Ⓑ Ⓒ Ⓓ Ⓔ   35. Ⓐ Ⓑ Ⓒ Ⓓ Ⓔ

2. Ⓐ Ⓑ Ⓒ Ⓓ Ⓔ   19. Ⓐ Ⓑ Ⓒ Ⓓ Ⓔ   36. Ⓐ Ⓑ Ⓒ Ⓓ Ⓔ

3. Ⓐ Ⓑ Ⓒ Ⓓ Ⓔ   20. Ⓐ Ⓑ Ⓒ Ⓓ Ⓔ   37. Ⓐ Ⓑ Ⓒ Ⓓ Ⓔ

4. Ⓐ Ⓑ Ⓒ Ⓓ Ⓔ   21. Ⓐ Ⓑ Ⓒ Ⓓ Ⓔ   38. Ⓐ Ⓑ Ⓒ Ⓓ Ⓔ

5. Ⓐ Ⓑ Ⓒ Ⓓ Ⓔ   22. Ⓐ Ⓑ Ⓒ Ⓓ Ⓔ   39. Ⓐ Ⓑ Ⓒ Ⓓ Ⓔ

6. Ⓐ Ⓑ Ⓒ Ⓓ Ⓔ   23. Ⓐ Ⓑ Ⓒ Ⓓ Ⓔ   40. Ⓐ Ⓑ Ⓒ Ⓓ Ⓔ

7. Ⓐ Ⓑ Ⓒ Ⓓ Ⓔ   24. Ⓐ Ⓑ Ⓒ Ⓓ Ⓔ   41. Ⓐ Ⓑ Ⓒ Ⓓ Ⓔ

8. Ⓐ Ⓑ Ⓒ Ⓓ Ⓔ   25. Ⓐ Ⓑ Ⓒ Ⓓ Ⓔ   42. Ⓐ Ⓑ Ⓒ Ⓓ Ⓔ

9. Ⓐ Ⓑ Ⓒ Ⓓ Ⓔ   26. Ⓐ Ⓑ Ⓒ Ⓓ Ⓔ   43. Ⓐ Ⓑ Ⓒ Ⓓ Ⓔ

10. Ⓐ Ⓑ Ⓒ Ⓓ Ⓔ   27. Ⓐ Ⓑ Ⓒ Ⓓ Ⓔ   44. Ⓐ Ⓑ Ⓒ Ⓓ Ⓔ

11. Ⓐ Ⓑ Ⓒ Ⓓ Ⓔ   28. Ⓐ Ⓑ Ⓒ Ⓓ Ⓔ   45. Ⓐ Ⓑ Ⓒ Ⓓ Ⓔ

12. Ⓐ Ⓑ Ⓒ Ⓓ Ⓔ   29. Ⓐ Ⓑ Ⓒ Ⓓ Ⓔ   46. Ⓐ Ⓑ Ⓒ Ⓓ Ⓔ

13. Ⓐ Ⓑ Ⓒ Ⓓ Ⓔ   30. Ⓐ Ⓑ Ⓒ Ⓓ Ⓔ   47. Ⓐ Ⓑ Ⓒ Ⓓ Ⓔ

14. Ⓐ Ⓑ Ⓒ Ⓓ Ⓔ   31. Ⓐ Ⓑ Ⓒ Ⓓ Ⓔ   48. Ⓐ Ⓑ Ⓒ Ⓓ Ⓔ

15. Ⓐ Ⓑ Ⓒ Ⓓ Ⓔ   32. Ⓐ Ⓑ Ⓒ Ⓓ Ⓔ   49. Ⓐ Ⓑ Ⓒ Ⓓ Ⓔ

16. Ⓐ Ⓑ Ⓒ Ⓓ Ⓔ   33. Ⓐ Ⓑ Ⓒ Ⓓ Ⓔ   50. Ⓐ Ⓑ Ⓒ Ⓓ Ⓔ

17. Ⓐ Ⓑ Ⓒ Ⓓ Ⓔ   34. Ⓐ Ⓑ Ⓒ Ⓓ Ⓔ

Practice Exam 2 Answer Sheet

Address Checking

Directions: For each question, compare the address in the left column with the address in the right column. If the two addresses are exactly alike, mark A on your answer sheet. If they are different in any way, mark D on your answer sheet.

1. Ⓐ Ⓓ	23. Ⓐ Ⓓ	45. Ⓐ Ⓓ
2. Ⓐ Ⓓ	24. Ⓐ Ⓓ	46. Ⓐ Ⓓ
3. Ⓐ Ⓓ	25. Ⓐ Ⓓ	47. Ⓐ Ⓓ
4. Ⓐ Ⓓ	26. Ⓐ Ⓓ	48. Ⓐ Ⓓ
5. Ⓐ Ⓓ	27. Ⓐ Ⓓ	49. Ⓐ Ⓓ
6. Ⓐ Ⓓ	28. Ⓐ Ⓓ	50. Ⓐ Ⓓ
7. Ⓐ Ⓓ	29. Ⓐ Ⓓ	51. Ⓐ Ⓓ
8. Ⓐ Ⓓ	30. Ⓐ Ⓓ	52. Ⓐ Ⓓ
9. Ⓐ Ⓓ	31. Ⓐ Ⓓ	53. Ⓐ Ⓓ
10. Ⓐ Ⓓ	32. Ⓐ Ⓓ	54. Ⓐ Ⓓ
11. Ⓐ Ⓓ	33. Ⓐ Ⓓ	55. Ⓐ Ⓓ
12. Ⓐ Ⓓ	34. Ⓐ Ⓓ	56. Ⓐ Ⓓ
13. Ⓐ Ⓓ	35. Ⓐ Ⓓ	57. Ⓐ Ⓓ
14. Ⓐ Ⓓ	36. Ⓐ Ⓓ	58. Ⓐ Ⓓ
15. Ⓐ Ⓓ	37. Ⓐ Ⓓ	59. Ⓐ Ⓓ
16. Ⓐ Ⓓ	38. Ⓐ Ⓓ	60. Ⓐ Ⓓ
17. Ⓐ Ⓓ	39. Ⓐ Ⓓ	61. Ⓐ Ⓓ
18. Ⓐ Ⓓ	40. Ⓐ Ⓓ	62. Ⓐ Ⓓ
19. Ⓐ Ⓓ	41. Ⓐ Ⓓ	63. Ⓐ Ⓓ
20. Ⓐ Ⓓ	42. Ⓐ Ⓓ	64. Ⓐ Ⓓ
21. Ⓐ Ⓓ	43. Ⓐ Ⓓ	65. Ⓐ Ⓓ
22. Ⓐ Ⓓ	44. Ⓐ Ⓓ	66. Ⓐ Ⓓ

67. Ⓐ Ⓓ   77. Ⓐ Ⓓ   87. Ⓐ Ⓓ

68. Ⓐ Ⓓ   78. Ⓐ Ⓓ   88. Ⓐ Ⓓ

69. Ⓐ Ⓓ   79. Ⓐ Ⓓ   89. Ⓐ Ⓓ

70. Ⓐ Ⓓ   80. Ⓐ Ⓓ   90. Ⓐ Ⓓ

71. Ⓐ Ⓓ   81. Ⓐ Ⓓ   91. Ⓐ Ⓓ

72. Ⓐ Ⓓ   82. Ⓐ Ⓓ   92. Ⓐ Ⓓ

73. Ⓐ Ⓓ   83. Ⓐ Ⓓ   93. Ⓐ Ⓓ

74. Ⓐ Ⓓ   84. Ⓐ Ⓓ   94. Ⓐ Ⓓ

75. Ⓐ Ⓓ   85. Ⓐ Ⓓ   95. Ⓐ Ⓓ

76. Ⓐ Ⓓ   86. Ⓐ Ⓓ

Memory for Addresses

Directions: Allow yourself five minutes to study and memorize this grid. Then give yourself five minutes to answer as many of the 88 questions that follow. On your answer sheet, mark each question either A, B, C, D or E. DO NOT refer back to the grid once your initial five minute memorization time is up.

1. Ⓐ Ⓑ Ⓒ Ⓓ Ⓔ   15. Ⓐ Ⓑ Ⓒ Ⓓ Ⓔ   29. Ⓐ Ⓑ Ⓒ Ⓓ Ⓔ

2. Ⓐ Ⓑ Ⓒ Ⓓ Ⓔ   16. Ⓐ Ⓑ Ⓒ Ⓓ Ⓔ   30. Ⓐ Ⓑ Ⓒ Ⓓ Ⓔ

3. Ⓐ Ⓑ Ⓒ Ⓓ Ⓔ   17. Ⓐ Ⓑ Ⓒ Ⓓ Ⓔ   31. Ⓐ Ⓑ Ⓒ Ⓓ Ⓔ

4. Ⓐ Ⓑ Ⓒ Ⓓ Ⓔ   18. Ⓐ Ⓑ Ⓒ Ⓓ Ⓔ   32. Ⓐ Ⓑ Ⓒ Ⓓ Ⓔ

5. Ⓐ Ⓑ Ⓒ Ⓓ Ⓔ   19. Ⓐ Ⓑ Ⓒ Ⓓ Ⓔ   33. Ⓐ Ⓑ Ⓒ Ⓓ Ⓔ

6. Ⓐ Ⓑ Ⓒ Ⓓ Ⓔ   20. Ⓐ Ⓑ Ⓒ Ⓓ Ⓔ   34. Ⓐ Ⓑ Ⓒ Ⓓ Ⓔ

7. Ⓐ Ⓑ Ⓒ Ⓓ Ⓔ   21. Ⓐ Ⓑ Ⓒ Ⓓ Ⓔ   35. Ⓐ Ⓑ Ⓒ Ⓓ Ⓔ

8. Ⓐ Ⓑ Ⓒ Ⓓ Ⓔ   22. Ⓐ Ⓑ Ⓒ Ⓓ Ⓔ   36. Ⓐ Ⓑ Ⓒ Ⓓ Ⓔ

9. Ⓐ Ⓑ Ⓒ Ⓓ Ⓔ   23. Ⓐ Ⓑ Ⓒ Ⓓ Ⓔ   37. Ⓐ Ⓑ Ⓒ Ⓓ Ⓔ

10. Ⓐ Ⓑ Ⓒ Ⓓ Ⓔ   24. Ⓐ Ⓑ Ⓒ Ⓓ Ⓔ   38. Ⓐ Ⓑ Ⓒ Ⓓ Ⓔ

11. Ⓐ Ⓑ Ⓒ Ⓓ Ⓔ   25. Ⓐ Ⓑ Ⓒ Ⓓ Ⓔ   39. Ⓐ Ⓑ Ⓒ Ⓓ Ⓔ

12. Ⓐ Ⓑ Ⓒ Ⓓ Ⓔ   26. Ⓐ Ⓑ Ⓒ Ⓓ Ⓔ   40. Ⓐ Ⓑ Ⓒ Ⓓ Ⓔ

13. Ⓐ Ⓑ Ⓒ Ⓓ Ⓔ   27. Ⓐ Ⓑ Ⓒ Ⓓ Ⓔ   41. Ⓐ Ⓑ Ⓒ Ⓓ Ⓔ

14. Ⓐ Ⓑ Ⓒ Ⓓ Ⓔ   28. Ⓐ Ⓑ Ⓒ Ⓓ Ⓔ   42. Ⓐ Ⓑ Ⓒ Ⓓ Ⓔ

43. Ⓐ Ⓑ Ⓒ Ⓓ Ⓔ   59. Ⓐ Ⓑ Ⓒ Ⓓ Ⓔ   74. Ⓐ Ⓑ Ⓒ Ⓓ Ⓔ
44. Ⓐ Ⓑ Ⓒ Ⓓ Ⓔ   60. Ⓐ Ⓑ Ⓒ Ⓓ Ⓔ   75. Ⓐ Ⓑ Ⓒ Ⓓ Ⓔ
45. Ⓐ Ⓑ Ⓒ Ⓓ Ⓔ   61. Ⓐ Ⓑ Ⓒ Ⓓ Ⓔ   76. Ⓐ Ⓑ Ⓒ Ⓓ Ⓔ
46. Ⓐ Ⓑ Ⓒ Ⓓ Ⓔ   62. Ⓐ Ⓑ Ⓒ Ⓓ Ⓔ   77. Ⓐ Ⓑ Ⓒ Ⓓ Ⓔ
47. Ⓐ Ⓑ Ⓒ Ⓓ Ⓔ   63. Ⓐ Ⓑ Ⓒ Ⓓ Ⓔ   78. Ⓐ Ⓑ Ⓒ Ⓓ Ⓔ
48. Ⓐ Ⓑ Ⓒ Ⓓ Ⓔ   64. Ⓐ Ⓑ Ⓒ Ⓓ Ⓔ   79. Ⓐ Ⓑ Ⓒ Ⓓ Ⓔ
49. Ⓐ Ⓑ Ⓒ Ⓓ Ⓔ   65. Ⓐ Ⓑ Ⓒ Ⓓ Ⓔ   80. Ⓐ Ⓑ Ⓒ Ⓓ Ⓔ
50. Ⓐ Ⓑ Ⓒ Ⓓ Ⓔ   66. Ⓐ Ⓑ Ⓒ Ⓓ Ⓔ   81. Ⓐ Ⓑ Ⓒ Ⓓ Ⓔ
51. Ⓐ Ⓑ Ⓒ Ⓓ Ⓔ   67. Ⓐ Ⓑ Ⓒ Ⓓ Ⓔ   82. Ⓐ Ⓑ Ⓒ Ⓓ Ⓔ
52. Ⓐ Ⓑ Ⓒ Ⓓ Ⓔ   68. Ⓐ Ⓑ Ⓒ Ⓓ Ⓔ   83. Ⓐ Ⓑ Ⓒ Ⓓ Ⓔ
53. Ⓐ Ⓑ Ⓒ Ⓓ Ⓔ   69. Ⓐ Ⓑ Ⓒ Ⓓ Ⓔ   84. Ⓐ Ⓑ Ⓒ Ⓓ Ⓔ
54. Ⓐ Ⓑ Ⓒ Ⓓ Ⓔ   70. Ⓐ Ⓑ Ⓒ Ⓓ Ⓔ   85. Ⓐ Ⓑ Ⓒ Ⓓ Ⓔ
55. Ⓐ Ⓑ Ⓒ Ⓓ Ⓔ   71. Ⓐ Ⓑ Ⓒ Ⓓ Ⓔ   86. Ⓐ Ⓑ Ⓒ Ⓓ Ⓔ
56. Ⓐ Ⓑ Ⓒ Ⓓ Ⓔ   72. Ⓐ Ⓑ Ⓒ Ⓓ Ⓔ   87. Ⓐ Ⓑ Ⓒ Ⓓ Ⓔ
57. Ⓐ Ⓑ Ⓒ Ⓓ Ⓔ   73. Ⓐ Ⓑ Ⓒ Ⓓ Ⓔ   88. Ⓐ Ⓑ Ⓒ Ⓓ Ⓔ
58. Ⓐ Ⓑ Ⓒ Ⓓ Ⓔ

Number Series

TIME: 20 minutes, 24 questions

Directions: Each number series question consists of a series of numbers that follow some definite, precise order: the numbers progress from left to right, following some deterimed rule. One lettered pair of numbers (A, B, C, or D) for each question represents the correct answer: that is, the next series of numbers that should follow in the order, and thus conform to the rule. Choose this correct answer, and mark it on your answer sheet.

1. Ⓐ Ⓑ Ⓒ Ⓓ   7. Ⓐ Ⓑ Ⓒ Ⓓ   13. Ⓐ Ⓑ Ⓒ Ⓓ
2. Ⓐ Ⓑ Ⓒ Ⓓ   8. Ⓐ Ⓑ Ⓒ Ⓓ   14. Ⓐ Ⓑ Ⓒ Ⓓ
3. Ⓐ Ⓑ Ⓒ Ⓓ   9. Ⓐ Ⓑ Ⓒ Ⓓ   15. Ⓐ Ⓑ Ⓒ Ⓓ
4. Ⓐ Ⓑ Ⓒ Ⓓ   10. Ⓐ Ⓑ Ⓒ Ⓓ   16. Ⓐ Ⓑ Ⓒ Ⓓ
5. Ⓐ Ⓑ Ⓒ Ⓓ   11. Ⓐ Ⓑ Ⓒ Ⓓ   17. Ⓐ Ⓑ Ⓒ Ⓓ
6. Ⓐ Ⓑ Ⓒ Ⓓ   12. Ⓐ Ⓑ Ⓒ Ⓓ   18. Ⓐ Ⓑ Ⓒ Ⓓ

19. Ⓐ Ⓑ Ⓒ Ⓓ   22. Ⓐ Ⓑ Ⓒ Ⓓ   24. Ⓐ Ⓑ Ⓒ Ⓓ

20. Ⓐ Ⓑ Ⓒ Ⓓ   23. Ⓐ Ⓑ Ⓒ Ⓓ   25. Ⓐ Ⓑ Ⓒ Ⓓ

21. Ⓐ Ⓑ Ⓒ Ⓓ

Oral Instructions Exam

Directions: When you are ready to practice this section of the exam, ask a friend to help. Your friend will read you the specific instructions for answering each question, or if you have no one to read them to you, then read them yourself, one example at a time. The examples are numbered 1 through 12 and referenced in the directions.

1. Ⓐ Ⓑ Ⓒ Ⓓ Ⓔ   21. Ⓐ Ⓑ Ⓒ Ⓓ Ⓔ   41. Ⓐ Ⓑ Ⓒ Ⓓ Ⓔ

2. Ⓐ Ⓑ Ⓒ Ⓓ Ⓔ   22. Ⓐ Ⓑ Ⓒ Ⓓ Ⓔ   42. Ⓐ Ⓑ Ⓒ Ⓓ Ⓔ

3. Ⓐ Ⓑ Ⓒ Ⓓ Ⓔ   23. Ⓐ Ⓑ Ⓒ Ⓓ Ⓔ   43. Ⓐ Ⓑ Ⓒ Ⓓ Ⓔ

4. Ⓐ Ⓑ Ⓒ Ⓓ Ⓔ   24. Ⓐ Ⓑ Ⓒ Ⓓ Ⓔ   44. Ⓐ Ⓑ Ⓒ Ⓓ Ⓔ

5. Ⓐ Ⓑ Ⓒ Ⓓ Ⓔ   25. Ⓐ Ⓑ Ⓒ Ⓓ Ⓔ   45. Ⓐ Ⓑ Ⓒ Ⓓ Ⓔ

6. Ⓐ Ⓑ Ⓒ Ⓓ Ⓔ   26. Ⓐ Ⓑ Ⓒ Ⓓ Ⓔ   46. Ⓐ Ⓑ Ⓒ Ⓓ Ⓔ

7. Ⓐ Ⓑ Ⓒ Ⓓ Ⓔ   27. Ⓐ Ⓑ Ⓒ Ⓓ Ⓔ   47. Ⓐ Ⓑ Ⓒ Ⓓ Ⓔ

8. Ⓐ Ⓑ Ⓒ Ⓓ Ⓔ   28. Ⓐ Ⓑ Ⓒ Ⓓ Ⓔ   48. Ⓐ Ⓑ Ⓒ Ⓓ Ⓔ

9. Ⓐ Ⓑ Ⓒ Ⓓ Ⓔ   29. Ⓐ Ⓑ Ⓒ Ⓓ Ⓔ   49. Ⓐ Ⓑ Ⓒ Ⓓ Ⓔ

10. Ⓐ Ⓑ Ⓒ Ⓓ Ⓔ   30. Ⓐ Ⓑ Ⓒ Ⓓ Ⓔ   50. Ⓐ Ⓑ Ⓒ Ⓓ Ⓔ

11. Ⓐ Ⓑ Ⓒ Ⓓ Ⓔ   31. Ⓐ Ⓑ Ⓒ Ⓓ Ⓔ   51. Ⓐ Ⓑ Ⓒ Ⓓ Ⓔ

12. Ⓐ Ⓑ Ⓒ Ⓓ Ⓔ   32. Ⓐ Ⓑ Ⓒ Ⓓ Ⓔ   52. Ⓐ Ⓑ Ⓒ Ⓓ Ⓔ

13. Ⓐ Ⓑ Ⓒ Ⓓ Ⓔ   33. Ⓐ Ⓑ Ⓒ Ⓓ Ⓔ   53. Ⓐ Ⓑ Ⓒ Ⓓ Ⓔ

14. Ⓐ Ⓑ Ⓒ Ⓓ Ⓔ   34. Ⓐ Ⓑ Ⓒ Ⓓ Ⓔ   54. Ⓐ Ⓑ Ⓒ Ⓓ Ⓔ

15. Ⓐ Ⓑ Ⓒ Ⓓ Ⓔ   35. Ⓐ Ⓑ Ⓒ Ⓓ Ⓔ   55. Ⓐ Ⓑ Ⓒ Ⓓ Ⓔ

16. Ⓐ Ⓑ Ⓒ Ⓓ Ⓔ   36. Ⓐ Ⓑ Ⓒ Ⓓ Ⓔ   56. Ⓐ Ⓑ Ⓒ Ⓓ Ⓔ

17. Ⓐ Ⓑ Ⓒ Ⓓ Ⓔ   37. Ⓐ Ⓑ Ⓒ Ⓓ Ⓔ   57. Ⓐ Ⓑ Ⓒ Ⓓ Ⓔ

18. Ⓐ Ⓑ Ⓒ Ⓓ Ⓔ   38. Ⓐ Ⓑ Ⓒ Ⓓ Ⓔ   58. Ⓐ Ⓑ Ⓒ Ⓓ Ⓔ

19. Ⓐ Ⓑ Ⓒ Ⓓ Ⓔ   39. Ⓐ Ⓑ Ⓒ Ⓓ Ⓔ   59. Ⓐ Ⓑ Ⓒ Ⓓ Ⓔ

20. Ⓐ Ⓑ Ⓒ Ⓓ Ⓔ   40. Ⓐ Ⓑ Ⓒ Ⓓ Ⓔ   60. Ⓐ Ⓑ Ⓒ Ⓓ Ⓔ